Digital Identity Management

Series Editor
Jean-Charles Pomerol

Digital Identity Management

Edited by

Maryline Laurent
Samia Bouzefrane

ELSEVIER

First published 2015 in Great Britain and the United States by ISTE Press Ltd and Elsevier Ltd

ISTE Press Ltd
27-37 St George's Road
London SW19 4EU
UK

www.iste.co.uk

Elsevier Ltd
The Boulevard, Langford Lane
Kidlington, Oxford, OX5 1GB
UK

www.elsevier.com

Notices

For information on all Elsevier publications visit our website at
http://store.elsevier.com/

British Library Cataloguing in Publication Data
A CIP record for this book is available from the British Library
Library of Congress Cataloging in Publication Data
A catalog record for this book is available from the Library of Congress
ISBN 978-1-78548-004-1

Printed and bound in the UK and US

Contents

Foreword

Global computerization has entered a new phase. For 40 years, information technology has altered chains of value production, distribution and information access at a significant rate. These changes, although they have shaken up numerous economic models, have not so far radically challenged the bases of our society.

This in my view is changing. If banks, PayPal, etc., have taken advantage of technology and the current banking system to develop online payment and the necessary environment of trust, now "Bit coin" is establishing itself on another level as a currency in its own right (already recognized in Germany). If distance courses have benefitted from the Internet's multimedia possibilities, now *Coursera* is establishing itself as a true virtual university, offering diplomas (the value of which depends on the prestige of the universities involved).

Identity, and its representation in the digital world, is, in the same way, beginning to be shaken up:

– The Internet's (short) history shows that the freedoms acquired by the Internet user cannot be fundamentally challenged by the states. The illegal downloading of music has only been contained, and will only be undermined by adopting new legal models deployed by Internet stakeholders (unlimited access to catalogs via a subscription at a reasonable price). Internet users have acquired the freedom of anonymity, i.e. "pseudonymity". While civil identities are determined by their filiation within the bounds of legal regulations, the identity of the Internet user can be masked, manifold and self-determined.

– Mobile phone numbers and e-mail addresses are now more stable for the individual than a physical address. Changing of mobile telephone numbers or e-mail addresses has become much more difficult to manage than physical addresses.

– The major Internet stakeholders have a particular interest in this. Facebook, Google and several others are drawing on their very high penetration rate to provide "universal" identification services, thus allowing their client to be recognized throughout the digital world. The ergonomics, for both the users and the "acceptor" services, is such that the adoption of this type of connection is developing very rapidly.

We are beginning to experience a struggle for power between the states and the major digital stakeholders within the field of identity, a standoff where precedence must be given to general interest, in a delicate balance where the freedoms acquired by *homo numericus* should be preserved and serve the development of the digital economy, and the state should continue to maintain a level of control allowing it to exercise fundamental prerogatives in terms of policing, law enforcement, taxation, etc.

Within the European Union, in the movement which led to the implementation of biometric passports, several states have taken a chance on a robust digital identification (ID) managed by public authorities, taking the form of a digital identity card that can be used in numerous sectors of administration. The French government, initially tempted by this, saw its "identity protection" bill voted against by the *Conseil Constitutionnel* in March 2012 with regard to the creation of a biometric database and the use of digital services in association with this sovereign title. Does the implementation of digital ID in France conflict with the regulations that protect individual liberties stemming from the history of its nation?

A new way is currently being explored. It concludes that the development of electronic administration has been able to rely on sectorial digital ID (my tax ID, my social insurance ID, etc.) which could also be used in other instances. Rather than defining a new "unique" digital ID to gradually impose everywhere, it would be a matter of relying on existing digital ID that users are familiar with and which is already well trusted, but needs to be made interoperable, enriched with all the relevant attributes and gradually made available for all situations in which digital proof of identity is required, possibly even in the private sector. This process – intrinsically optional for the user – would have the advantage of not imposing centralized management on digital ID, restoring control of personal data which has been spread across various administrative silos back to the citizen and developing trust in the digital without needing to implement a grand, costly and risky deployment project for a system that flattens everything out.

In order to have a better understanding of the underlying technological, judicial and societal elements of this vast issue which affects each of us according to our own daily lives and outlooks, and in order to potentially understand these changes that are taking place, we require a scientific appraisal which examines the issue of digital ID. This is what this book proposes.

Mathieu JEANDRON
December 2014

List of Acronyms

AaaS	Authentication as a Service
AN.ON	Anonymity.Online
API	Application Programming Interface
APPEL	A P3P Preference Exchange Language
B2C	Business to Consumer
BYOD	Bring Your Own Device
CA	Certification Authority
CBEFF	Common Biometric Exchange Formats Framework
CHAP	Challenge Handshake Authentication Protocol
CISO	Chief Information Security Officer
CNIL	Commission nationale de l'informatique et des libertés
CoT	Circle of Trust
CPU	Central Processing Unit
CRCs	Cyclic Redundancy Checks
CRM	Customer Relationship Management
CSP	Cloud Service Provider
DDoS	Denial of Service
DNS	Domain Name Service
ECC	Elliptic Curve Cryptography
EDM	Electronic Document Management

EPC	Electronic Product Code
ERP	Enterprise Resource Planning
FOAF	Friend of a Friend
HMI	Human–Machine Interface
HTTP	HyperText Transfer Protocol
I2P	Invisible Internet Project
IaaS	Infrastructure as a Service PaaS: Platform as a service
IAM	Identity and Access Management
ICEMAN	Intercloud Identity Management
ICIMI	Intercloud Infrastructure Management Identity
ICT	Information and Communication Technologies
ID	Identity
IDaaS	IDentity as a Service
IDP	Identity Provider
IETF	Internet Engineering Task Force
IP	Internet Protocol
ISO	International Organization for Standardization
JAP	JonDonym Anonymous Proxy
MAC	Media Access Control/Message Authentication Code
MITM	Man in the Middle
OASIS	Organization for the Advancement of Structured Information Standards
OTP	One Time Password
P3P	Platform For Privacy Preferences
PAP	Password Authentication Protocol
PKCS	Public-Key Cryptography Standards
PKI	Public Key Infrastructures
PRNG	Pseudo-Random Number Generator
RFID	Radio Frequency Identification

RPC	Remote Procedure Call
RSA	Rivest Shamir Adleman
SaaS	Software as a Service
SAML	Security Assertion Markup Language
SNS	Social Network Services
SOA	Service-Oriented Architecture
SOAP	Simple Object Access Protocol
SPs	Service Providers
SSO	Single Sign-On
STS	Security Token Service
TLS	Transport Layer Security
TOR	The Onion Router
URI	Uniform Resource Identifier
URL	Uniform Resource Locator
USB	Universal Serial Bus
VPC	Virtual Private Cloud
VPN	Virtual Private Network
W3C	World Wide Web Consortium
WIFI	Wireless Fidelity
WP29	Article 29 Data Protection Working Party
WS	Web Services
XML	Extensible Markup Language

Digital Identity

1.1. Introduction

According to the records on "digital trust" from ACSEL [ACS 13], which is an acronym for the French Digital Economy Association, French Internet users used an average of 16.4 digital IDs[1] in 2013, compared to 12.2 in 2009. By digital ID, we mean information – like login and password – needed to activate an account, but also any traces left by an individual due to their activities or technological devices (IP address, photos, types of purchase, etc.). Ninety percent of Internet users use their digital IDs to access e-administration and e-commerce services, 8% for online banking, and 77% for social networks. The same ACSEL study measures the risks perceived by Internet users with regard to their digital ID and observes that 42% of them fear errors with their ID (compared to 34% in 2009) and 40% misuse of their data. It is important to know that the French are victims of 400,000 identity thefts per year on average. ACSEL argues that an Internet user's "breaking point with regards to trust" occurs "when the risks perceived by the user are considered to be greater than the use value of a digital service".

The level of user trust in a system is also mentioned by Catherine Kherian in *Les Focus de Solucom* [KHE 13], as one of the three conditions to be met for the wider adoption of digital ID, namely: universality of use, user trust in the system (made possible through user control over personal information),

---

Chapter written by Maryline LAURENT, Julie DENOUËL, Claire LEVALLOIS-BARTH and Patrick WAELBROECK.
1 Online survey conducted among 772 Internet users.

and service providers (SPs), trust in using the same system (based on the information reliability). A step in this direction was made by the European Commission in 2012 with its project on the regulation of "electronic identification and trust services for electronic transactions in the internal market" (eIDAS Regulation) which would see each member state identify the "electronic identification systems that they accept under their jurisdiction when electronic identification is required for public services". In this sense, the French government – which aborted numerous projects considered as violation of individual freedoms – revived the project *IDéNum* in 2013 which is funded by a joint public–private partnership.

The topic of digital ID is an extremely sensitive and pervasive subject. On the one hand, the Internet has been built up over the years as a space of unregulated freedom for the individual, where everyone is free to exhibit themselves, consume, educate themselves, have a social life, etc. This *"métamorphose numérique"* [digital metamorphosis], as named by Francis Jutand [JUT 13], is not without consequences: economic consequences, with a large volume of transactions evading tax regulations, and consequences in terms of security, for citizens who are subject to harmful upshots (identity theft, e-pornography and harassment). In this context, the state whose mission is to protect its citizens, and to ensure a public service via a sufficient treasury, has no alternative but to intervene in this digital world, in order to implement a regulation that will protect the interests of the state and its citizens, and to define an adequate investigation, identification and sanction system. As such, digital identity is a challenging and critical topic, especially due to its international range, its huge economic stakes and the targeted objective of our society to find its place within this digital metamorphosis.

In this chapter, three research professors, Patrick Waelbroeck, Doctor of Economic Sciences, Julie Denouël, Doctor of Linguistics, and Maryline Laurent, Doctor in Network and Computer Science, will share their views and personal reflections on how to comprehend digital identity, how difficult it is to manage them, and the remaining challenges in their respective disciplines. These works related to digital identity are part of the activities of the multidisciplinary chair on values and policies of personal information[2] at the Mines-Télécom Institute in France. This chair aims to help businesses,

---

2 http://cvpip.wp.mines-telecom.fr/.

citizens and public authorities in their reflections on the collection, use and sharing of personal information, namely information relating to individuals (their private lives, professional activities, digital identities, and contributions on social networks, etc.) including the information collected by the communicating devices surrounding them (smartphones, smart meters, smart televisions and smart NFC games, etc.). Authors Maryline Laurent and Patrick Waelbroeck are cofounders of that chair along with Pierre-Antoine Chardel. Claire Levallois-Barth is the coordinator.

1.2. The social dimension of online self-representation

Since personal web pages in the course of the 1990s up to more recent blogs and social network sites, the democratization of the Internet has been accompanied by the dissemination of communication devices "functionally dedicated to the presentation of self" [HON 07], which have allowed composite and plural *identity elements* to become visible (from physical characteristics to identity traits, tastes and/or personal content). In this section, we intend to address the issue of self-presentation online by drawing upon research which, coming from the sociology of uses [DEN 11, JAU 11], is interested in social uses of these technical devices and have been able to provide numerous insights into the different approaches based on digital identity.

1.2.1. *Digital identity: at the crossroads of platform configuration and Internet user tactics*

1.2.1.1. *Personal identity through the prism of the sociology of uses*

If the sociology of uses is based on a combination of approaches and fields of research for the least plural[3], we nevertheless notice that the work carried out on this all pays particular attention to the *socio-technical processes*, observing the reflexive relations that take place between the

---

3 Initially created "in the absence of incorporated theoretical references and of models to be applied" [JOU 00], the sociology of uses has never ceased to borrow from a range of theoretical methods (ethnomethodology, pragmatics, sociology of innovation, interpretive and critical sociologies, etc.) in order to explore social territories (family, specific friendship circles, professional environment, etc.) and at the very least a wide variety of ICTs (landline and mobile telephones, computers, online communication apps, etc.).

technical configuration of the device and the organization of interactional and social practices. Because it is necessarily sensitive to the process of "double mediation" both technical and social [JOU 00], the research in sociology of uses which is interested in personal identity has thus addressed this problem by carefully observing the prescriptive part of Information and Communication Technologies (ICTs) in the organization of self-presentation practices. Throughout the 1990s, the massification of the use of personal web pages offered, for example, fertile ground for the analysis of what we will call *self-expression*. However, many studies have highlighted the fact that the affordances specific to personal web pages tend to frame the way in which Internet users present or reveal themselves online [BEA 99, DOR 02]. Self-presentation, produced in (and via) these services, thus appears to be a composite phenomenon. It is *intrapersonal*, because a personal web page is conducive to self-narrative or the exposure of the facets of the self, *interpersonal*, because it allows links to other pages to be integrated and *dynamic* since the page can be enriched and updated at will.

1.2.1.2. *Identity and Web 2.0*

More recently, the dissemination of the use of Web 2.0, and more particularly of socio-digital networks [COU 11], has allowed these initial questions to develop. In fact, today, we have moved on from the issue centered on *the means of online self-presentation* and *self-expression*, to analysis centered on the processes for *making oneself visible, self-deprivatization*, or even *self-exposure*. These analytical categories, which are the result of qualitative research based on the detailed examination of empirical data, also show researchers' marked increase in attention to the relationship between the configuration of Web 2.0 platforms, identity practices implemented by Internet users, but also changing social cultures.

In 2008, Danah Boyd and Nicole Ellison gave an initial definition of social network sites (SNS) as web services which allow users to: (1) construct a public or semi-public profile within a defined system, (2) maintain a list of users with whom they have friendships, (3) be able to see and browse their list of friendships and those set up by other individuals via the same platform. As it marks the central role of user profiles, this first definition is interesting, but regrettably it takes a very formal point of view which fails to consider the activities carried out by Internet users on these platforms. As within these social networking sites, it is in fact possible to distinguish between at least two groups of devices: interpersonal platforms that are linked to networking activities (e.g. *Facebook, Twitter* or *LinkedIn*) and self-production platforms more dedicated to the storage and sharing of recycled or self-produced content (e.g. *Youtube, Soundcloud, Tumblr*). In terms of the different formats of activities that these two types of platform make possible, the new analysis that Ellison has recently proposed seems to take better account of the diversity of practices carried out on these sites [ELL 11]. In this context, Ellison stresses that an SNS is above all "*a platform for networked communication* in which participants: (1) have *profiles which can be uniquely identified* that are created via a combination of content provided by the user, content provided by 'friends' and system data; (2) can publicly expose relationships that are likely to be viewed and consulted by others; (3) can access *streams of content including content generated by the user* – particularly combinations of texts, photos, videos, Website updates and/or links – provided by their contacts on the site" [ELL 11]. By highlighting the fact that each profile (even private ones) presents a minimum degree of visibility and that includes content produced by the Internet user, but also by their "friends", Ellison correlatively draws out one of the most recent characteristics of digital ID: it can be produced by the Internet user by uploading statutory elements on their profile (name, age, gender, profession, domicile, self-portrait, etc.) and more expressive elements on their "wall" (status, texts – notes and comments, interpersonal network, photos, videos, links, etc.); but it can also be deployed independently of the self, via content published by others and to whom it is possible to provide different forms of ratification – the "like" is undoubtedly the most simple expression of this.

Consequently, we are interested in different socio-technical logics which appear to participate in the structuring of digital identities in the era of Web 2.0.

1.2.2. *Different approaches*

1.2.2.1. *Expressive approach*

Many studies underline that the use of Web 2.0 services, and more particularly of SNS, has fully contributed to the "expressivist" movement on the Internet [ALL 03], insofar as interpersonal platforms and self-generation devices promote the construction and increasing online visibility of subjective, singular, personal and original content. Retaining the hypothesis of *expressive individualism* which aims to understand the different methods used by individuals in order to construct themselves as individuals; this research is interested in the "expressive work through which individuals *perform* their identities via the latest digital technology" [ALL 09]. These different studies show that, far from being a homogeneous phenomenon, digital expressivism consists of a variety of practices and dynamics, ranging from self-expression in intimate narratives, the affirmation of independent living choices, to the eclectic assortment of cultural and media products, displaying amateur activities, the quest for reputation, or even citizen engagement and participation in digital public debates. Therefore, this research reveals that identity work implemented by individuals to become singular individuals is based on different creative activities (online) whose final objective is the construction of self via the production of content and the recognition of this content by an audience [ALL 07].

1.2.2.2. *Technicist approach*

The issue of influence (or at least of the implication) of technical apparatus in the organization of digital identity practices was also addressed by Fanny Georges [GEO 09]. After examining the "cultural grip" of an interpersonal platform such as Facebook, she observes that digital identity is deployed in three ways: "declarative identity", which corresponds to elements which have been captured and uploaded by users (e.g. sections filled in on the profile or blog entries posted on the wall); "active identity", which refers to messages generated by the system concerning the user's activities (e.g. "X and Y are now friends"); "calculated identity" which groups together the figures recorded in the system (e.g. number of friends, number of groups, etc.). In addition, we note that it is from this calculated identity that practices, which are still very marginal but nevertheless noteworthy, of quantified-self develop (i.e. "self-knowledge through numbers"[4]). For those who are avid about quantified-self, these practices involve daily observation of statistics provided by applications on certain platforms, allowing them to have a distanced rereading of their ordinary activities and to gain a better understanding of their own lives [GRA 13].

---

4 A detailed presentation of this movement's activities can be accessed via the following link: http://quantifiedself.com/.

1.2.2.3. *Visibility approach*

Visibility also seems to be a key-component of self-expression. In this sense, Dominique Cardon remarks that we can see "very different elements on a *Meetic* page which intends to seduce, on a student's *Facebook* page, on a collage of tastes on *MySpace*, or in the imaginative iconography of *Second Life* avatars" [CAR 08]. Studying at the same time the identity elements posted by users of SNS, the mode of visibility afforded by the selected platforms and the methods allowing other users to access their profiles, Cardon has proposed a typology of different modes of online self-visibility ("to hide, to be seen", "to be seen hidden", "to appear hidden", "everything shown, everything seen"). Through this classification, he finally demonstrates that digital identity must be seen as a "co-production where the strategies of platforms and the tactics of users meet" [CAR 08].

1.2.2.4. *Logic of self-deprivatization*

In fact, we observe that the construction of digital identities on SNS is based most frequently on processes of externalizing one's own singularities, even of "self-deprivatization" [GRA 10a]. On this point, the *Sociogeek* enquiry, conducted at the end of 2008 with a wide range of Internet users, offers valuable insights, as it highlights five ways of online self-exposure: "modest exposure" (involving a search for discretion and caution in the construction of online identities), "mainstream exposure" (framed by conventional norms of self-restraint in public), "bodily immodesty" (consists of uploading nude images, or representations with sensual or sexual connotations), "playful exhibitionism" (involving caricatured or theatrical representations which clearly intend to deviate from standards of good taste and decency) and, finally, "trash provocation" (originating from *trash culture* and involving provocative representations of advanced states of intoxication, physical disgraces and heightened emotions). This study thus reveals that, far from resulting from a naïve and unthinking attitude, the riskiest processes of self-deprivatization (the last three in the typology in particular) fall within the framework of tactics and strategies which both aim to create an audience and demands for recognition.

1.2.2.5. *Interpersonal approach*

For many authors, this tendency for expression or self-deprivatization is evidently a matter of a pathological exacerbation of the ego, which is the consequence of the narcissistic culture prevalent in advanced capitalist societies [TWE 09]. But as it is too focused on the individual, this perspective probably lacks consideration for "the otherness and desire for social connectedness" which characterizes the use of Internet users [JOU 11]. The self-expression occurrences that can be observed on SNS reflect the personal (even intimate) *identity elements* that are linked to the personal subjectivity, but they continue to be directed toward the Other, from whom, a reaction is expected, even some sort of evaluation (even if it is derogatory). Thus, self-expression online is part of a process that is both *relational* [CAR 09] and *extimate* [TIS 11], knowing that extimacy refers to a "process by which fragments of the intimate self are put forward in relation to others in order to be validated. This is not exhibitionism. (...) On the contrary, the desire of extimacy is inseparable from the desire to encounter oneself through the other and to take risks" [TIS 11].

1.2.2.6. *A risk-seeking approach for the purposes of recognition*

Thus, many researchers agree on the fact that "in contrast with all the concerns about digital surveillance and respect of privacy, (...) users take a lot of risks with their identity" [CAR 08, GRA 10b]. It must be stated that the presentation of self on SNS often tends to involve the uploading (and thus increasing visibility) of very personal *identity elements*, which, in even more recent times, were used in the limited context of "social lives behind the scenes" and reserved for a single circle of close or even intimate individuals. If risks are observable, they are thus largely linked to the opening up of private spheres but also to the expansion of audiences, insofar as the expression of individual singularities on SNS requires that these elements be available to a more or less broad public, the members of which are not always clearly identified or even known [LIV 08].

However, to better understand the substantial risks that can sometimes be taken, it can be useful to address the issue of recognition which, for a number of Internet users, seems at the heart of the process of expression and increasing self-visibility. In a study that we carried out with Fabien Granjon [GRA 10b], we were interested more specifically in "bodily immodesty" (one of the five means of self-exposure highlighted by *Sociogeek*), as it is reasonable to assume that this poses a significant risk for Internet users who "reveal themselves"[5]. However, it appeared that the forms of self-exposure observed were part of an inter-subjective and dialogic relationship, aimed at the *recognition of subjective singularities*, that is to say, "the recognition of particular qualities via which individuals are characterized in their plural identity" [GRA 10b]. In this case, the recognition of *online* subjective singularities favors the positive construction process of their *offline* self: because they carry specific normative validity, these subjective singularities in fact have much socially valuable potential in other places (particularly offline), involving a concomitant demand for subjective and social self-esteem.

Going through the different approaches involved in identities displayed in the digital age, it seems obvious that online identities must be addressed with respect to a context that is not only linked to digital cultures, but more widely to current social logic; the very logic which has a tendency to value an individual who is an entrepreneur of their own existence and whose success essentially stems from the qualities of their person [BRO 07].

1.3. Socio-economic dimension

A survey conducted in October 2011 for the *Journal du Net* reveals that an Internet user has 13 digital identities on average to purchase products online, to email, to access e-government Websites, to join social networks or to consult online bank accounts. The majority of Internet users prefer identifiers specific to each use. Internet users are maintaining an increasing number of passwords to secure their accounts, more than a third uses more than five passwords.

Digital identity is the collection of traces that we leave behind us (ID, IP address, email, passwords, pseudonyms, personal, administrative and banking data, photos, avatars, tags, links, publications) as well as the reflection of these traces stored and analyzed by search engines and web browsers.

---

5 In fact, our attention focused on the Facebook profile of young women, allowing people to see relatively unclothed forms of self-demonstration, intended primarily for adult audiences familiar with the codes of new-burlesque and fetishistic mediums. The increasing visibility of the self on Facebook for a wide unidentified and potentially uninformed audience, seems to us to be a significant risk, all the more so as the decision to open a Facebook page is tied up with the desire for self-worth.

Identification (authentication), online identity and personal data are necessary to access various online services. We leave traces as soon as we open a web browser. These traces are related to the various identities that we maintain in a more or less active manner. On the one hand, some people prefer to remain completely anonymous, which makes it impossible to reconstruct the complete image of the identity puzzle. At the other end, others decide to reveal their true name as well as numerous elements of their private life on socio-digital networks such as Facebook.

1.3.1. *Introduction*

1.3.1.1. *Why study the economics of digital identities? Does it have an impact on the real economy?*

The first question this section attempts to answer focuses on the economic importance of the notion of digital identity: (1) Is identity an economically significant phenomenon? (2) Do events that happen online have an influence on the real economy?

The response to these two questions is affirmative for three reasons. First, the way in which people manage their online identities fundamentally influences the development of online communities as well as the reliability of information that circulates. On the one hand, communities such as those on Amazon.com or ebay.com are very active in generating ratings on products and sellers on these platforms. These ratings allow Internet users to make informed decisions both online and in the physical world and therefore have an economic value.

Second, events that occur online can have a significant impact in the real world. For instance, online dating sites allow people to make contact online in order to potentially meet in real life. The relationship between the real world and the online world is reciprocal, since a difference in point of view during a physical encounter may have repercussions online; conversely, embarassing photos or messages exchanged on Facebook can have enormous impact in the real world. Finally, more and more often, a physical encounter is preceded by a "virtual contact" (for a job interview for example). Knowledge of the identity of an Internet user and of his or her "e-reputation" is therefore increasingly essential for professional recruitment. The development of professional networking sites such as LinkedIn witnesses this evolution.

Third, the way in which people manage their identities can have an impact on companies such as Google or Facebook who sell personal data to advertisers. Personal data represent considerable financial stakes for these companies. Google was valued at 200 billion dollars at the beginning of 2012, mainly due to the amount that advertisers are willing to pay to access targeted audiences using personal data. Similarly, Facebook was valued at 100 billion dollars when it went public due to the way in which the company markets the personal data of its users. These social networks are financed by advertising and therefore fundamentally depend on the behavior of its Internet users in terms of the traces that they leave behind throughout their clickstream. More personal data allows advertisers to better target their customers with customized offers and prices. Targeted advertising is based on the onion metaphor, which postulates that the identity of a person consists of successive layers left by past socio-cultural influences. It would suffice to better target users in order to peel off the different layers in order to arrive at its core. Active identity management questions this metaphor. Hui and Png [HUI 06] and Rochelandet [ROC 10] review the literature on the economics of privacy protection. This section questions this crude vision of targeted advertising.

Finally, there are other issues related to big data. More and more companies develop services based on the large-scale exploitation of personal data collected online. To what extent is this data representative of the reality of the individuals concerned?

1.3.1.2. No direct interaction between economic agents in the reference model (general equilibrium)

Unfortunately, the economics literature on digital identity is scarce. There are two reasons for this. First, economists are ill-equipped to analyze the formation of tastes. Economic theory postulates the existence of a utility function, which measures the well-being or satisfaction of an individual, but does not explain how it is constructed (construction of social identity, construction of tastes and cultural references). Second, digital identities are constructed through interaction with others, and again, economic theory hardly addresses direct interactions between economic agents.

This point of view is shared by Kirman [KIR 04] who would like the economics to focus more on interactions between agents and on identity. In fact, for more than 30 years, the economic sciences have built theories on the paradigm of general equilibrium. In this model, all consumers and businesses are isolated atoms without identities which interact only through a price system. They also all have the same information. Thus, the notion of identity is useless and has therefore not been addressed within this framework. There are however recent models based on game theory that assume that people understand perfectly the identity of other individuals with whom they interact. These local interactions often lead to herd behavior, network effects and multiplicities of equilibria. The aggregate behavior of a population is then different from individual behavior, which challenges the notion of a representative agent in economics. Thus studying interactions and identity is economically important.

1.3.1.3. *Organization of the discussion*

Users reveal their personal data to develop close and meaningful relationships through reciprocal exchange. This desire to communicate personal information is counterbalanced by the risk of losing anonymity. This can lead to risks in terms of privacy protection: there is a connection between the virtual world and the material world that some are attempting to break. This can lead to disappointment and stigma (due to age or physical disability for example) and therefore to lying. The physical world therefore appears to be a constraint on the management of digital identities. Reputation can lead people to juggle between multiple identities. People develop their identities as a response to personal motivations and to external demands from social contexts.

The numerous motivations behind the management of digital identities are clearly summarized by Kaplan [KAP 10]:

– the construction of self;

– the control of information;

– convenience (personalization of services, password reminders, bookmarks, etc.);

– self-worth.

This section is organized into two large parts. Section 1.3.4 summarizes two sociological approaches to digital identities, which are both complementary and in opposition. Section 1.3.5 critically analyzes the economics literature that touches directly or indirectly on the notion of identity. Section 1.3.6 concludes this discussion.

1.3.2. Digital identities: two sociological approaches

Digital identity seems to result from a cognitive process of identification which results from the processing of a sometimes imperfect signal such as a pseudonym or avatar, or even an image on a dating site. The process of online identification is more complex than that carried out every day in the physical world where one's body is a relatively precise signal. A writing style, a pseudonym are imperfect signals that can mask an identity. The different degrees of anonymity associated with the disappearance of a physical body create a mediated environment where new identities can emerge.

The notion of identity is closely linked to that of privacy in the sense that people tend to control the information that they share and receive. Although much information is not *a priori* personal, it can become so *a posteriori* with data mining (exploitation of data to find regularities) and big data (connecting public, private and corporate data) which can be used to reveal private information. Furthermore, the notion of identity is an objective notion, while reputation is a subjective notion. However, these two notions coexist on the Internet. Digital identity then becomes the lowest common denominator of the traces and their interpretation.

There are two opposing visions of digital identity in the marketing and sociology literature. The first assumes that people use the Internet tools to construct their identity; they therefore try avatars different from their real personality. According to Turkle [TUR 06], people use characters different from their true identity. These identities depend on technology, social contexts (arising for example from social norms established in online communities) and cultural contexts. The second vision assumes, on the contrary, that Internet users present themselves online as they are in real life, but that they actively manage the information that they share with people from their communities.

1.3.2.1. *The identity laboratory*

Turkle [TUR 06] shows that new forms of identities are tethered to the technology used and to the social context: mobile phones, the Internet, and instant messaging. Users frequently rotate between these different tools and thus create a continuous state of co-presence. Thus a person travelling can check the news and weather for the city where they live by calling someone who is geographically very far away: it is possible to be in two places at the same time. Virtual worlds such as *Second Life* offer the ability to reinvent ourselves in different and changing social contexts. The choice of avatar in these virtual worlds is often related to issues of sexuality or intimacy: anonymity allows them to construct their identity. Thus, socio-digital networks represent a new filter through which we can discover and explore our own limits. Online identities can take numerous forms: the choice of an avatar on World of Warcraft, participation in discussion forums or learning communities, the construction of music playlists, etc. These tools can also be used to validate an opinion. Ultimately, the user is looking to construct and test their identity.

Technology has a continuous and absorbing nature which is conducive to the construction and destruction of multiple identities. However, technology can modify behavior and identity if users participate in a beauty contest for example, where people attempt to know what others think before making their decision. The search for validation from others can create a problem in the construction of identity. More generally speaking, computers and new technologies change the way we reflect on and view the right to privacy, and how we interact in real life when we are used to virtual encounters.

According to Kaufmann [KAU 04], identity is the result of a work in which an individual opts for an image of themselves. Kaufmann uses the theory of Hazel Markus (social psychology) and Sheldon Stryker (sociology). He develops the notion of narrative identity and proposes the idea of Immediate Contextualized and Operative (ICO) identity. Identity would develop like a double helix: the first reflects the norms and habits, and the second is characterized by subjectivity, inventions and ambitions.

Kafai *et al.* [KAF 10] illustrate this concept of the identity laboratory. They study the way in which young adolescents construct their avatars and identities in a virtual social game called Whyville. Users can buy face parts to create an interface with the rest of the community. They look specifically at the resources used to construct their faces as well as the choice of facial characteristics and the social and institutional constraints. Social status is established by the "beauty" of the face. The users chose certain characteristics for their avatars for numerous reasons: aesthetic beauty, the desire to join a group or to meet another person, real life characteristics, to adhere to or to protest against a fashion, to disguise themselves. Some users frequently modify the face of their avatar or even create several avatars ("alts"). The social constraints seem to be very strong in Whyville and the appearance of an avatar is the subject of numerous lines of discussion. Social norms emerge, even though there are numerous possibilities for personalization made available by the interface.

In conclusion, social norms structure identities; people attempt to recreate their cultural norms, but are constrained by the communities to which they belong.

1.3.2.2. *Active management of multiple identities, demonstration and self-projection*

In contrast to the notion of the identity laboratory, the concept of self-projection (to borrow a term used by the *Fing*[6]) builds on the idea that people seek to communicate, share, expose themselves, get personalized services and thus actively manage their digital identity by divulging more or less information to others. For example, Merzeau [MER 09] believes that the practice of targeting and matching the supply with the demand is evolving from a phase of a (stable and reproducible) type of identification toward a (idiosyncratic and contextual) "token" model. Personal data is no longer a probability but a proof of presence. We thus move from a targeting model to a screening model where only information validated by the user is retained.

According to Cardon [CAR 08], Internet users divulge a lot of personal information and explore new communities. This reflects a tension between being (gender, age, marital status, etc.) and doing (works, projects and productions). Identities characterize the tension between real life and self-projection. Cardon believes that visibility can take four forms: to hide, to be

---

6 Acronym for the *French Fondation pour l'Internet Nouvelle Génération* [Foundation for the New Internet Generation].

seen (dating site); to be seen hidden (avatar); to appear hidden (skyblog, Friendster); everything shown, everything seen.

Therefore, there is a strong link between the real and the virtual worlds on dating sites, social networks where existing physical networks are reinforced online, post-it platforms (Twitter) where geolocation data are often displayed eliminating the boundary between the real and the virtual.

Coutant and Stenger [COU 10] also emphasize that the offline and online boundaries are indeed porous: individuals recognize that their online profile represents an improved version of themselves not necessarily at odds with the real world. The authors criticize Cardon's analysis. First, the real/projected axis does not truly reflect the interactive aspect of the identity process and the fact that the individual is not always in control of this process. The being/doing axis is in contradiction with the literature on the techniques of the self and the writing of the self (rite of passage, extreme acts).

The various manifestations of oneself are clearly illustrated on dating sites. Chester and Bretherton [CHE 07] show that on these sites characteristics that are desirable online are similar to those that are desirable in the physical world. Some people are willing to present themselves as their true self, believing that other strategies are dishonest. However, according to Toma *et al.* [TOM 08], 86% of members of online dating sites believe that other users do not communicate their true physical appearance. Moreover, there are technological constraints linked to the fact that some sites group their users according to their age category. Numerous users try to get around these constraints by pretending to be younger than they really are. Ultimately, evaluating someone else's identity is a complex process related to the interpretation of sometimes contradictory signals. Therefore, some clues such as misspellings and sexual references are thoroughly analyzed.

Strategies of self-presentation reflect the tension between the desire to present oneself in the best light and the need to reveal true identity in order to attract a soul mate. The asynchronous nature of dating sites allows a user to present himself/herself based on what others expect. However, the anticipation of future interactions reduces deception. Ultimately, users are relatively honest on dating sites.

Therefore, there is a paradox. People are willing to divulge more information about themselves in an intimate environment with close friends but it is easier to share intimate feelings with strangers.

To conclude, the virtual dating world does not correspond to the identity laboratory metaphor described in the previous section. Basically, the online world is not different from the physical world. The user is thus incited to cloud his/her identity: anonymity, pseudonyms, withholding information, false statements. Internet users manage their digital identity.

1.3.2.3. *Interactive loop between self-construction and projection*

The two approaches described in the previous sections are not necessarily contradictory, as Internet users move from one to the other in a dynamic process involving self-construction and self-projection. Thus, according to Stenger and Coutant [COU 11], individuals construct their identities via both a collective and an individual process

This interactive loop is clearly established on virtual worlds such as Second Life and on social networks such as Facebook. McLeod and Leshed [MCL 11] study the way in which people manage their identities in Second Life: from complete anonymity to the full disclosure of information on their real life. Members of Second Life therefore choose their degree of exposure. Anonymity can paradoxically lead to more intimacy than when people who are relatively close share feelings. Anonymity can reveal the true self. Furthermore, people define their identity according to their social group. However, active participation in social groups can reduce anonymity, because it becomes easier to identify someone. The physical world can be a constraint on what we wish to reveal about ourselves. People connect on Second Life to meet new people and to express their ideas and opinions while maintaining their reputation. There is a tension between anonymity and the desire to develop social relations and to construct their identity in relation to others. The development of the virtual world depends on tolerance and experimentation.

1.3.3. *Economic approaches*

While sociological approaches have pushed the analysis of digital identity quite far, the economics literature is scarce. We can distinguish several strands of the literature that address issues related to identity and personal information. They are summarized in this section. Very few economists have directly modeled the notion of identity. They contribute to a difficult theoretical literature which is summarized in section 1.3.3.1, but which can be skipped by the uninterested reader. Some behavior can therefore be explained, like the choice of giving money to the university that someone attended, for example. The literature on the economics of privacy is resumed in section 1.3.3.2. This literature addresses the notion of identity in terms of price discrimination: companies seek to collect personal information related to an individual in order to find the best price at which they can sell their service and product according to the potential customer's willingness to pay. Customers then benefit from personalized services (that the *Fing* calls customization). Media and the Internet economics also justifies the economic value linked to the collection of personal information when this information is exchanged on a multi-sided market where an intermediary collects personal information and sells it to advertisers, such as Google or Facebook. This literature, which is summarized briefly in section 1.3.3.3, explains why Internet users participate in this type of market: they can use the service free of charge, while the intermediary is funded by advertisers. Section 1.3.3.4 summarizes the literature on informational asymmetries that analyzes the notion of online identity through the notion of reputation. The development of a good reputation explains why it is important to manage personal information on e-commerce platforms, such as eBay or Amazon Marketplace: there is a premium for reputation which can be used to charge a higher price than their competitors.

1.3.3.1. *Economics literature on identity*

Within the literature on identity, the approach of Akerlof and Kranton [AKE 00] extends the neoclassical analysis by including social categories. The approach of Sen [SEN 02] and of Kirman and Teschel [KIR 06a] departs from this analytical framework and proposes alternatives based on limited rationality. Davis's approach [DAV 10] is more theoretical and philosophical, as it does not claim to analyze an equilibrium between economic agents. Finally, Castronova [CAS 03] is the only article to deal with the notion of online digital identity. It explicitly acknowledges the multiple identities associated with a single individual.

1.3.3.1.1. Akerlof and Kranton

The authors propose to include two new dimensions of identity in the utility function: C, for social categories and P, for prescriptions. The prescriptions indicate the behavior appropriate for individuals in different social categories or the ideal image. Individual actions can affect the prescriptions and social categories.

In the Akerlof and Kranton model, social categories have an influence on individual actions depending on norms and prescriptions. Kirman and Teschel [KIR 06a] call this analytical framework a model of the "where" of identity (where is the agent situated in the social space). Not conforming to norms gives rise to two types of cost: anxiety and reprisals. The model improves upon the neoclassical model of the "what" of identity which assumes that individuals choose according to given preferences. This analytical framework according to its authors can still be used to explain relatively paradoxical situations for standard neoclassical models: self-mutilation (tattoos, piercings, steroid abuse, plastic surgery and circumcision), the choice of job according to gender, donations to a school or university attended.

Akerlof and Kranton's social preference approach seems too atomistic and static. They do not address the management of multiple online identities, even if the authors acknowledge that some people choose their identity. For example, a woman can decide to pursue a professional career or stay at home to look after her children. Parents can decide to put their children into a public or private school. However, the authors think that the choice of identity is often very limited.

1.3.3.1.2. Sen

Sen [SEN 02] considers that the set of choices faced by an individual is too broad. The economic theory underlying general equilibrium models makes a strong rational hypothesis called an axiom of revealed preferences, which states that individuals are capable of making perfect choices. From this follows the existence of a utility function that rationalizes these choices. Sen does not think in terms of utility but more in terms of "capabilities". Sen assumes that individuals have incomplete preferences in the sense that people have difficulty in making perfect choices. Instead, they chose something that is not worse than other potential choices. Capabilities reflect the freedom that everyone has to live the life which suits them and which they value.

The notion of social identity appears in Sen's analysis when he speaks about individual commitment. These are part of the social context in which people live. Therefore people can have objectives which take the well-being of others into account, such as the notions of justice and fairness.

Sen's critics point to the fact that people should choose for themselves and not be influenced by a social norm if it is disadvantageous to them. And more importantly, how do we assess their well-being if there is no relationship between their actions and a utility function? Beyond these criticisms, Sen's approach barely addresses the choice of identity and the management of multiple identities.

1.3.3.1.3. Kirman, Horst and Teschl

Kirman *et al.* [KIR 06b] proposes a dynamic model where agents choose what they want to become, while interacting with other people within social groups. They call this analytic framework the model of the "who" of identity. This theory is based on the work of Higgins [HIG 87] who posits that individuals act to reduce inconsistencies between who they are ("actual self"), who they should be ("ought-to self") and who they wish to be ("ideal self").

Kirman, Horst and Teschl's model is built around a triangle of identity ("what", "where", "who") where people choose the social groups to which they belong. Their own characteristics are then modified, as well as the group's characteristics. Each individual has the possibility of changing group, but in equilibrium, the group's characteristics as well as the proportion of individuals in each group stabilize. This equilibrium occurs when two conditions are met: an individual's future characteristics and participation in a group does not overly depend on the current state of affairs, and the individual is not overly influenced by the different social groups.

Davis [DAV 10] criticizes this theory because it yields unsatisfactory results, such as the constant development of identity depending on the group to which an individual belongs. This approach also ignores the management of multiple identities.

1.3.3.1.4. Davis

Davis [DAV 10] considers two types of social identity: categorical and relational. Categorical identity is socially constructed and can relate to skin color for example. It represents what people in a group have in common.

Relational identity results from the various social roles that each person plays and with which they identify themselves: for example, the relationship between an employee and an employer. This identity is self-constructed.

According to the theory of social psychology, social identity results from identification with individuals that we meet in social contexts or identification with members of other groups without interaction.

This static approach based on categorized self-selection does not take the dynamics of small groups into account. It also eliminates the individual and the differences within a group. Overall, Davis believes that individuals construct their identity by using social groups, while being constrained by norms and culture.

According to Davis, personal identity is both subject to social norms and is self-constructed. Individuals respond to stigmatization by weighing up the different social identity categories that they include themselves in. These individuals can then be at the intersections of several social groups. Consequently, social groups are heterogeneous and individuals may rank their various social identities. So the social context and people's commitment to their social roles are both important. It is then a question of assessing our proximity in relation to members of the group and to members of other groups.

Teschl criticizes Davis' approach because it relies too little on what motivates the choices of an agent. How to allocate resources between individuals who have several identities? How to choose between different ways of developing certain identities? Davis' approach is nevertheless interesting as it questions the notion of an individual as a collection of social identities. On the contrary, identity according to Davis relates to the way in which an individual can develop during multiple interactions with others and the conflicts that may arise.

1.3.3.1.5. Castronova – theory of the avatar

Castronova [CAS 03] proposes to model the choice of an avatar as the choice of the time spent occupying various avatars within a period of no longer than 24 h per day. If we assume that our physical representation is one avatar among others, the rise of the Internet has allowed the set of possible choices to expand and therefore overall well-being. The ultimate utility depends on the interaction between the avatar and the virtual world in which it develops. However, the choice of worlds is itself endogenous since it depends on the player's choices. The choice of avatar may be dictated by economic conditions such as the division of labor. For example, players of World of Warcraft form teams composed of members with complementary skills (close combat fighting, healing, remote fighting, etc.). In this case, the choice of identity is no longer an individual choice but instead dictated by the choice of the other members of the team or society.

1.3.3.2. *The economics of privacy protection*

1.3.3.2.1. Justification for the protection of privacy

This section follows the presentation of Rochelandet [ROC 10] in order to justify the protection of privacy: individual autonomy on the one hand, and intimacy and social peace on the other hand. Numerous empirical studies show that:

– individuals monitored in prison can lose the autonomy of thinking and acting in a singular independent manner;

– privacy allows people to construct their identity;

– privacy allows people to develop self-confidence;

– sharing personal information enables the construction of a circle of friends and of a social network;

– privacy allows people to establish independent moral judgment.

The concept of autonomy is however not addressed in economics except by Hirschleifer [HIR 80]. Economic literature concentrates on the notion of secrecy developed by the Chicago school which postulates that people seek to conceal information about themselves, which can lead to inefficiencies insofar as companies must commit more resources to obtain additional information. The protection of privacy is then only a way to conceal one or several hidden defects. This results in costs for the collection of information which affects prices. A lack of information can also lead to decisions which are not optimal. This argument is clearly illustrated by Turner and Vargese [TUR 10] who study the credit market in developing countries. In such markets where there are informational asymmetries between the market participants, Akerlof showed that when only the average quality can be assessed, the good records risk being eliminated and there remains nothing but "lemons" (to borrow the term used for cars of a very poor quality). The price mechanism is not sufficient in itself to prevent the rationing of good records. Thus when banks only use incomplete information on a potential borrower (typically negative information relating to the number of times that the loan candidate has, in the past, been late in paying their monthly payments), they refuse good candidates more often than when they use all available information on the potential candidate (including positive information such as the number of past successful business ventures). Lack of information can therefore lead to inefficiencies which could be eradicated with more information.

1.3.3.2.2. Protection of privacy and externalities

However, the Chicago school's approach ignores two fundamental issues. First, too much information can destroy some markets such as insurance, as the insurance companies only insure good profiles who may not necessarily need insurance. Second, the Chicago school's argument denies the existence of positive and negative externalities linked to the use of personal data by third party companies. Positive externalities (beneficial for companies) can lead to under-production of personal information. Examples of positive externalities include:

– better forecasting of market trends, and the development of individual preferences;

– better targeting of offers, the development of niche products;

– new business models such as big data and marketing of personal data.

Negative externalities (for the consumer) lead to too much data gathering. Examples of negative externalities include:

– identity theft;

– other forms of third party data use for questionable purposes such as spamming or direct marketing;

– loss of personal data such as credit card numbers due to a lack of security of the servers where the data are stored.

Are market forces enough to discipline companies to protect personal data and the privacy of their clients? Acquisti [ACQ 10] argues that we cannot leave the market on its own if consumers are not completely rational.

He develops theories based on behavioral economics where the rationality of consumers is not expected *a priori*.

1.3.3.2.3. Protection of privacy and price discrimination

If businesses have more information on their clients, they can practise price discrimination: they can price the same product or service at different net prices. The net price includes net delivery and production costs. Thus, for digital products, the most widespread form of discrimination is where businesses can identify several consumer groups and propose different versions of the same product or service. For example, a software manufacturer proposes different versions of their product with different functions: a complete professional version and a simpler (or student) version for which certain functions are unavailable. Each version can be used to extend their market to new consumers. However, each new version also encourages some consumers from a more profitable market toward a segment that is less profitable for the company. The number of versions marketed thus depends on the equilibrium between these two forces. The collection of information can therefore be used to customize offers for targeted customers, at often a very low cost for companies producing digital goods. What is the effect of this practice on firms' profits and on customer satisfaction? Surprisingly, total surplus does not necessarily decrease when a monopoly practises price discrimination, particularly when the quantities consumed on the market increase. Thus, an increase in the collection of information is not necessarily bad for consumers who are given targeted offers, even if there is a risk of clientelism (a seller offers prices to its clients based on non-objective criteria).

1.3.3.3. *Two-sided markets and the value of personal data*

Many social networks can be characterized by what the economics literature calls two-sided markets. These are characterized by network externalities between different groups of agents. For example, a search engine, such as Google.com, let Internet users access content free of charge, and the site is funded by advertising. The site therefore puts potential consumers and advertisers in contact with one another. The utility of the consumer when he or she uses the search engine depends on the number of targeted ads that he or she finds to be relevant. Similarly, an advertiser benefits from a large number of users who search on the platform. There is therefore a positive externality between Internet users and advertisers. This is also true for news sites (online newspapers for example) which are funded by advertising. The dynamics of two-sided markets where Internet users and advertisers interact implies that the platforms which manage to earn a small initial comparative advantage can find themselves in a positive feedback loop while others are caught in a downward spiral. Thus, the markets for search engines and news sites can be highly concentrated. The theory of multisided markets shows that the intermediary has incentives to subsidize the cost of the side of the platform that is essential for the development of the platform. Thus the services of Google and Facebook are free for users, while the advertisers pay to access their audiences. This practice also explains why users find it difficult to place a value on their personal data, since they do not pay for the service. Taken together, personal data are valued at hundreds of billions of dollars by financial markets.

What would happen if the cost of collecting information were increased? Tucker [TUC 12] provides a partial answer. In a comparative study between the choices of advertisers in the United States and Europe, they show that in a more regulated environment such as Europe, advertisers prefer to finance specialized sites rather than more general sites.

1.3.3.4. *Informational asymmetry and reputation*

The economic theory on reputation also sheds light on people's motivations in their way of actively managing their identities. Reputation is defined as a "goodwill": it is something which increases with positive experiences. A good reputation has economic value that is nevertheless difficult to measure. First, Internet users have a higher probability of giving a good rating to a transaction if the price/quality ration is good. In this case, the rating depends on the price: a buyer who has paid a price judged to be too high will give a lower rating to the transaction than a buyer who has paid less for the same product. So, it is common to see a transaction with a higher price assessed with a lower rating. If we seek to use this rating as a measure of reputation, there is a risk to estimate a negative reputation premium. Second, sellers who carry out a high volume of transactions are also those who receive more evaluations. But they also benefit from economies of scale and can therefore offer discounts and promotions more easily than their smaller competitors. If we use the "number of ratings" to assess the reputation of a seller, we once again risk estimating a negative reputation premium. Third, reputation can be manipulated. There are even reputation markets where sellers pay to receive a good rating (see for example Dini and Spagnolo [DIN 07] and Lumeau *et al.* [LUM 10]). It is then up to the buyer to assess reputation as an imperfect signal of a seller's true reliability. Cabral [CAB 12] provides a brief overview of the economic models for reputation. Fourth, all transactions are not necessarily rated. In fact, rating a buyer or a seller contributes to the overall knowledge of an online community (on eBay or Amazon for example). But the person who leaves the rating does not receive a reward for his contribution. This results in a less than optimal contribution from each individual, a problem known in economics as free-riding. Furthermore, Internet users rate a transaction for different reasons (to correct an injustice, to develop a community, in anticipation of reciprocal evaluation, just for pleasure, etc.). If it turns out that the characteristics of people who contribute are different from those who do not contribute, then we find ourselves confronted with a selection bias due to the non-random nature of the sample that is used to estimate the reputation premium.

Despite these issues, a large number of studies show that there exists a positive but low reputation premium. Reputation does however have an effect on the likelihood (for a seller) of finalizing a transaction. For example, Cabral and Hortasu [CAB 10] have shown that an increase in the percentage of the number of negative evaluations on eBay.com leads to a decrease of 7.5% of the sale price. They also show that when a seller receives their first negative evaluation, their sales decreases by 13%. A seller who receives several negative evaluations is more likely to leave the e-commerce platform. Similarly, Bounie *et al.* [BOU 11] show that there is a positive reputation premium that can reach 10% on Amazon Marketplace. Thus, active management of the seller profile has economic value and explains why people wish to show themselves in the best light.

1.3.4. *Conclusion*

There are different reasons why people manage their digital identities. Sociological research shows on the one hand that certain Internet users wish to construct their identity or to share intimate experiences via anonymity and pseudonyms. Others wish to build up relationships in social networks and do not hesitate to communicate their true identity, while others strictly limit the information that the rest of the online community can access. Even if the Internet has multiplied these different manifestations of identity, managing online identities is undoubtedly not so different from managing encounters in the physical world when we evolve in different social circles.

Research in economics must build upon sociological studies in order to extend models of targeted advertising and theories of choices and reputation.

This section raises some important limitations in the general use of data collected online and also in the use of big data. First of all, individuals can present themselves under false identities or partial or desired identities or identify themselves as little as possible in order to remain as anonymous as possible. Second, they can contribute a little or a lot to open projects (open source, Wikipedia, forums and other knowledge communities). Therefore, certain opinions and characteristics may be over-represented. These data problems can be solved by explicitly modeling identity choices and individual contributions.

1.4. Technological dimension

The notion of digital identities refers to several technical notions such as attributes, identifiers, credentials, pseudonyms and aliases, etc. In this section, we intend to describe, from a technical point of view, an overview of techniques associated with digital identities with inherent properties, existing identity management solutions, existing standards and risks.

A digital identity can be defined as a set of digital data which represents an entity in the digital virtual world (Internet, information systems, etc.). It can also be known as "computer representation". The entity is not necessarily a person; it can be a group of people, an organization, or any (software or hardware) device capable of carrying out a transaction (server, PC, computer process). A natural person can also create several digital identities which correspond to them in order to compartmentalize their activities as a professional, a family member, a contributor to a social network or a blog, buyer or seller, etc.

The digital data which makes up this digital identity is commonly called "attributes". These attributes can be given in different ways, to specify their date of birth, their postal address, etc. They can be declarative, that is to say, simply declared without proof brought by the owner, or certified in which case the attributes are proven to be valid by a trusted third party. They can be derived from existing attributes; thus the age or age range of an individual can be inferred from their "date of birth" attribute; similarly the post code of their place of residence can be inferred from the "postal address" attribute. Some other attributes can also be collected thanks to electronic transactions carried out by the entity, namely the list of visited Websites, favorite hobbies, etc. Everything which characterizes an entity in an immaterial way can be recorded in one or several attributes. We then speak of "profiles". Beyond preferences enriched according to an entity's transactions, profiles can keep track of an entity's habits, their behavior, the tools that they use, periods of time when they carry out a particular action. Research is being carried out in this area within the scientific community [OLE 14, OUA 10]. Efforts are made to link attributes to an entity where attributes are dynamically evolving according to their behavior, transaction history, current geolocation, an individual's geolocalized movements, etc. The idea is to refine an individual's profile so as to better customize the services, access network, workspaces, but also advertising spaces, spam, etc. With the emergence of ontologies, semantics is introduced into computer networks, interpretation of information by a computer program is made possible, thus we can imagine that profiles will gain in accuracy in order to, let's hope, be beneficial to the user.

A digital entity's attributes have market value and the companies which, in order to fulfill an online service, collect attributes and perform profiling on their clients, can obtain a return on this collection by selling, without their client's consent, their attributes. Thus, sometimes, you just need to book a hotel by the coast in order to begin receiving targeted adverts on promotional flights in your inbox just a few hours later. The entity to whom this information belongs must usually be informed of this collection and transmission of attributes to a third-party company. It is up to the entity to reject the contract if it does not meet their demands for respect of privacy.

An identifier is a specific attribute which can be used to uniquely identify a digital identity in an application domain relying on its own naming space. Thus, a mobile telephone number (country code included) is a unique identifier in the reference system provided by fixed and mobile telephone operators. An IP address is also unique to the local access provider. An email address is unique within the Internet system. A URL (for example ericgautierguitar.com) is unique within the Domain Name System (DNS). A pseudonym or an alias is also unique to Facebook. A large number of identifiers are available to us and allow us to identify a service, a Website, individual, etc. Without being exhaustive, here is a list of other possible identifiers: identity card number, social security number, tax number, identifier of a computer process, Skype identifier, Twitter identifier, etc. Incidentally, if earlier the use that we make of our different identifiers was compartmentalized and it was difficult to link them together, now, with the convergence of computing, telephony and the digital, these identifiers (surname, forename, mobile telephone number, e-mail addresses, home address via the GPS navigation system, etc.) are currently grouped within the same device which can be secure to greater and lesser degrees. Collaborative online services, such as those offered by public services (mon.service-public.fr), can collect several identifiers throughout our transactions (tax code number, child benefit number – called CAF number in France and social security number).

An identifier as defined above can have a shorter or longer lifetime depending on the type of transaction, service, or the properties desired in its implementation (see section 1.4.1). In fact, a social network where an individual wishes to remain anonymous, considers his identifier (known as an "alias") valid for the duration of the connection. However, an individual has an interest in retaining their mobile telephone number, even when they change operators, as they want to remain reachable.

Finally, the decision to revoke an identifier can be done to erase the traces of a past that no longer corresponds to an individual's life, which has become a nuisance or unproductive. Changing email address because your inbox is polluted with undesirable messages or with messages of harassment from an ex-husband is not difficult. But on the other hand, with duplication systems used by search engines on the Internet, it is a lot harder to erase some undesirable traces of a past life left on Facebook. Some companies (for example Reputation Defender) have found a promising market and offer their services to help individuals or businesses to create a reputable image for themselves in the digital world.

Note that some digital identities are used under an authentication procedure as they provide access to a range of customized services, with service access rights, depending on the individual's status, the subscription, etc. This authentication is given by an operator, a banking authority, a government agency, a business, etc. For the authority, it consists of verifying the authenticity of the identifier given by the entity requiring proof. This proof provided electronically is conventionally called a Credential. It can take the form of either a one-time or static password, an electronic signature, a response given to a random number provided by the system... It is most often a static password that is required, with an average of 5 passwords per Internet user to access different online accounts [DEL 13].

The advantage of an authenticated entity is that it allows the authority to impute an action to an entity and thus to take legal action in case of malicious acts. It is therefore necessary to pay attention to credential and identity thefts that may ensue. We should also note that, even under the guise of an unauthenticated identity, a malicious act (downloading of illegal content, cyber-attacks, etc.) will certainly be subject to more thorough investigation in order to trace it back to the responsible entity. This investigation can be made much simpler if the individual responsible has used their own cable line from their residence in order to carry out the criminal act.

Various software solutions based on architectures, and various economic models share digital identity management today. This management includes the creation of these identities (enrollment) – a fundamental step which secures the more or less strong link between digital identity and the natural person or legal entity who owns the identity, authentication of these identities, management of associated personal data, the commitment contract concerning the management of this data (use, disclosure to third parties), and revocation of these identities.

If the field of digital identity is experiencing rapid growth in today's society, some major efforts are still required to manage these identities, to provide comfort to users while ensuring their safety and privacy. The diversity of uses associated with digital identity (see section 1.4.2), properties which are antithetical to their objectives and their implementation (see section 1.4.1), the range of solutions for identity management (see section 1.4.3), still unsatisfactory standards (see section 1.4.4) and significant risks in challenging privacy, and fraud (see section 1.4.5), make the field of digital identity exciting for researchers and industrials. More technically focused research tracks, particularly on the preservation of privacy, will be presented in Chapter 4.

1.4.1. *Important notions*

The notions and properties associated with digital identity are listed below. Some of these definitions are derived from the terminology of [ISO 11] and [WP 14].

– Identifier: an identifier is a set of attributes that allows an application domain to link the declared identity to a digital entity previously known to the system.

– Uniqueness: an identifier is unique within the naming space of an application domain (email inbox, mobile phone, etc.), thus enabling a direct linking to a single entity in the domain.

– Authentication: a digital identity proves by stating their identifier and digital proof of identity (Credential) that they are truely the declared identity.

– Anonymity: characteristic of information which cannot be used to directly or indirectly identify the individual to whom the information pertains.

– Unlinkability: inability to connect at least two separate pieces of information (messages, URLs, actions, identifiers) to one individual, or a group of individuals.

– Linkability: this is the opposite of unlinkability. It is particularly useful when tracing something back to the identity of a cybercriminal.

– Pseudonymity: information which is associated with a pseudonym. A pseudonym can be used to reference a digital identity in an application domain without knowing their true identity. In this way, unlike anonymity, linkability is possible.

– Trust: an application domain can test depending on the transaction, the honest or dishonest behavior of a digital identity, whether this entity is authenticated or not, and thus, assign it a level of trust. This trust reflects the application domain's perception of the entity, and not the perception of the other entities.

– Reputation: multiple digital identities can interact within the same application domain and, after transaction, rate each other to make the quality of the relationship and service provided public. This rating contributes to an entity's overall rating. Other entities will tend to favor entities with a good reputation to obtain a service. Overall, this system encourages entities to adopt good behavior, but is vulnerable to Sybil attacks (see section 1.4.6). This reputation system is a transposition of word-of-mouth as practiced in the real world.

1.4.2. *The various digital identifiers*

Among the digital identifiers typically listed, we can list [IT 10]:

– Main identifier: an identifier associated with his/her own identity in the real world. It is common to have several main identifiers depending on the context of use: professional, family-related, childhood friends, etc.

– Pseudonym: alias or name assumed to conceal their identity. The same individual can have several pseudonyms.

– Alias: an identifier enabling its owner to benefit from the properties of anonymity, and unlinkability. The current tendency is to associate an alias with an avatar, that is to say, a more or less graphic self-representation highlighting certain aspects of their personality. The avatar may be similar to the world of role-playing games where everyone can have fun impersonating a real or imaginary person.

A pseudonym or alias may or may not be authenticated by an application domain. A pseudonym is often used within social networks (Twitter, Facebook), collaborative sites (Wikipedia), sites for classified ads (leboncoin.fr), sites which facilitate transactions and sales (eBay, Amazon) while an alias is more frequently reserved for social networks. Note that, to open an account under a pseudonym (Twitter, leboncoin.fr), most of the time, it is necessary to provide an email address that is mainly used to communicate content related to the service, to monitor the offered service and to issue a new password if it has been forgotten. It is the only identifier to be provided. It is not necessarily attached to their main identity (gmail) and can have a very short lifetime. On the other hand, for other accounts involving a financial transaction (Amazon, Quelle, etc.), whether you are a buyer or seller, you are often obliged, during a transaction, to provide a bank card number with a name (or Paypal identifier), and postal address to receive a package. Thus, pseudonymity is preserved with other participants in the service (Amazon vendors), but not for the SP (Amazon).

Finally, note that an alias is generated by a natural person. A pseudonym can be generated by a person or by the federated identity management system in order to preserve the secret of the individual's real identity (see section 1.4.3.3). In the latter case, the pseudonym has a lifetime limited to the transaction. Another transaction involving the same stakeholders will result in the generation of another pseudonym, the aim being to protect themselves against SP linkability operations.

1.4.3. *Digital identity management*

Identity management systems have evolved significantly over the past 10 years. While the first generation of systems (isolated or silo model) for users consisted of managing in total isolation their identifiers and attributes according to the service, the next generation (centralized model) introduced centralized management thus providing users with ease of use. More recently, with the emergence of collaborative and distributed services, two new models have emerged: the federated model and the user-centered model. In this section, we intend to present these different models along with their advantages and disadvantages and a list of existing software solutions.

To unify the description of identity management models, we define the following entities:

– a user: a natural person with at least one digital identity wishes to conduct a transaction;

– an identity provider (IdP): an entity in charge of digital identity management and of the execution of the authentication mechanism. It enrolls any new user by registering their identifier(s) and some of their attributes. During enrollment, according to its policy, it may be necessary to verify the veracity of the identity provided with the help of an identity card, proof of residence, or even mere proof of receipt of an email;

– a service provider (SP): an entity providing users with a service usually a Web service, and relying on the IdP in order to verify the identity given by the user.

1.4.3.1. *Isolated or silo model*

In this historic model, the user must manage as many identifiers (ID) and credentials (for example passwords) as service providers SP1, SP2, SP3, etc. Note that in this model (see Figure 1.1), the attributes associated with each identifier are managed in isolation by each SP. Still today, a large number of Web services do operate in this way.

The big drawback of this model is the large number of logins and passwords to be memorized by the user. Therefore, there is a significant risk that the user will choose the same logins and passwords for several of their accounts, which reduces the level of security. In fact, a cyber-attacker may be more likely to attack servers known to be vulnerable to recover passwords, and then use these same passwords to access several user accounts hosted on more robust sites.

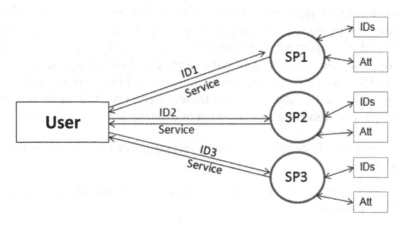

Figure 1.1. *Identity management – isolated or silo model*

1.4.3.2. *Centralized model*

This model introduces an IdP that centralizes digital identity management (see Figure 1.2). Thus the user can authenticate themselves with SPs with the same identity, the same credential and all this without having to repeat authentication for each new SP requested. We speak of a "Single Sign On" mechanism as a single instance of authentication grants access to all SPs depending on the same IdP. OpenAM (successor to Open SSO) [OPE 14a] in its simple version offers an open source software solution to this model. If ease of use is undeniable with regard to the isolated model, the centralized model is vulnerable as disclosure of one identifier with the associated credential (provided it is static) is sufficient for giving at once unauthorized access to all services. Furthermore the centralized aspect of this model does not make it suitable for a large number of users or SPs.

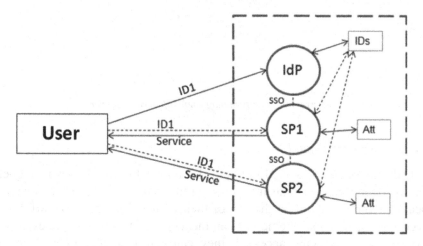

Figure 1.2. *Identity management – centralized model*

1.4.3.3. *Federated model*

The model illustrated in Figure 1.3 assumes that the IdP and SPs group together to form a federation of identities and are bound by relations of trust due to commercial agreements and a common technology platform (OpenID Connect [OPE 14b], Shibboleth [SHI 14], WS-Federation [WS 07], OpenAM [OPE 14a]). This federation is called a Circle of Trust (CoT). Just like in the centralized model, SSO mechanisms can be implemented so that the user can authenticate himself/herself a single time with the IdP to access the services of SPs that are members of the CoT. On the other hand, the user who accesses an SP is then referenced by the SP with the help of a pseudonym. In fact, all exchanges between SPs and IdP that are related to a user are done on the basis of these pseudonyms. This model is suitable for a large number of users and SPs. It is particularly interesting within the context of distributed and collaborative services. As in the previous model, the user assigns their attributes and identifier to the IdP and SPs and they are forced to trust them to respect their privacy.

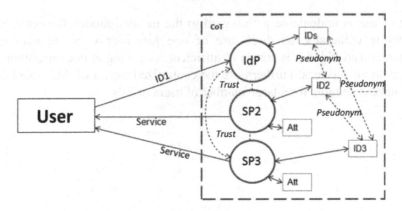

Figure 1.3. *Identity management – federated model*

1.4.3.4. *user-centric model*

Only the model presented in Figure 1.4 allows the user to have complete control over their personal attributes. From their workstation, in either a local or remote fashion on the IdP of their choice, they have a portfolio of electronic identities and sometimes an identity selector. At the request of the services and SPs being accessed, they can select an identity and decide whether to issue certain attributes. U-Prove [PAQ 13] is a software solution of this type involving an IdP responsible for signing a token proving the validity of the user's attributes. Note that the SPs act individually in this model and can, albeit not without difficulty, offer collaborative services. SPs are increasingly inclined to propose authentication of user by leaving them to decide on the choice of IdP. This is, for example, the case with Yahoo who offers the possibility of authenticating users with their Facebook or Google account.

The web community (W3C – World Wide Web Consortium [W3C 14]) is currently specifying a user-centric solution, but with different properties. This approach is known as both names: WebID for the approach used to identify a user and WebID-TLS for the protocol used to authenticate them [WEB 14]. WebID allows a user (or even an organization) to be uniquely identified by a Uniform Resource Identifier (URI) [BER 05] and to manage their profile in an online storage space at the same URI location, management being under their full control. The user's profile is defined on the basis of a vocabulary defined by Friend of a Friend (FOAF) [FOA 14] and is enriched with the user's electronic public key and an electronic signature (potentially self-signed) for their WebID-TLS authentication. Thus, user authentication to an SP is pretty much like TLS protocol as the user transmits their certificate and an electronic signature. The difference with TLS is the form of certificate and the verification of the certificate by the SP. In fact, with WebID-TLS, the certificate carries the identifier corresponding to the profile's URI location and their verification consists of ensuring that the certificate received is the same as the one stored at the URI. Thus the WebID-TLS authentication has the sole purpose of verifying that the requesting user is the owner of the URI. The advantage of the WebID approach is that it leaves profile management up to the owner. On the other hand, by leaving all attributes of the personal space without access control, it does not so far offer any means for protecting user privacy.

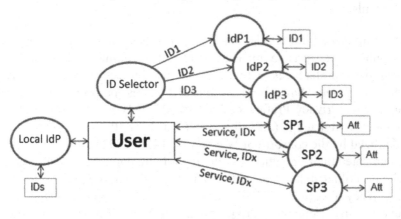

Figure 1.4. *Identity management – user-centric model*

1.4.5. *The norms*

The majority of identity management systems are based on web standards, in order to achieve entity authentication, exchange attributes, express particular policies regarding privacy. It is possible to split these standards into two categories:

– the language supporting authentication and exchange of attributes;

– the language for expressing privacy policies.

Security Assertion Markup Language (SAML 2.0) [MIS 05] was standardized in 2005 by OASIS (Committee of the Organization for the

Advancement of Structured Information Standards) [OAS 14]. It defines a structure based on XML to allow for the exchange of authentication and authorization data, and of attributes between an IdP and an SP, this structure can itself be secured by the Simple Object Access Protocol (SOAP) protocol [SOA 14] which can implement encryption and electronic signature mechanisms. SAML is very flexible with regard to the content of the exchanges between IdP, SP and user and identifies the different exchange patterns in the form of profiles (for example Web browser SSO, Single Logout, Basic Attribute Profile). The profile is selected according to the use scenario. Finally OAuth 2.0 [OAU 14] provides the user with the advantage of delegating rights to an application which will act on behalf of the user. Readers interested in this area may wish to refer to Chapter 2 for more details.

In compliance with regulations [EC 14], it has become necessary for an SP to publish their privacy management practices online, and for the user to express their preferences with regard to the protection of their privacy. Several languages have been designed for this purpose, most notably "Platform for Privacy Preferences" (P3P) [P3P 14] and "A P3P Preference Exchange Language" (APPEL) [APP 14]. P3P and APPEL were standardized by the consortium W3C [W3C 14] in 2002 to allow Websites to communicate their practices with regard to the collection, use and distribution of attributes received from users, and to allow the user to specify their privacy preferences. P3P refers to an XML syntax which can be understood by computer programs so that a browser can compare the practices of a Website with a user's preferences before continuing with the transaction. Note that P3P and APPEL are like a set of responses to multiple choice questions and do not make it easy to specify certain combinations, particularly what is acceptable. Readers interested in the technical and legal aspects associated with privacy in networks today may wish to refer to Chapter 4.

1.4.6. *The risks related to digital identity*

In the case of a main identity, just like in the real world, a cybercriminal may be interested in committing identity theft for profit or even in order to access advantageous services or confidential information whether private or professional. This cyber-attack [LAU 11] can be achieved by theft of identifier and credential obtained by social engineering (for example you receive a telephone call from your network administrator who convinces you to provide your login/password), via phishing (for example: an e-mail indicating a computer problem invites you to connect to a site with your login/password), or through the installation of a keylogger Trojan on the victims machine which can capture and record the keys struck on a keyboard. The motives for such offences are as diverse as in the real world: bank transfers, the sale of trade secrets to competitors, fraud, etc. However, with our increasing tendency to entrust more and more of our private life on our computer, the theft of intimate data (photos and correspondence) could go further and lead to an increase in harassment, blackmail, etc.

As we have seen, the risk may also come from the owner of a main identity. Through negligence, they may divulge certain personal information on a social network, blog, or on a large distribution network such as DailyMotion or YouTube. It will then be difficult for them to control the disclosure and replication of this data and to have the right to be forgotten.

Finally, it is easy for a cyber-attacker to evolve when they are anonymous or using a pseudonym. In fact nothing stops them from creating several identities and, once identified as undesirable, from changing and disturbing the service operations again (e.g. a social network). This Sybil attack where the attacker has several identities is problematic for maintaining the quality of service (QoS) and for reputation systems that can see their rating system distorted. For instance, a cyber-crook can wear the hat of both the buyer and the seller so as to give positive reviews of completely fictitious sales transactions and thus favorably increase their seller rating.

1.5. Conclusions

This chapter has highlighted the multidisciplinary nature of the digital identity field. Researchers have proposed their own understanding and analysis about the self-representation in the digital world, the new economic models and challenges, and existing technical solutions along with their limitations.

Digital identities are the result of the major technological advancements that we have experienced during the last 20 years. They have given way to a virtual world in which individuals, groups and businesses need to find their place. The emerging area of digital identities is constantly and rapidly changing and growing. As such, it brings together a community of scientists, philosophers, lawyers, industrials, educators, politicians, etc., who attempt to provide answers in order to build a regulated economically viable, secure and trusted digital world that society can appropriate.

1.6. Bibliography

[ACQ 10] ACQUISTI A., "The economics and behavioral economics of privacy: a note", *Proceedings of the Third International Conference on Ethics and Policy of Biometrics and International Data Sharing*, Hong Kong, Springer LNCS, vol. 60059, 2010.

[ACS 13] ACSEL (Association de l'Economie Numérique), relation numérique de confiance; des enjeux des identités numériques, June 2013. Available at:http://www.acsel.asso.fr/2013/version-numerique-du-cahier-la-relation-numerique-de-confiance-des-enjeux-des-identites.

[AGU 09] AGUITON C., *et al.*, "Does showing off help to make friends? Experimenting a sociological game on self-exhibition and social networks", *Proceedings of the 3rd International ICWSM Conference*, San Jose, pp. 10–17, 2009.

[AKE 00] AKERLOF G.A., KRANTON R.E., "Economics and identity", *Quarterly Journal of Economics*, vol. 115, no. 3, pp. 715–753, 2000.

[ALL 03] ALLARD L., VANDENBERGHE F., "Express yourself! Les pages perso. Entre légitimation technopolitique de l'individualisme expressif et authenticité réflexive peer to peer", *Réseaux*, vol. 21, no. 117, pp. 191–220, 2003.

[ALL 07] ALLARD L., "Blogs, podcast, tags, mashups, cartographies, locative medias : le tournant expressiviste du web", *Médiamorphoses*, no. 21, pp. 57–62, 2007.

[ALL 09] ALLARD L., "Pragmatique de l'Internet mobile. Technologies de soi et culture du transfert", in DERVIN F., ABBAS Y., (eds.), *Technologies numériques du soi et (co-)constructions identitaires,* coll. Questions contemporaines, L'Harmattan, Paris, pp. 59–82, 2009.

[APP 14] APPEL, *APPEL 1.0: A P3P Preference Exchange Language 1.0*, http://www.w3.org/TR/P3P-preferences/, 2014.

[BEA 99] BEAUDOUIN V., VELKOVSKA J., "Constitution d'un espace de communication sur Internet (forums, pages personnelles, courrier électronique…)", *Réseaux*, vol. 17, no. 97, pp. 121–178, 1999.

[BER 05] BERNERS-LEE T., MASINTER L., BERNERS-LEE R., Uniform Resource Identifier (URI): GenericSyntax, Standards Track, RFC 3986, January 2005.

[BOU 11] BOUNIE D., EANG B., SIRBU M., *et al.*, "Une analyse empirique de la dispersion des prix sur Internet", *Revue Française d'Economie*, vol. 25, pp. 121–145, 2011.

[BOY 08] BOYD D., ELLISON N., "Social Network Sites: definition, history and scholarship", *Journal Of Computer Mediated Communication*, vol. 13, no. 1, pp. 210–230, 2008.

[BRO 07] BRÖCKLING U., *Das unternehmerische Selbst. Soziologieeiner Subjektivierungsform*, Frankfurt, Suhrkamp, 2007.

[CAB 10] CABRAL L., HORTASU A., "The dynamics of seller reputation: theory and evidence from eBay", *Journal of Industrial Economics*, vol. 58, pp. 54–78, 2010.

[CAB 12] CABRAL L., "Reputation on the internet", *Oxford Handbook of the Digital Economy*, Oxford University Press, 2012.

[CAR 08] CARDON D., "Le design de la visibilité. Un essai de cartographie du Web 2.0", *Réseaux*, vol. 26, no. 152, pp. 93–137, 2008.

[CAR 09] CARDON D., "L'identité comme stratégie relationnelle", *Hermès*, no. 53, pp. 61–66, 2009.

[CAS 03] CASTRONOVA E., Theory of the Avatar, CESIfo Working paper 863, 2003.

[CHE 07] CHESTER A., BRETHERTON D., "Impression management and identity online", in JOINSON A., MCKENNA K., POSTMES T., *et al.* (eds.), *Oxford Handbook of Internet Psychology*, Oxford: Oxford University Press, pp. 223–236, 2007.

[COU 10] COUTANT A., STENGER T., *Processus identitaire et ordre de l'interaction sur les réseaux socionumériques*, Mime, 2010.

[COU 11] COUTANT A., STENGER T., (eds.), "Ces réseaux numériques dits sociaux", *Hermès*, no. 59, 2011.

[DAV 10] DAVIS J.B., *Individuals and Identity in Economics*, Cambridge University Press, 2010.

[DEL 13] DELOITTE, Technology, Media & Telecommunications Predictions, 2013. Available at http://www2.deloitte.com/content/dam/Deloitte/global/ Documents/ Technology-Media-Telecommunications/gx-TMT-Predictions2013-Final.pdf

[DEN 11] DENOUËL J., GRANJON F., (eds.), *Communiquer à l'ère numérique. Regards croisés sur la sociologie des usages*, Paris, coll. Sciences sociales, Presses de l'école des Mines, 2011.

[DIN 07] DINI F., SPAGNOLO G., *Buying Reputation on eBay*, QuadernoConsip VIII, 2007.

[DOR 02] DÖRING N., "Personal home pages on the web: a review of research", *Journal of Computer-Mediated Communication*, vol. 7, no. 3, 2002.

[EC 14] Proposal for a regulation of the European Parliament and of the Council on the protection of individuals with regard to the processing of their personal data and on the free movement of such data (General Data Protection Regulation) (COM(2012)0011 – C7-0025/2012 – 2012/0011(COD)) (Ordinary legislative procedure: first reading), A7-0402/2013

[ELL 11] ELLISON N., "Réseaux sociaux, numérique et capital social", *Hermès*, no. 59, pp. 21–23, 2011.

[FOA 14] FOAF, http://www.foaf-project.org/, 2014.

[GEO 09] GEORGES F., "Représentation de soi et identité numérique. Analyse sémiotique et quantitative de l'emprise culturelle du Web 2.0", *Réseaux*, vol. 27, no. 154, pp. 165–193, 2009.

[GRA 13] GRANJON F., NIKOLSKI V., PHARABOD A.N., "Métriques de soi et self-tracking: une nouvelle culture de soi à l'ère du numérique et de la modernité réflexive?", *Recherches en Communication*, pp. 13–26, 2013.

[GRA 10a] GRANJON F., "Expositions de soi sur les SNS. Les déplacements numériques de l'impudeur", in AGOSTINELLI S., AUGEY D., LAURIE F., (eds.), *Entre communautés et mobilité. Actes du colloque Médias 09, Marseille*, Presses Universitaires de Marseille, pp. 95–112, 2010.

[GRA 10b] GRANJON F., DENOUËL J., "Exposition de soi et reconnaissance des singularités subjectives sur les sites de réseaux sociaux", *Sociologie*, no.1, vol. 1, pp. 25–43, 2010.

[HIG 87] HIGGINS E.T., "Self-discrepancy: a theory relating self and affect", *Psychological Review*, vol. 94, pp. 319–340, 1987.

[HIR 80] HIRSCHLEIFER J., "Privacy: its origin, function, and future", *Journal of Legal Studies*, vol. 9, no. 4, pp. 649–664, 1980.

[HON 07] HONNETH A., *La lutte pour la reconnaissance*, Paris, Cerf, 2007.

[HUI 06] HUI K.L., PNG I.P.L., "The economics of privacy", in HENDERSHOTT T., (ed.), *Economics and Information Systems*, Handbooks in Information Systems, vol. 1, Elsevier, 2006.

[IDE 13] IDENTITY FRAUD REPORT 2013: Data Breaches Becoming a Treasure Trove for Fraudsters, Javelin Strategy & Research, February 2013.

[ISO 11] International Standard, Information Technology– Security techniques – Privacy framework, ISO/IEC29100, 1st ed., December 2011.

[IT 10] AURAY N., LEVALLOIS-BARTH C., CUPPENS F., *et al.*, "Identités numériques", *Les cahiers de veille de la Fondation Télécom*, April 2010.

[JAU 11] JAURREGUIBERRY F., PROULX S., *Usages et enjeux des technologies de communication*, Edition Eres, Toulouse, 2011.

[JOU 00] JOUËT J., "Retour critique sur la sociologie des usages", *Réseaux*, vol. 18, no. 100, pp. 487–522, 2000.

[JOU 11] JOUËT J., "Des études sur la télématique aux Internet studies", in DENOUËL J., GRANJON F., (eds.), *Communiquer à l'ère numérique. Regards croisés sur la sociologie des usages*, Paris, coll. Sciences sociales, Presses de l'école des Mines, pp. 44–90, 2011.

[JUT 13] JUTLAND F., *La métamorphose numerique: vers une société de la connaissance et de la coopération*, Edition Alternatives, collection Manifesto, April 2013.

[KAF 10] KAFAI Y.B., "World of Whyville: an introduction to tween virtual life", *Games and Culture 2010*, vol. 5, p. 3, 2010.

[KAP 10] KAPLAN D., *Informatique, libertés, identités*, FYP Editions, coll. La fabrique des possibles, 2010.

[KAU 04] KAUFMANN J-C., *L'invention de soi. Une théorie de l'identité*, Armand Colin, 2004.

[KHE 13] KHERIAN C., "Identité numérique: créer la confiance pour libérer les usages", *Les Focus Solucom*, October 2013. Available at: http://www.solucom.fr/wp-content/uploads/2013/10/focus_identite_numerique_solucom.pdf.

[KIR 04] KIRMAN A., "The structure of economic interaction: individual and collective rationality", in BOURGINE P., NADAL J.-P., (eds.), *Cognitive Economics: An Interdisciplinary Approach*, Springer-Verlag, 2004.

[KIR 06a] KIRMAN A., TESCHL M., "Searching for identity in the capability space", *Journal of Economic Methodology*, vol. 13, no. 3, pp. 299–325, 2006.

[KIR 06b] KIRMAN A., HORST U., TESCHL M., Changing Identity: The emergence of social groups, Working paper GREQAM, 2006.

[LAU 11] LAURENT M., "Introduction à la Sécurité des Systèmes d'Information", *Techniques de l'Ingénieur*, Sécurité des systèmes d'information, 2011.

[LIV 08] LIVINGSTONE S., "Taking risky opportunities in youthful content creation: teenagers' use of social networking sites for intimacy, privacy and self expression", *New Media and Society*, vol. 10, no. 3, pp. 393–411, 2008.

[LUM 10] LUMEAU M., MASCLET D., PENARD T., "Les conséquences de la manipulation de la réputation dans les systèmes d'évaluation en ligne", *Revue Economique*, vol. 61, no. 6, pp. 1123–1133, 2010.

[MCL 11] MCLEOD P.L., LESHED G., "As long as they don't know where I live: information disclosure strategies for managing identity in second life", *Reinventing Ourselves: Contemporary Concepts of Identity in Virtual Worlds*, Springer, 2011.

[MER 09] MERZEAU L., "Du signe à la trace: l'information sur mesure, 'Traçabilité et réseaux'", *Hermès*, no. 59, pp. 23–29, 2009.

[MIS 05] MISHRA P., MALER E., *et al.*, Conformance Requirements for the OASIS Security Assertion Markup Language (SAML) V2. 0, Language (SAML), vol. 2, 2005.

[OAS 14] Oasis consortium, http://www.oasis-open.org/, 2014.

[OAU 14] http://oauth.net/documentation/getting-started/, 2014.

[OLE 14] OLEJNIK L., CASTELLUCCIA C., JANC A., "On the uniqueness of web browsing history pattern", *Annals of Telecommunications,* Special issue on "Privacy-aware electronic society", vol. 69, nos. 1–2, 2014.

[OPE 14a] OPENAM Project, http://openam.forgerock.org/, 2014.

[OPE 14b] OPENID, http://openid.net/, 2014.

[OUA 10] OUANAIM M., HARROUD H., BERRADO A., *et al.*, "Dynamic user profiling approach for services discovery in mobile environments", *Proceedings of the 6th International Wireless Communications and Mobile Computing Conference (IWCMC'10) ACM,* New York, NY, 2010.

[P3P 14] P3P, *P3P: Platform for Privacy Preferences,* http://www.w3.org/TR/P3P11/, 2014.

[PAQ 13] PAQUIN C., U-Prove Technology Overview V1.1 (Revision 2), Microsoft, April 2013.

[PFI 10] PFITZMANN A., HANSEN M., A terminology for talking about privacy by data minimization: anonymity, unlinkability, undetectability, unobservability, pseudonymity, and identity management, August 2010. Available at http://dud.inf.tu-dresden.de/Anon_Terminology.shtml.

[ROC 10] ROCHELANDET R., *Économie des données personnelles et de la vie privée,* La Découverte, coll. Repères, Paris, 2010.

[SEN 02] SEN A., *Rationality and Freedom,* Harvard Belknap Press, 2002.

[SHI 14] SHIBBOLETH, http://shibboleth.net/, 2014.

[SOA 14] SOAP, http://www.w3.org/TR/soap/, 2014.

[TIS 11] TISSERON S., "Intimité et extimité", *Communications,* no. 88, pp. 83–92, 2011.

[TOM 08] TOMA C., HANCOCK J., ELLISON N., "Separating fact from fiction: an examination of deceptive self-presentation in online dating profiles", *Personality and Social Psychology Bulletin,* vol. 34, pp. 1023–1036, 2008.

[TUC 12] TUCKER C.E., "The economics of advertising and privacy", *International Journal of Industrial Organization,* EARIE Conference Papers and Proceedings, vol. 30, no. 3, pp. 326–329, 2012.

[TUR 06] TURKLE S., "Tethering", in CAROLINE A.J., (ed.), *Sensorium: Embodied Experience, Technology, and Contemporary Art*, Cambridge, MA: List Visual Art Center and MIT Press, 2006.

[TUR 10] TURNER M.A., VARGHESE R., *The Economic Consequences of Consumer Credit Information Sharing: Efficiency, Inclusion, and Privacy*, Mimeo, 2010.

[TWE 09] TWENGE J.M., CAMPBELL K.W., *The Narcissism Epidemic, Living in the Age of Entitlement*, Free Press, New York, 2009.

[W3C 14] W3C consortium, http://www.w3.org, 2014.

[WEB 14] WebID Specifications, https://dvcs.w3.org/hg/WebID/raw-file/tip/spec/index.html, 2014.

[WP 14] WORKING PARTY 29, Opinion 05/2014 on Anonymisation Techniques onto the web, WP216, 10.04.2014.

[WS 07] *Understanding WS-Federation*, IBM and Microsoft, 28 May 2007.

[ZEN 06] ZENATI-CASTAING F., REVET T., *Manuel de droit des personnes*, PUF, no. 33, 2006.

The Management of Identity by the Federation

2.1. The fundamentals of the identity federation

2.1.1. *Identity: a set of personal attributes*

A user's identity can be defined as a set of personal attributes. For example, a forename, surname and date of birth are personal attributes. These attributes can be used to define an identity.

Each application defines its users' identities according to its needs (see Figure 2.1).

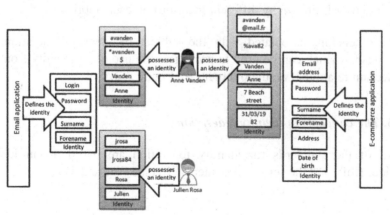

Figure 2.1. *Identity: a set of personal attributes*

Chapter written by Augustin DE MISCAULT.

For example, an email application defines an identity via a login, password, a surname and a forename. An e-commerce application can define an identity via an email address, a password, a surname, a forename, an address and a date of birth.

The user possesses an identity on each application. For example, in Figure 2.1, Anne Vanden has an identity on the email application (avanden; *avanden$; Vanden; Anne) and an identity on the e-commerce application (avanden@mail.com; %ava82; Vanden; Anne; 7 Beach Road; 31/03/1982).

From a technical perspective, a user account on an application can be considered equivalent. A user, then, possesses as many identities as they have accounts.

The user's identifier is an identity attribute. The identifier has to be unique. The identifier allows the application to find one user out of all of the application's users. For example the login (avanden) is the identifier for Anne Vanden on the email application, and the email address (avanden@mail.com) is the identifier for Anne Vanden on the e-commerce application.

2.1.2. *Identity federation: propagating identity*

Identity federation allows a set of applications to refer to a single user, while the user is known by different identities on each application.

By extension, associated with the subject of identity federation, are mechanisms which can be used to propagate the use of an identity from one application to another on the Internet (see Figure 2.2).

2.1.3. *The concepts of identity federation*

All of the standards for identity federation are based on an identity provider (IdP) and the service providers (SP) (see Figure 2.3).

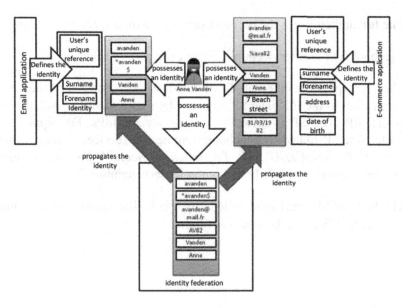

Figure 2.2. *Identity federation: propagating identity*

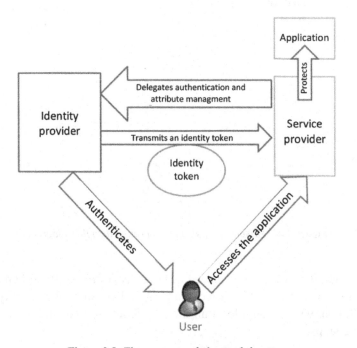

Figure 2.3. *The concepts of identity federation*

The IdP authenticates the user and propagates their identity.

Facebook and monservicepublic.fr are examples of IdPs.

The SP protects the application. The SP delegates the user's authentication to the IdP. The SP requests the user's identifier and attributes from the IdP. The SP is linked to one or several IdPs. Foursquare is an example of a SP linked to Facebook. Online tax services, *Chèque Emploi Service Universel (CESU)* and *Prestation d'Accueil du Jeune Enfant (PAJE)* are examples of SPs linked with monservicepublic.fr.

The IdP and SPs exchange an identity token. The identity token contains the user's identifier and the user's attributes.

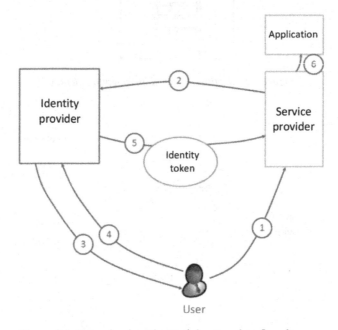

Figure 2.4. *Example of an identity federation data flow diagram*

Each identity federation standard defines the format of the token and the request-response protocol in order to obtain and consume the identity token. Figure 2.4 shows an example of an identity federation mechanisms with the following steps:

1) The user seeks to access an application.

2) The SP intercepts the request. The user is not yet authenticated on the SP. The SP requests that the IdP authenticate the user and propagate the user's identity.

3) The user is not yet authenticated on the IdP, which requests that the user authenticates.

4) The user authenticates.

5) The IdP validates the authentication and transmits the identity token containing the user's identifier and attributes to the SP.

6) The SP validates the identity token and extracts the identifier and attributes. The user accesses the application.

2.1.4. *Trust: a prerequisite for identity federation*

Identity federation is based on a relationship of trust between the IdP, the SPs and the user:

– the SPs trust the IdP in his ability to authenticate the user and propagate reliable and up-to-date identity attributes. For example, if the IdP transmits the user's address and telephone number, the SPs expect this information to be accurate and up-to-date;

– the IdP trusts the SPs with regard to what they decide to do with the user's identity. For example, the IdP ensures that the SPs do not send personal information to third parties without the user's consent;

– the user trusts the IdP's ability to protect their identity and privacy. These relationships of trust are conceptualized by the circle of trust (see Figure 2.5);

– the circle of trust is centred on an IdP. The IdP propagates the user's identity to the SPs;

– the circle of trust may have a governance structure. The IdP and the SPs within a circle of trust are committed to complying with a set of rules and procedures which dictate the way in which exchanges must be carried out;

– the circle of trust can help to contractualize trust.

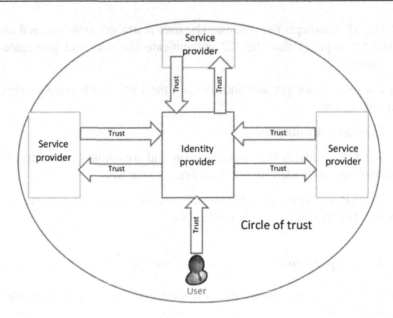

Figure 2.5. *Circle of trust*

2.1.5. *Stakeholders in identity federation*

Identity federation involves several stakeholders:

The *corporate user* seeks to access computer applications.

The accessed applications are for example the Enterprise Resource Planning (ERP)[1] or an Electronic Document Management (EDM)[2]. Applications are inside the company or outside the company.

The user's identity is propagated to the applications by the IdP's identity federation.

---

1 ERP stands for Enterprise Resource Planning. ERP is a piece of software which can be used to manage all of the company's operational processes, such as, for example, the management of human resources, accounting, finances, but also sale, distribution, procurement and e-commerce.
2 EDM stands for Document Management System. An EDM is a piece of software which can be used to manage document content.

The *home user* seeks to access applications on the Internet.

The home user has a user account on the application that he/she wishes to access. The user accounts are for example mail accounts, or accounts on e-commerce sites or public administration sites.

The home user is also called the internet user.

The *IT manager* is responsible for the company's computer system. The IT manager provides solutions to the company's computer problems.

The IT manager usually makes the decision to implement an IdP within the company.

The *application manager* is responsible for the application that the user seeks to use. The application manager is responsible for the administration and development of the application.

The application manager decides whether to link the application to an IdP or not.

The *Chief Information Security Officer* (CISO)[3] is responsible for the company's computer security.

The CISO ensures the security of exchanges. With regard to identity federation, it ensures that the user's identity is protected. For example, the attributes of the identity must not be seen by a malevolent and the identity must not be usurped by a malevolent.

2.2. The technical limitations of solutions before identity federation

Identity federation enables several technical limitations to be overcome. Namely:

– using WebSingle Sign-On (WebSSO) and propagating the identity beyond a Domain Name Service (DNS) domain;

– propagating the user's identity during the use of web services.

---

3 CISO: Chief Information Security Officer.

2.2.1. *Using WebSSO beyond a DNS domain*

2.2.1.1. *The advantages of WebSSO: ergonomics, security and administration*

If a user seeks to access several applications, typically, each application requires authentication.

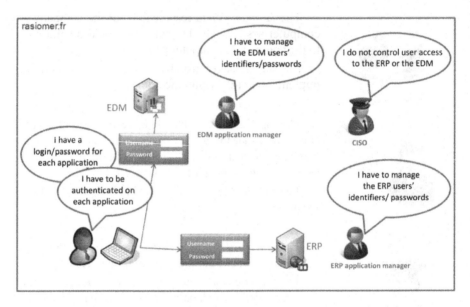

Figure 2.6. *Accessing applications without WebSSO*

This set-up has several drawbacks (see Figure 2.6):

– the user must be authenticated on each of the applications;

– the user has a password for each application;

– the application manager has to manage the users' login/passwords. They must, for example, define a password policy, manage the resetting of passwords in case of loss, and ensure that the password is protected;

– the CISO cannot centralize access management. The application managers are the only ones in charge of access management.

WebSSO is set up within companies to remedy these drawbacks (see Figure 2.7).

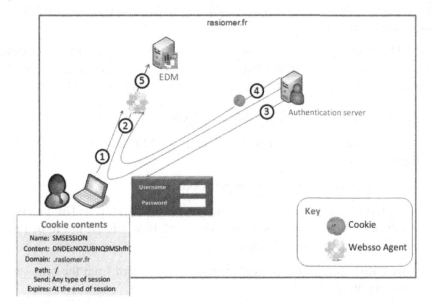

Figure 2.7. *WebSSO data flow diagram*

The steps of WebSSO are as follows (see Figure 2.7):

1) The user seeks to access an application. A WebSSO agent, in front of Web application, intercepts the request.

2) The WebSSO agent redirects the user toward the authentication server.

3) The user authenticates on the authentication server which places a session cookie[4] on the user's browser. The cookie contains the user's identifier (if the user already has a valid session cookie for the authentication server, then this step is skipped).

---

4 A cookie is a file stored on the user's hard drive. The cookie allows the application to recognize the user from one webpage to another. For example the applications use the cookies to store user preferences.

Cookies are part of the HTTP protocol specifications. HTTP requests and responses contain headers. The cookies are sent in an HTTP header.

The main information transmitted by a cookie is: the name of the cookie, the content of the cookie (for example the user's encrypted identifier), the cookie's domain name, the path to the directory where the cookie is stored, and the cookie's expiry date.

4) The authentication server redirects the user to the application. The WebSSO agent, in front of Web application, intercepts the request, verifies the cookie's validity (signature and expiration date) and retrieves the user's connection identifier.

5) The WebSSO agent transmits the user's identifier to the application. The user accesses the application. The user has been authenticated on the application without having to enter their username and password.

There are many benefits in using a WebSSO:

– the user has a single password, which is used to authenticate themselves on the authentication server;

– the user only has to enter their password once;

– the CISO can implement a company password policy. The password policy defines the composition of the password, how often it has to be reset, the means to reset in case of loss, etc;

– the CISO can limit the circulation of the password from the browser to the authentication server;

– the CISO can extend the authentication methods to smart card or One Time Password (OTP)[5] authentication, etc;

– the application manager no longer needs to manage the user's connection identifiers.

2.2.1.2. The limits of WebSSO: the DNS domain

The WebSSO solutions propagate the user's identity via a cookie.

The HyperText Transfer Protocol (HTTP) protocol limits the cookie to a DNS domain. The user cannot use WebSSO to access applications outside of the DNS domain, for example applications in Software as a Service (SaaS) mode (see Box 2.1) or applications hosted by partners (see Figure 2.8).

---

5 OTP: One Time Password is a security mechanism that requires a new password for each user authentication. The password is either generated by a pocket calculator that the user possesses, or sent to the user via an SMS or an email.

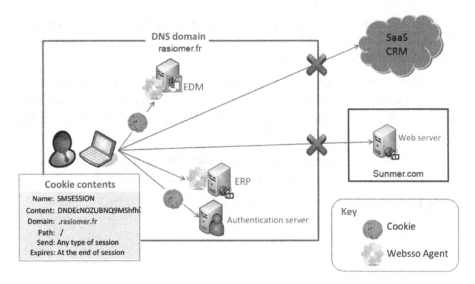

Figure 2.8. *Using WebSSO on the Internet*

The application in SaaS mode is used by an operator. The operator commercializes the use of the application to several companies. The application is standardized to facilitate its maintenance by the operator. There is only one version of the application that runs for any companies requesting use.

The operator relies on a multi-tenant architecture in which the application is shared by several clients. This facilitates the tasks related to operations such ashigh availability management, version upgrades and backups.

Box 2.1. *Description of an application in SaaS (Software as a Service) mode*

2.2.1.3. *Workarounds before the discovery of identity federation*

2.2.1.3.1. The cross-domain cookie

Propagation of a cookie on different DNS domains can be achieved due to a mechanism which is based on several cookies. This is what we call the cross-domain cookie.

Figure 2.9 shows how the cross-domain cookie works:

1) The user is authenticated in the domain Rasiomer.fr and has a valid session cookie in the domain Rasiomer.fr. The user seeks to access a Web application in the domain Sunmer.com.

2) A WebSSO agent, in front of the Web application Sunmer.com, intercepts the request. The WebSSO agent redirects the user toward the authentication server of the domain Rasiomer.com.

3) The authentication server authenticates the user due to their Rasiomer.fr cookie. The Rasiomer.fr authentication server redirects the user toward the WebSSo agent and transmits the authentication information in the HTTP request.

4) The WebSSO agent validates the user authentication and places a session cookie on the user's browser in the Sunmer.com domain.

5) The user accesses the web application.

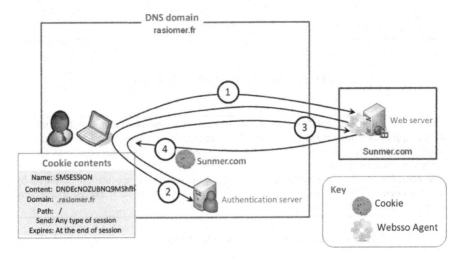

Figure 2.9. *The cross-domain cookie*

The cross-domain cookie has several drawbacks:

– the mechanism is not standardized and assumes that the authentication server and the WebSSO agent are compatible. In practice they are often from the same publisher;

– poorly implemented, the cross-domain cookie poses synchronization problems for users logging off. When the user logs off the authentication server, all his sessions setup with the applications must be informed of the disconnection and terminate the sessions.

2.2.1.3.2. Extension of WebSSO through dedicated line

A second solution to propagate the user's identity on the Internet is available by installation of a WebSSO agent in front of the partner's application (see Figure 2.10).

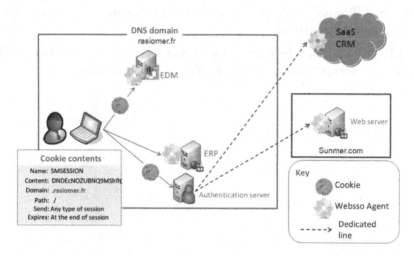

Figure 2.10. *Solution with a WebSSO agent hosted by the partner and a dedicated line*

A dedicated line[6] connects the WebSSO agent to the authentication server in order to transmit the cookie. The partner's installation of the WebSSO agent raises support issues. As for renting a dedicated line, this incurs costs.

2.2.1.4. *Identity federation: WebSSO beyond a DNS domain*

SAML is an Identity federation standard that provides an appropriate response for WebSSO beyond a DNS domain.

Identity federation requires the company to install an IdP and the partner to install a SP (see Figure 2.11).

The application access process is as follows:

1) The user seeks to access the application; the SP intercepts the request.

---

6 A dedicated line is a dedicated physical line. The dedicated line is separated from the public network, so the data does not flow on the Internet. The main advantages of dedicated lines are the guaranteed bandwidth and the security.

2) The user has no valid session on the SP; the SP redirects the user towards the IdP.

3) If the user has no valid session on the IdP, then the idP authenticates the user.

4) The IdP sends an identity token to the SP; the identity token contains the user's identifier and attributes.

5) The SP validates the identity token, and transmits the identifier and the attributes to the application. The user accesses the application.

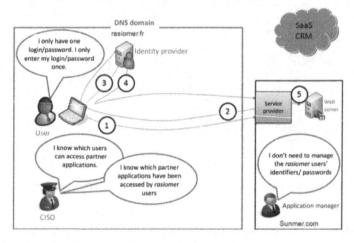

Figure 2.11. *Solution with identity federation*

The identity token can be embedded for example either in the body of the HTTP messages, or in the body of the Simple Object Access Protocol (SOAP) messages (see Box 2.2), or in the redirection Uniform Resource Locators (URLs).

SOAP is used to transmit messages between remote objects which means that it authorizes an object to invoke methods of objects physically situated on another server. The transfer is most often carried out with the help of the HTTP.

The SOAP protocol consists of two parts:

– an envelope, containing information on the message itself in order to allow for its delivery and processing;

– a data model defining the format of the message, that is to say the information to be transmitted.

Box 2.2. *Description of SOAP protocol*

Identity federation is not therefore limited to a DNS domain:

– identity federation does not require a dedicated line;

– identity federation is standardized and its use allows for independence with regard to publishers.

Identity federation retains the advantages in terms of ergonomics, security and WebSSO administration (see Figure 2.11) and extends them beyond the DNS domain.

Identity federation allows for the use of WebSSO and the propogation of the user's identity beyond the DNS domain.

2.2.2. *Propagating user identity for the needs of web-services*

2.2.2.1. *The limits of web services: the need for a user account*

From an architecture perspective, services are the building blocks of the system and make a particular service which is *a priori* mutualized.

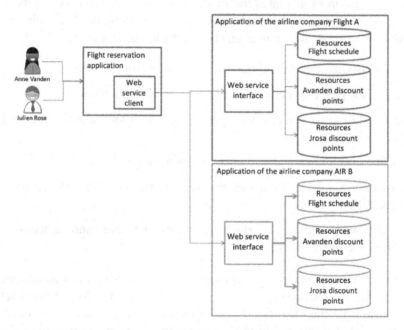

Figure 2.12. *Diagram of an SOA*

A resource posseses a web service interface (see Figure 2.12). The web service interface is invoked by a web service client, which is itself used by another user via an application.

For example in Figure 2.12, an application allows users to reserve flights on several airline companies.

Each airline company has an application which can be used to consult schedules and to benefit from a discount depending on the number of points accumulated. The flight schedules and the points accumulated by each user can be accessed via a web service interface.

The flight reservation application has a web service client. The web service client uses the airline company's web service interface in order to access the airline company's resources.

Some of the resources used by the web service client are public. For example, the flight schedules.

Other resources are intended to be consumed via the user account, for example checking points accumulated per hour of flight. The web service client has to propagate the user identity to the targeted resources.

2.2.2.2. *Workarounds before the discovery of identity federation*

2.2.2.2.1. Propagating the identifier via an *ad hoc* architecture

One solution consists of propagating the identifier the web services (see Figure 2.13):

1) The user authenticates themselves on the application.

2) The web service client uses the web service interface and transmits the user identifier.

3) The web service interface identifies the user and transmits the resources relating to the user.

However, the manner of transmitting the identifier is not standardized. The application managers of each service must then develop an architecture for transmitting the identifier. Each application manager must then have the means to develop this architecture. The architecture that is implemented may turn out to be difficult to develop.

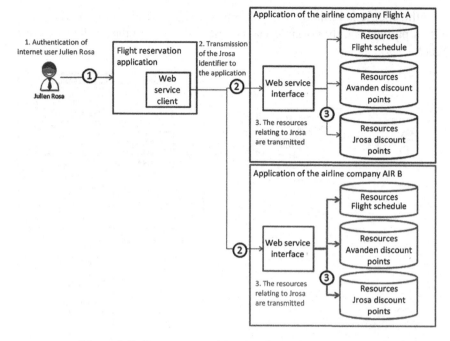

Figure 2.13. *Transmission of the identifier to the web services*

2.2.2.2.2. Propagating the cookie when using web services

Another solution relies on cookie propagation, as described in Figure 2.13:

1) The user authenticates themselves on the application. The application deposits a cookie on the user's browser.

2) The web service client uses the web service interface and transmits the user cookie.

3) The web service interface extracts the user's identifier from the cookie and transmits the resources relating to the user.

This cookie-based solution has several drawbacks:

– an agent must be installed in front of web service interfaces;

– the cookie is limited to a DNS domain. The use of a hosted web service with a partner is only possible via a dedicated line and the deployment of an agent.

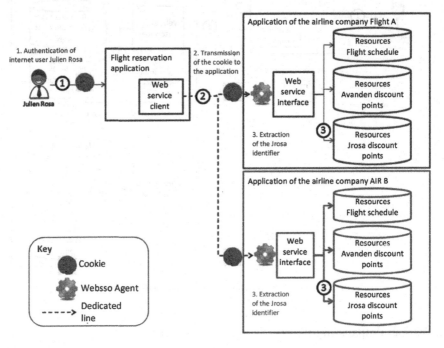

Figure 2.14. *Propagating the user's identity via a cookie to web services*

2.2.2.3. *Identity federation: the propagation of the identity for web services*

Identity federation offers standards such as OAuth and WS-*, which propose web service architectures in order to access resources on behalf of a user.

OAuth defines the means for authorizing access to private resources in a REST architecture.

WS-* defines how to propagate the user's identity in a SOAP architecture (see Figure 2.15):

1) The user authenticates themselves on a portal's Human Machine Interface (HMI). The portal places a cookie on the user's browser in order to

maintain the session on the portal. While the session is valid, the user does not need to authenticate again. Between the user and the portal, the authentication information is transmitted in the HTTP header.

2) The portal embeds the cookie in a SOAP header. The SOAP header is embedded in the HTTP load. The portal's web service client propagates the cookie in a SOAP header to the Security Token Service (STS). The STS normalizes the received authentication format; for example, it converts the cookie into a Security Assertion Markup Language (SAML) token. The SAML token contains the user's identity, that is to say an identifier and attributes.

3) The web service client transmits the user's identity to the web service interface via the SAML token.

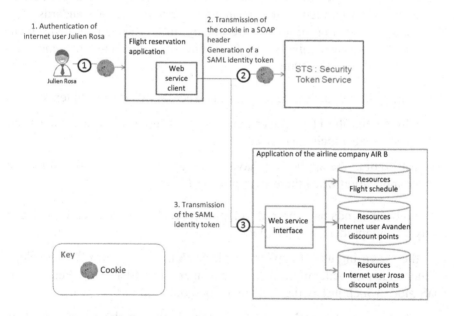

Figure 2.15. *The user's identity is propagated to web services*

Identity federation can be used to propagate the user's identity to web services.

– identity federation can be used to eliminate constraints with regard to design, and flexible evolution of *ad-hoc* architectures;

– identity federation allows the identity to be transmitted beyond a DNS domain.

2.3. The use value of identity federation

2.3.1. *Identity federation catalysts*

The first identity federation standards appeared in the early 2000s: Liberty Alliance has been launched in 2001, OASIS[7] standardizes SAML 1.0 in 2002 and WS-Federation in 2003, the OpenID Foundation launches OpenID in 2005 and the Internet Engineering Task Force (IETF)[8] standardizes OAuth1.0 in 2007.

The adoption of identity federation by the market and the first real uses of it have not been correctly carried out with the approval of standards. The first identity federation projects were mainly pilot projects and government projects. Monservicepublic.fr has been one of the precursors, since the service was launched in 2006.

The adoption of identity federation came across two main problems:

– why should the IT manager have to invest in an IdP when there were not any SPs with which to connect?

– why should the application have to add an identity federation interface to their application when there were not any IdPs?

Two basic trends have been developing since the 2010s and are used as a catalyst to adopt identity federation:

– the increasing use of applications in SaaS mode (see Box 2.1) develops business identity federation. The IT manager finds SPs in applications in SaaS mode which justify the implementation of an IdP;

– the success of social networks is contributing to the development of identity federation in the public sphere. The application managers see social networks as IdPs, which justifies the addition of an identity federation interface.

---

7 OASIS: Organization for the Advancement of Structured Information Standards. OASIS is a standardization body.
8 IETF: Internet Engineering Task Force. The IETF is a standardization body.

2.3.2. *Use cases for identity federation*

Use cases for identity federation can be found in the business sphere and the public sphere (see Figure 2.16).

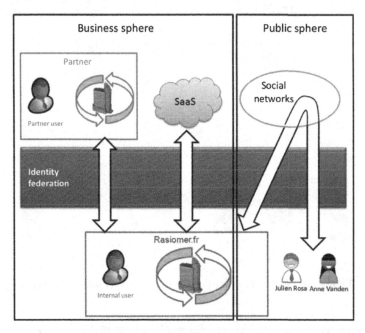

Figure 2.16. *Use cases for identity federation*

Identity federation is used in companies to facilitate and secure access of:

– users to applications in SaaS mode (see Box 2.1);

– partner users to company applications.

In the public sphere, for example, identity federation allows the user of a social network to subscribe and quickly access new e-commerce applications.

2.3.3. *Accessing applications in SaaS mode*

2.3.3.1. *Accessing applications in SaaS mode without identity federation*

Currently companies frequently use applications in SaaS mode (see Box 2.1).

Companies can be brought to consume several applications in SaaS mode, such as CRM[9], ERP, HR applications, email, etc.

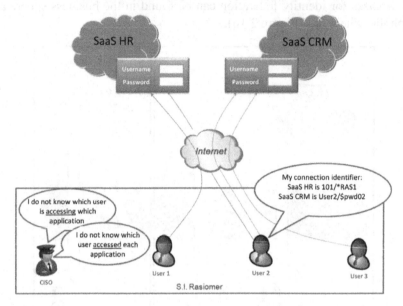

Figure 2.17. *Use case: accessing a SaaS application without federation*

A company that consumes several applications in SaaS mode restricts its users to have one connection identifier per application in SaaS mode (see Figure 2.17).

The user must:

– authenticate on each of the applications in SaaS mode;

– remember each of their connection identifiers.

Access control to applications in SaaS mode is carried out locally by the application, access control is not centralized in the company.

9 CRM stands for Customer Relationship Management and is a set of tools and techniques to collect, process and analyze the information relating to current and prospective customers, in order to retain them by offering the best service. In terms of IT applications, the associated package software enables direct interactions with the customer, either for sale, marketing or service activities. It is often known under the term "front-office", which is defined in opposition to "back-office" tools corresponding to ERP software.

The CISO does not know:

– which user is accessing the SaaS application;

– or which user has accessed the SaaS application.

The application manager must be notified of the transference or departure of a user (see Figure 2.18).

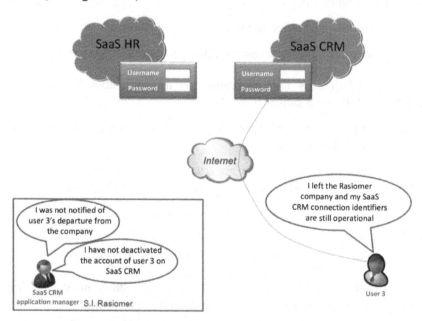

Figure 2.18. *Use case: departure out of company and access to a SaaS application without federation*

The application manager must ensure that the user account has been deactivated on the SaaS application; otherwise the user will still be able to access the SaaS application even though they have left the company.

2.3.3.2. *Prerequisites for using identity federation*

Identity federation requires the following prerequisites:

– the application in SaaS mode must support an identity federation protocol;

– the IT manager must implement an IdP;

– the application manager and the IT manager must link the IdP and the SP of the SaaS. They exchange URLs, the signature and encryption certificates.

The user must meet the following prerequisites in order to access the application in SaaS mode:

– the user must be authorized to use the application;

– the user must have an account on the application in SaaS mode.

A standard process for registration on an application in SaaS mode includes the following steps:

1) The application manager implements a workflow to request authorization to the application.

2) The user needs to use the application in SaaS mode. He makes an authorization request and obtains the right to use the application.

3) User authorization is stored in the identity and company access repository.

4) The user account is created on the application in SaaS mode.

The CISO can audit the identity and access repository in order to know which user is authorized to use which application in SaaS mode.

2.3.3.3. *Accessing applications in SaaS mode with identity federation*

2.3.3.3.1. The user is not yet authenticated and accesses the SaaS

Identity federation involves the following steps in order to access the first application in SaaS mode (see Figure 2.19):

1) The user seeks to access an application in SaaS mode.

2) The SP redirects the user towards the IdP.

3) The IdP requests that the user authenticate.

4) The user enters their connection identifiers: U8834 / *passWD.

5) The IdP authenticates the user and verifies that the user is authorized to use the requested SaaS application. The IdP sends the user's identifier in an identity token to the SP.

6) The SP verifies the validity of the token and transmits the user's identifier to the application.

7) The user accesses the application.

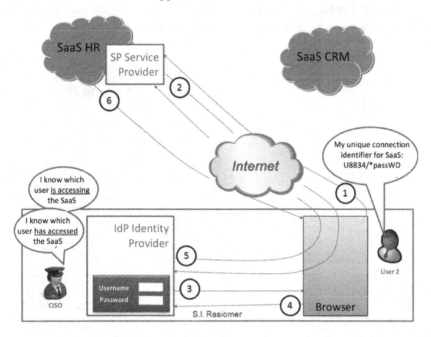

Figure 2.19. *Use case: access to the first SaaS application via identity federation*

The CISO can analyze the log files on the IdP to know which user has accessed which application in SaaS mode.

2.3.3.3.2. The user is already authenticated and accesses the SaaS

Identity federation allows a user already authenticated by the IdP to access other SaaS applications without having to authenticate again (see Figure 2.20).

The steps are as follows:

1) The user seeks to access an application in SaaS mode.

2) The SP redirects the user toward the IdP.

3) The user is already authenticated on the IdP. The IdP verifies that the user is authorized to use the requested SaaS application. The IdP sends the user's identifier in an identity token to the SP.

4) The SP verifies the token's validity and transmits the user's identifier to the application. The user accesses the application.

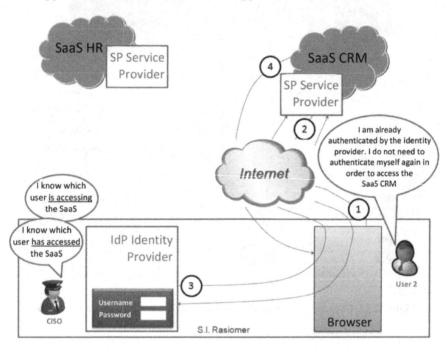

Figure 2.20. *Use case: access to a second SaaS via identity federation*

2.3.3.3.3. The user leaves the company

If the user leaves the company, the IT manager deactivates the user account in the identity and access repository. The user can no longer be authenticated on the IdP.

The user can no longer use the SaaS application, even if the application manager does not deactivate the user account on the SaaS application (see Figure 2.21).

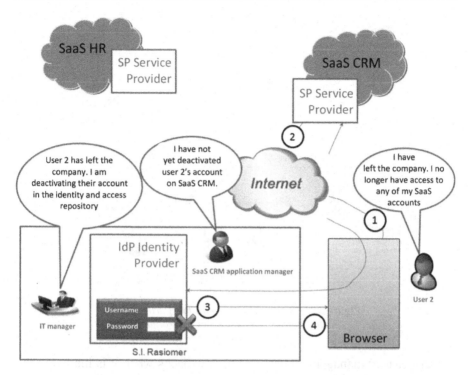

Figure 2.21. *Use case: departure from of the company and access to a SaaS application via federation*

2.3.4. *Exchange between trading partners and subsidiaries*

2.3.4.1. *Granting access to its partners without identity federation*

Every company is led to trade with partners or subsidiaries.

The partner users need to access certain company applications. Conversely, internal users, whether they are employees or contractors, need to access the applications of partner companies (see Figure 2.22).

The IT manager must adapt their company's information system to allow exchanges with partners and subsidiaries. The IT manager and the application managers implement the necessary means to enable partners to access the company's applications.

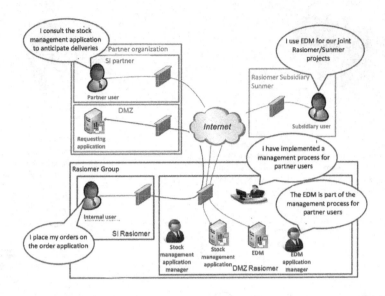

Figure 2.22. *Exchange between trading partners and subsidiaries without identity federation*

Partner user management has several drawbacks when it is limited to the creation and deletion of an account:

– the IT manager must provide mechanisms in case of loss and resetting of connection identifiers;

– the IT manager must be notified immediately of the partner user's departure in order to delete the account. A user account which remains active after the user has left is a security risk; the user may, for example, access the resources through their account from their new employer;

– The user has as many connection identifiers as it has partners.

2.3.4.2. *Granting access to partners via identity federation*

Identity federation addresses the drawbacks mentioned in Figure 2.23, namely:

1) The partner user seeks to access the company's application.

2) The SP intercepts the access request and redirects the user toward their IdP.

3) The IdP sends the partner user's identifier in an identity token to the SP.

4) The SP verifies the token's validity and transmits the user's identifier to the application.

5) The user accesses the application.

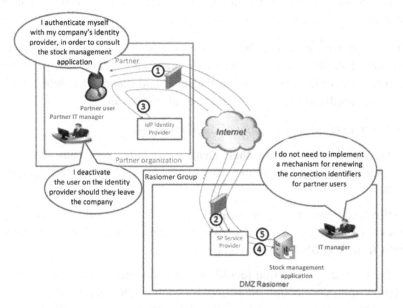

Figure 2.23. *Exchange between trading partners via identity federation*

The partner user does not authenticate on the application. When identity federation has been implemented, the partner user authenticates himself on his IdP:

– the user does not have a connection identifier to access their partner applications;

– the IT mananger does not have to provide a mechanism to reset connection identifiers;

– the partner IT manager deactivates the user account when the user leaves the company;

– the partner user can no longer authenticate and can no longer access federated applications;

– the partner IT manager does not need to immediately inform their counterpart of the user's departure.

2.3.5. *Public sphere: register with and access an application in three steps*

2.3.5.1. *On average internet users in France have 12 accounts*

The barometer of digital trust for the French shows that in 2011 users in France possessed an average of 12 accounts.

Each application stores the connection identifiers (login/password) and the user's identity attributes (forename, surname, email address, address, etc). The user's identities are often the same and managed independently on each of the applications. This is what we call silo mode.

Silo mode presents a number of disadvantages:

– the user has to re-enter their identity attributes each time they register on a new application and may be tempted to abandon the registration process;

– the user has to authenticate themself in order to access each application, which makes surf sessions unergonomic. The user does not benefit from WebSSO mechanisms;

– the user has connection identifiers for each application. The user has to remember their connection identifiers for each of the applications. This often means that many users use the same connection identifiers on each application. This behavior poses a security risk, since if a connection identifier for an application is compromised, it is then easy to access all the other applications on which the user has an account.

2.3.5.2. *Internet browsers as a solution for storing identities?*

Internet browsers provide solutions for storing logins and passwords.

However, Internet browser storage of logins and passwords has several drawbacks:

– the user must first enter their login and password on each browser that is being used. For example, a user who accesses their applications from their PC and smartphone must enter their login and password on their PC's browser(s) and on their smartphone's browser.

– The logins and passwords are stored in plain-text by the Internet browser. Following an attack on the browser, there is a risk that the logins and passwords will be divulged. Storage of logins and passwords by the Internet browsers is not secure.

2.3.5.3. *Registering on an application via identity federation*

With identity federation, the steps for registration on an application are as follows:

1) The user is registered in an IdP, for example Facebook. The user's identity attributes are stored on the IdP (surname, forename, email address, and date of birth).

2) The user registers on a SP linked to the IdP, for example Foursquare. The SP requests that the user register with their IdP, for example via the "Sign up with Facebook" button (see Figure 2.24). The SP requests the user's identifier and identity attributes from the IdP.

Figure 2.24. *A user registers on a new application, and uses identity federation (Step 2)*

3) The IdP authenticates the user, if they have not been authenticated. The IdP requests the user's consent, in order to authorize the SP to access identity information (see Figure 2.25). The user gives their authorization.

4) The IdP transmits the identity token to the SP. The identity token contains the identifier and the user's identity attributes.

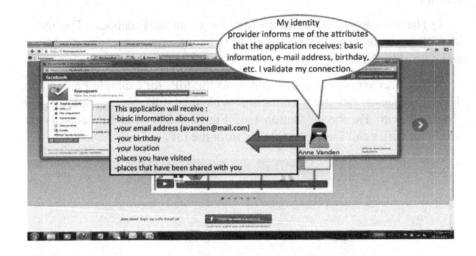

Figure 2.25. *The user registers on a new application, and uses identity federation (Step 3)*

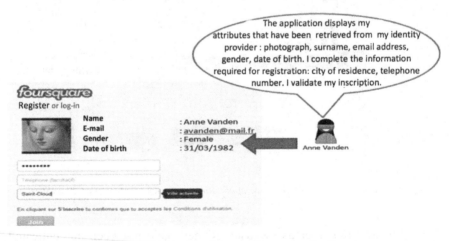

Figure 2.26. *A user registers on the new application and uses identity federation (Step 5)*

5) The SP validates the identity token, the application autofills the registration form with the user's identity attributes. The user enters the information specific to the application (see Figure 2.26)

6) The user is registered on the application.

Identity federation limits the user's contribution as little as possible when they register on a new application: the user authorizes propagation of their identity with the SP, and enters additional information required for registration.

2.3.5.4. Accessing an application via identity federation

With identity federation the steps for accessing an application are as follows:

1) The user is authenticated by their IdP.

2) The user wants to access an application that they linked to their account by the IdP. The user selects the authentication via their IdP.

For example the user wants to access Foursquare, and is already authenticated on Facebook. They select the Facebook connection button on Foursquare (see Figure 2.27).

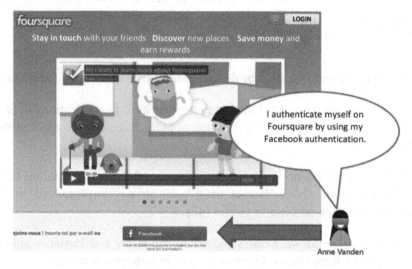

Figure 2.27. *A user accesses an application via identity federation*

Figure 2.28. *A user accesses an application* via *identity federation*

3) The SP requests user authentication from the IdP. The IdP transmits the user's identifier. The user accesses the application (see Figure 2.28).

In summary, the user only needed to select authentication via their identity user to access the application. The user did not enter a connection identifier and benefits from SSO.

2.4. SAML 2.0 and OAuth 2.0: de facto standards of identity federation

Identity federation is used to propagate identities, to applications in SaaS mode (see Box 2.1), partner applications or public e-commerce applications, for example.

The choice of identity federation standard is often made according to the identity federation standards that have been already implemented by the SaaS operators, the partners or public IdPs.

SAML 2.0 is the *de facto* standard in the SaaS and business sphere. OAuth 2.0 is a leader in social networks and in smartphone access.

2.4.1. *SAML 2.0*

SAML 2.0 is a mature standard that was created in 2005 and maintained by OASIS.

SAML 2.0 was adopted by the market:

– the major publishers of Identity and Access Management (IAM)[10] solutions offers SAML 2.0 identity federation solutions including: CA, Oracle, Ping Identity, IBM, etc;

– applications in SaaS mode (see Box 2.1) offer SAML 2.0 interfaces, for example: Salesforces, HR Access, Google, etc.

SAML 2.0 is a modular standard. SAML 2.0 consists of a set of components that define how identity and SPs can exchange identities.

2.4.1.1. *Main components*

The main compenents of SAML 2.0 are:

– the identity provider (IdP): this manages user authentication and the propagation of user identity;

– the service provider (SP): this protects the application. It delegates user authentication to the IdP and requests user identity from the IdP. It transmits the user identity to the application;

– assertion: an assertion is an identity token.

2.4.1.2. *Specifications overview*

SAML can be broken down into several specifications:

– assertion specification describes the identity token. Assertions are expressed in Extensible Markup Language (XML)[11];

– the SAML protocol specification describes SAML messages. The messages, for example, can be used to:

---

10 IAM: Identity and Access Management is a security system which authorizes users to access company systems and information. It can be used to prevent unauthorized access to data and its misuse, which could harm the company, their partners or even their customers.

11 XML: eXtensible Markup Language. XML is a computer language. XML can be used to structure the data. XML facilitates the exchange of data between heterogeneous applications.

- request an assertion;

- delegate authentication;

- resolve an artifact. An artifact is a reference to an SAML assertion. The IdP generates an assertion, retains the assertion and transmits an artifact to the SP. The SP requests the assertion from the IdP and transmits the artifact to them. The IdP validates the artifact and transmits the assertion to the SP;

- Request a single logout which is synchronized between sessions. During the same session, the user accesses several applications via identity federation. The single logout allows the user to log out in one click from all of the sessions setup with applications.

SAML messages are expressed in XML:

– the SAML "bindings" specification. A binding defines how the SAML messages are transported via an underlying protocol. SAML defines as an underlying protocol:

- HTTP redirect, HTTP POST, HTTP URI;

- HTTP artifact;

- SOAP.

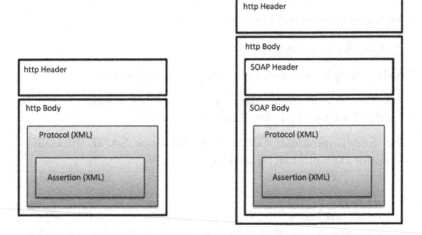

Figure 2.29. *Sending SAML meesages with HTTP and SOAP*

– the SAML bindings detail how the different SAML protocol messages are inserted in the HTTP and SOAP request bodies (see Figure 2.29);

– the SAML profiles specification. An SAML profile defines an SAML use case. The SAML profile defines the assertion, messages and bindings of the use case. The Web Browser SSO, IdP Discovery, and the Single Logout are examples of SAML profiles.

2.4.1.3. *Examples of the Web Browser SSO profile*

The "Web Browser SSO" profile can be implemented in several ways:

– with HTTP POST;

– with HTTP redirect and HTTP artifact.

2.4.1.3.1. WebSSO HTTP POST profile

The WebSSO HTTP POST profile is shown in the diagram of Figure 2.30.

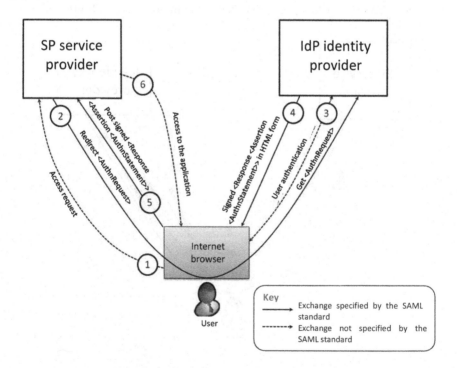

Figure 2.30. *WebSSO HTTP POST profile*

Figure 2.30 includes the following steps:

1) The user attempts to access an application. The SP intercepts the access request.

2) The SP redirects the user to the IdP with a authentication request.

3) If the user has not yet been authenticated in this web session, then follows a dialogue with the IdP to authenticate them. This dialogue is not specified by SAML.

4) The IdP sends a form to the web browser. The form contains the authentication assertion.

5) The internet browser sends the html form to the SP. The SP receives the authentication assertion contained in the html form.

6) The user accesses the application.

2.4.1.3.2. WebSSO artifact profile

The WebSSO artifact profile is shown via the diagram in Figure 2.31.

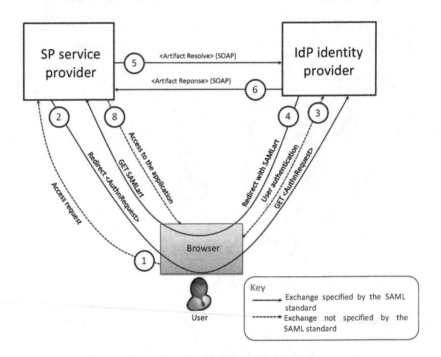

Figure 2.31. *WebSSO artifact profile*

Figure 2.31 presents the following steps:

1) The user attempts to access an application. The SP intercepts the access request.

2) The SP redirects the user toward the IdP with an authentication request.

3) If the user has still not been authenticated in this web session, then follows a dialogue with the IdP to authenticate them. This dialogue is not specified by SAML.

4) The IdP and SP redirects the user to the SP. The redirection contains an artifact, that is to say a reference to the assertion. The assertion is stored on the IdP.

5) The SP resolves the artifact. The SP sends the artifact's reference to the IdP. The artifact resolution is based on the SOAP binding.

6) The IdP sends the authentication assertion.

7) The user accesses the SP.

2.4.2. OAuth 2.0: accessing a resource on behalf of a user

OAuth 2.0 is widely adopted by social networks. The "sign in with Facebook, Google" buttons operate due to OAuth 2.0.

2.4.2.1. Password antipattern

An application has to access a user's resource with a username and with their authorization.

For example in Figure 2.32, the flight reservation application must access Julien Rosa's discount points for companies A and B.

Before OAuth2.0, the reservation application had to:

– request the login and password from the user for the applications of companies A and B;

– store the user's login and password so as not to request the login and password for each new access.

This approach is called "password anti-pattern". It has many drawbacks:

– the applications for companies A and B are restricted to use login and password as means of authentication;

– the flight reservation application obtains complete access to the user's resources for companies A and B. The flight reservation application accesses the "discount points" resource but also their "dietary requirements". The user does not have the means to restrict this parameter to the "discount points" resource;

– the user cannot simply revoke the flight reservation application access;

– the theft of login/passwords on the flight reservation application raises the issue of compromising resources.

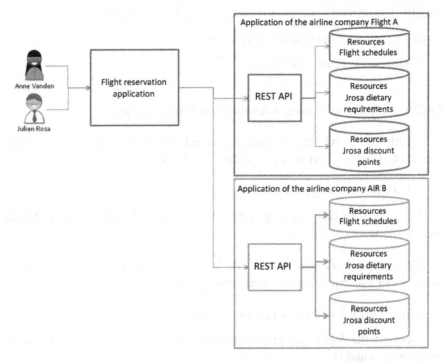

Figure 2.32. *OAuth2.0*

2.4.2.2. *OAuth 2.0*

OAuth 2.0 allows the flight reservation application to use the username for the resources of company A and B's applications. Access to resources is achieved via the use of REST APIs[12] of company A and B's applications.

OAuth 2.0 introduces the notions of resource owner, client, resource server and authorization server. In our example, the resource owner is Julien Rosa, the client is the flight reservation application and the resource servers are the applications of companies A and B. The authorization server is a component provided by OAuth 2.0, which allows the owner to give the client permission to access the resource.

The operation of OAuth 2.0 is based on two steps:

– the retrieval of an access token;

– the use of an access token to access resources.

2.4.2.2.1. The three types of client

OAuth 2.0 identifies three types of client:

– *web applications*: the client's code is executed on a web server. In this case, access to the client is carried out via a web browser:

- the user's web browser requests the client;

- the client constructs the web page and sends it to the web browser;

- the web browser displays the page.

– *applications based on a user-agent*: the client's code is downloaded from a web server and executed in the user-agent. A web browser is a user-agent. For example:

- the user's web browser requests a web server and downloads the JavaScript included in a web page. The client is the downloaded JavaScript;

---

12 From a technical point of view an API is a set of operations, procedures or classes made available by a software library, an operating system or application. The knowledge of APIs is essential for interoperability between applications.

- the client's JavaScript code is executed in the user's web browser and constructs the page to be displayed;

- the web browser displays the page.

– *native applications*: the client is an application installed on the user's terminal. The client's code is executed on the user's terminal.

2.4.2.2.2. The four grants

OAuth 2.0 proposes four grants, that define how a client can obtain an access token. These four grants are:

– the authorization code grant;

– the implicit grant;

– the resource owner password credentials grant;

– the client credentials grant.

The three more significant grants are described in the following paragraphs.

2.4.2.3. *The authorization code grant: OAuth 2.0 and the web applications*

Figure 2.33 shows the operation of OAuth 2.0 when the client is a web application.

Figure 2.33 presents the following steps:

1) The flight reservation application transmits an authorization request to the authorization server to access Julien Rosa's discount points.

2) The authorization server authenticates Julien Rosa. The authorization server ensures that Julien Rosa's authorizes the flight reservation application to access his discount points on the application of airline company A.

3) The authorization server sends an authorization code[13] to the flight reservation application.

---

13 The authorization code is the authorization granted by the owner to access their resources. This concession is required to obtain an access token.

4) The flight reservation application requests an access token[14] from the authorization server. The authorization code is transmitted in the query for an access token request.

5) The authorization server validates the access token request. The authorization server sends an access token.

6) The flight reservation application presents the access token to the application of airline company A.

7) The application of airline company A validates the access token and grants access to the flight reservation application for Julien Rosa's discount points.

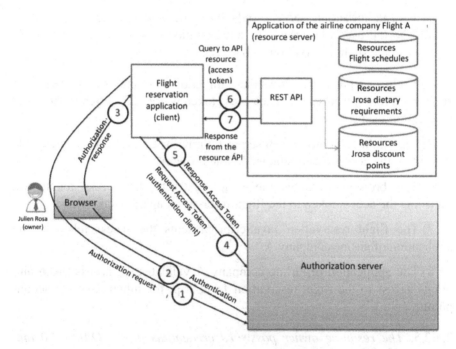

Figure 2.33. *OAuth2.0 and web applications*

---

14 The access token allows a client to access the resource. It is valid on a perimeter and for a given duration. The access token is designed to prevent the replay of the owner's login/password and identity attributes retrieval.

2.4.2.4. The implicit grant: OAuth 2.0 and applications based on a user-agent

Figure 2.34 shows the operation of OAuth 2.0 when the client is an application based on a user-agent. The steps are as follows:

1) The flight reservation JavaScript is a JavaScript downloaded from the flight reservation web server. The JavaScript's code is executed in the user's (Julien Rosa's) browser. The flight reservation JavaScript initiates an authorization request with the authorization server.

2) The authorization server authenticates the user. The authorization server ensures that Julien Rosa authorizes the flight reservation JavaScript to access his discount points on the airline company A application.

3) The authorization server sends the access token and its period of validity to the user's browser. The authorization server redirects the user's browser to the flight reservation web server.

4) The user's browser follows the redirection instructions and queries the flight reservation web server. The access token is not transmitted to the flight reservation web server.

5) The flight reservation web server returns for example, a script capable of reading the access token retained by the browser.

6) The browser executes the script, extracts the access token and transmits the access token to the flight reservation application.

7) The flight reservation JavaScript presents the access token to the application of airline company A.

8) The application of airline company A validates the access token and grants access to the flight reservation JavaScript for Julien Rosa's discount points.

2.4.2.5. The resource owner password credentials grant: OAuth 2.0 and native applications (smartphone)

OAuth 2.0 for native applications is suitable for smartphone applications. For example, the user (Julien Rosa) downloads the flight reservation application on his smartphone.

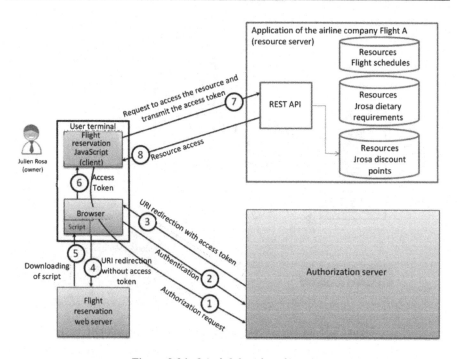

Figure 2.34. *OAuth 2.0 and applications based on a user-agent*

Figure 2.35 includes the following steps:

1) The user (Julien Rosa) provides his login/password to the flight reservation smartphone application.

2) The flight reservation smartphone application requests an access token from the authorization server and sends the user's login/password.

3) The authorization server validates the user's login/password and returns an access token.

4) The flight reservation smartphone application presents the access token to the application of airline company A.

5) The application of airline company A validates the access token and grants access to the flight reservation smartphone application for Julien Rosa's discount points.

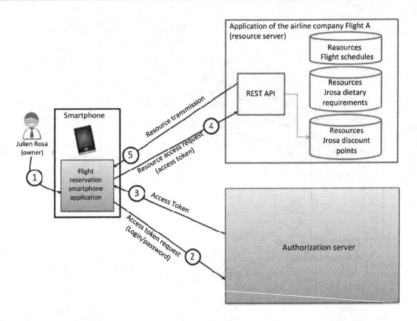

Figure 2.35. *OAuth 2.0 and native (smartphone) applications*

2.5. Conclusion

In the business sphere, identity federation is used to propagate the identity securely outside the boundaries of the firm.

The user authenticates themself on their firm's IdP in order to access remote applications, for example, applications in SaaS mode or applications of trading partners.

The IdP is administered by the user's company which helps to improve security:

– for example, if the user leaves their company, the deactivation of the user on the company's IdP is sufficient to prevent the user from accessing any of the remote applications;

– the CISO is able to know which user is accessing which remote application.

Identity federation allows the user, once authenticated on the IdP to reauthenticate themselves in order to access remote applications (SSO function).

SAML 2.0 is the standard of identity federation in companies. SAML 2.0 is adopted both by the publishers of IAM solutions and by the main applications in SaaS mode.

Corporate deployment of an identity federation solution is driven by the development of SaaS solutions.

In the public sphere, identity federation allows an application, with the internet user's consent, to read or modify some of their personal data.

Identity federation allows:

– internet applications to offer a shortened registration process to their customers. For example personal data is already autofilled;

– the internet user to navigate from one internet application to another without having to authenticate themself again (SSO function).

OAuth 2.0 is frequently used by social networks.

The rise of social networks is contributing to the development of identity federation in the public sphere.

2.6. Bibliography

[OAS 05] OASIS http://saml.xml.org/saml-specifications/, 2005.

[OAS 12] OASIS http://en.wikipedia.org/wiki/Security_Assertion_Markup_Language, 2012.

[OAU 12a] OAUTH http://oauth.net/documentation/getting-started/, 2012.

[OAU 12b] OAUTH http://tools.ietf.org/html/draft-ietf-oauth-v2-31/, 2012.

[OAU 12c] OAUTH https://developers.google.com/accounts/docs/OAuth2/, 2012.

3

Authentication Systems

3.1. Introduction

The notion of digital identity cannot be fully understood without considering the concept of authentication. The aim of digital identity is simply to formalize the individualization of access to computer networks, conditional by the existence of means of verifying the digital identity of users or objects. We therefore need to be able to authenticate equipment, services and individual users, whether for local or broader networks, wired or wireless systems and client-server or distributed architectures. All aspects relating to private access, i.e. access control to information and resources reserved to certain entities, are dependent on authentication.

The generic term "authentication" covers a wide range of protocols, systems and architectures, with varying levels of robustness (i.e. the capacity to resist to attacks) and complexity. Generally speaking, the aim of designing an authentication system is to reach a compromise between these criteria, as high levels of robustness generally imply high levels of complexity that may limit, or even prevent, use of the system.

For this reason, the most widespread authentication system in current use (notably for online authentication) is, unsurprisingly, the simple combination of a username and password, i.e. the sending of the simplest possible identity model, generally over an unprotected connection. The limitations of

Chapter written by Christophe KIENNERT, Samia BOUZEFRANE and Pascal THONIEL.

this system in terms of security are well known. Efforts have been made to prevent the simplest forms of attacks, such as password harvesting through network eavesdropping; however, the principle of permanent passwords remains inherently weak. This is made clear by the success of social engineering, or *phishing* attacks, and dictionary attacks, used to obtain the simple passwords selected by large numbers of users.

In this chapter, we shall provide a detailed description of authentication and the general principles used for authentication systems. We shall then give a general and critical overview of existing solutions, with the aim of highlighting real alternatives to the "user name/password" system. Finally, we shall consider authentication in the context of broader identity management systems for access to Web services.

3.1.1. *Authentication: definition and key issues*

3.1.1.1. *Identification, authentication and authorization*

Identification simply consists of declaring an identity. Authentication, on the other hand, requires *proof* of this identity. We have chosen to use the following, more formal definition: authentication is the security function that consists of providing and checking proof of the identity of a person, the sender of a message, a program, a logical server or a device.

At this point, we wish to highlight two elements of this definition:

1) The notion of proof is not itself defined. The term should be understood in the broadest possible sense, as an element which only the authenticating entity would be able to know or physically possess. A user password is therefore considered to be a form of proof, due to its status as a confidential element, whether or not it is particularly robust. Initial registration of a user name and confidential proof by a system is known as enrollment; this requires prior verification of the identity of a user and is a critical aspect of the process.

2) Successful user authentication in no way guarantees access to protected system resources. This access is dependent on another function, known as *authorization*, which provides authenticated users with access to different system resources.

The notion of *access control* in its broadest sense thus includes identification, authentication, authorization and access logging.

3.1.1.2. *Simple authentication and mutual authentication*

The term "authentication" is often used to mean *simple* authentication. The authentication operation always involves two entities, but the relationship between these entities may be established in one of two ways:

– *simple authentication* consists of authenticating one of the two entities to the other entity. The relationship between the two is therefore asymmetric, as one of the two does not need to prove its identity to the other.

– *mutual authentication* requires the authentication of each entity to the other entity. The relationship between the entities is therefore symmetrical.

Most protocols, including password-based systems, use the simple authentication mode. However, two entities may be authenticated via two independent simple authentication protocols. For example, this technique is used for bank Websites: the Web server is authenticated to the user via the Transport Layer Security (TLS) protocol (see section 3.2.5), while the client is authenticated using "username/password"-type data, protected by the TLS session. Note that the TLS protocol is also able to manage mutual authentication, but this would require complex procedures on the part of the client (notably the management of an X.509 certificate) and is therefore very rarely used on the Internet.

3.1.1.3. *Authentication issues*

The aim of authentication systems is to guarantee that an entity attempting to access protected resources is genuine. In concrete terms, this consists of preventing two main types of attack, both of which may have serious consequences:

– fraudulent access to a system, allowing access to sensitive data;

– identity theft, which may result in an innocent individual being considered to be responsible for the actions of the attacker.

Clearly, identity theft leads to fraudulent entry into the computer system by the attacker, who holds all of the access rights allocated to the victim. However, fraudulent entry to a computer system alone via a weakness in the authentication system (or its implantation) does not necessarily imply user identity theft.

Identity theft presents a major threat, both for companies, which may suffer serious consequences in terms of both finances and reputation, and for users, who may become implicated in illegal acts committed by the usurper of their identity. While robust authentication systems present significant resistance to identity theft, simple "username/password" systems are highly vulnerable, particularly in cases where users (with low-risk awareness) choose simple passwords.

The issues surrounding the implementation of system authentication therefore require careful consideration, and we need to find alternatives to the ubiquitous "username/password" authentication method.

3.1.2. Individual authentication factors

As we have seen, authentication is essentially based on the notion of proof of an identity. The nature of this proof may vary; for individual identities, these may be divided into four categories that are known as *authentication factors*:

– something the person is (biometrics: finger printing, iris or retina recognition, voice, DNA, etc.);

– something the person possesses (an authentication device, such as a key, chip card, etc.);

– something the person knows (a code, password, etc.);

– something the person can do (e.g. a handwritten signature).

The combination of at least two of these factors is one (but not the only) condition in creating a strong authentication system.

An authentication system will be considered *strong* if it is hard to usurp the identity of an authorized user who has previously been supplied with a means of authentication. If an authentication system can be easily worked around, biased, fooled or broken by an attacker, however, as in the case of "username/password" combinations, we speak about *weak* authentication.

3.1.3. *Basic security in network protocols*

3.1.3.1. *Security services*

Network protocols may be classified according to the security services they offer. Authentication is one of these security services, but protocols using authentication are generally designed to provide other additional services in order to add robustness. These security services will be covered in the remaining chapter, and include:

– *data confidentiality*: the ability to make a message incomprehensible, and therefore inaccessible, to any potential attacker or spy. Only the author and legitimate recipients of the message are able to access the contents. Confidentiality is essentially ensured using cryptography.

– *data integrity*: this guarantees that a message has not been altered during communication, between the moment of sending and the moment of reception, either accidentally or intentionally. Hashing functions (see section 3.1.4.3) or other techniques (for example parity bits or cyclic redundancy checks, less reliable than hashing) may be used for these purposes.

– *non-repudiation*: the ability to certify that the author of a message cannot pretend not to have sent it or not to be the real author, and that the recipient cannot deny reception of the message. This also includes guaranteeing the integrity of the message, without which a third party would be able to modify the message in the course of communication. Non-repudiation is implemented using an electronic signature, an asymmetrical cryptographic operation that will be described in more detail in section 3.1.4.2. In different cases, an electronic signature may be applied to the sent message (proof of origin) or to proof of delivery.

– *time stamping*: this is the ability to provide the accurate date (generally to the nearest second) when a message was sent.

These security services are not always necessary for an authentication protocol, depending on the nature of the protocol itself. For example, when using an authentication method based on sending static passwords, the use of a protocol including a confidentiality aspect (e.g. Hypertext Transfer Protocol Secure (HTTPS)) is strongly recommended. However, this element is less useful for authentication methods using one-time passwords (OTPs, see section 3.2.3); even if an attacker were to obtain the value of a password by spying on the network during a transaction, this password could not be used for authentication in the victim's name during a later transaction.

3.1.3.2. *Typology of network attacks*

Attacks on networks may be classified and differentiated by type in order to obtain a more detailed judgment of the solidity of protocols and architectures, notably those used for authentication. These attacks may be grouped into two complementary categories: active attacks, which involve an injection of traffic by the attacker, and passive attacks, based on spying on communications.

Passive attacks are relatively scarce from a classification perspective, but can be carried out with relative ease, particularly if the traffic is not encrypted. There are two types of passive attacks:

– *eavesdropping (tapping)*: the attacker simply listens to messages exchanged by two entities. For the attack to be useful, the traffic must not be encrypted. Any unencrypted information, such as a password sent in response to an HTTP request, may be retrieved by the attacker.

– *traffic analysis*: the attacker looks at the metadata transmitted in traffic in order to deduce information relating to the exchange and the participating entities, e.g. the form of the exchanged traffic (rate, duration, etc.). In the cases where encrypted data are used, traffic analysis can also lead to attacks by cryptanalysis, whereby the attacker may obtain information or succeed in unencrypting the traffic.

Active attacks take a wider variety of forms, with an almost endless number of possibilities. In an active attack, the attacker is involved in a communication, either by sending or modifying messages. The main types of active attacks are as follows:

– *replay*: this attack consists of recording a series of messages exchanged by two entities, typically a client (the victim) and a server, in order to play them back as-is to the same server with the aim of obtaining access to protected resources, for example. This attack type works on encrypted conversations, unless additional countermeasures have been taken. These countermeasures generally take the form of random number exchanges or time stamping.

– *denial-of-service*: in this case, the attacker aims to exhaust the network or system resources of a machine. One well-known variant is the *distributed denial of service* (DDoS), where a large number of zombie (malware-compromised) machines are used to generate a very large amount of traffic for a given target.

– *man in the middle* (MITM): in this case, the attacker relays communications between victims, in each case pretending to be the other legitimate correspondent. The attacker therefore intercepts all messages and is able to modify them before transmission to the true recipient, as shown in Figure 3.1. MITM attacks are hard to prevent from a theoretical perspective. When designing a protocol including countermeasures, these measures lead the protocol to question the identity of the correspondent during the authentication process itself; this prevents production of a proof of identity. By definition, all password-based protocols, including OTPs, are therefore vulnerable to MITM attacks.

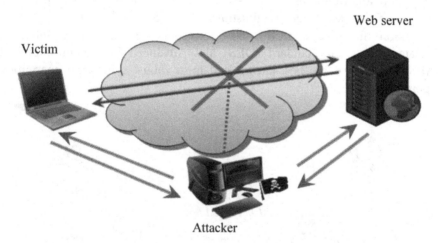

Figure 3.1. *Man in the middle principle*

Brute force attacks also fall into this category. In this case, the attacker aims to obtain a secret code by testing all possible combinations; this is only efficient in cases with a relatively limited number of possibilities. Dictionary attacks also fall into this category, targeting passwords by testing dictionary terms and close derivatives.

3.1.4. *Cryptography principles*

The authentication protocols discussed in this chapter often make use of cryptography; in this section, we shall provide a brief (and informal) overview of the principles involved.

Cryptography involves two broad categories of algorithms, relating to *symmetric* and *asymmetric cryptography*.

3.1.4.1. *Symmetric cryptography*

In symmetric cryptography, two entities, traditionally known as Alice and Bob, share a key. When Alice wishes to encode a message to send to Bob, she uses a symmetric algorithm, using the secret key and the message as parameters. When Bob receives the message, he applies the corresponding decryption algorithm, using the same key as a parameter. The principle of symmetric encryption is illustrated in Figure 3.2, where E is the encryption function and E^{-1} the corresponding decryption function. 3 Data Encryption Standard (DES) and Advanced Encryption Standard (AES) are two of the best-known and most robust symmetric encryption algorithms.

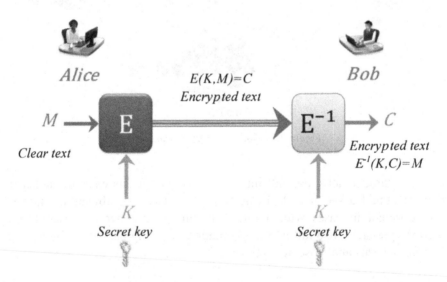

Figure 3.2. *Principle of symmetric encryption*

Despite the existence of robust algorithms and strong performances in terms of calculations, symmetric cryptography presents two main limitations:

– the number of keys to manage: a different symmetric key is needed for each pair of correspondents. Thus, the number of keys required increases in line with the square of the number of individuals;

– the exchange of the secret key: we know that Alice and Bob share a key, but the way in which this key is exchanged is not specified. Security at this stage is a significant issue; asymmetric cryptography offers one possible solution.

3.1.4.2. *Asymmetric cryptography*

In asymmetric cryptography, each entity has a *pair of keys*: the first key is public, accessible to all, and the other is private, and should only be known to the legitimate holder. These two keys are specific to a given algorithm and are related in a very specific manner; essentially, if one key is used for encryption, then the other will be used for decryption. If Alice wishes to send an encrypted message to Bob, she uses Bob's public key for encryption; Bob then decrypts the message using his own private key, as shown in Figure 3.3.

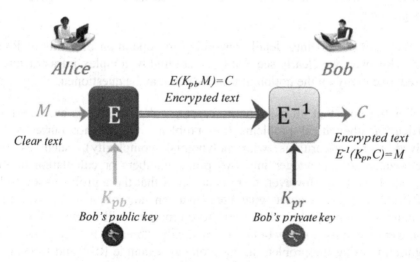

Figure 3.3. *Principle of asymmetric encryption*

Using this model, we no longer need to consider the way in which the key is common, and the number of keys is no longer an issue. However, other problems arise, including:

– performance: significantly reduced when compared to symmetric algorithms, making it impractical to encrypt large volumes of data. For this reason, asymmetric cryptography is often used to transport a symmetric key. This symmetric key then allows much faster encryption of data. This is known as a hybrid cryptosystem;

– guaranteeing the connection between a public key and the identity of the holder: we must ensure that an individual is, in fact, the legitimate holder of the public key he or she claims to possess. If this is not the case, there is nothing to prevent Bob from declaring that he has Alice's public key.

This second issue is particularly tricky and no simple solution has been found. Currently, the association between a public key and its holder is managed by *public key infrastructures* (PKIs); roughly speaking, the principle behind PKIs involves creating a certificate to confirm this association. The certificate is supplied to the holder of the public key by a certification authority (CA), acting as a trusted third party, and is digitally signed using the authority's own private key. The authority's public key is universally acknowledged to be trustworthy, and is not questioned, meaning that any individual may verify that a certificate has been signed by a recognized CA.

We shall not go into detail concerning the operation or limits of PKIs here. However, we clearly see that these are highly complex infrastructures, based essentially on the notion of trust, which may be questioned.

Finally, note that all asymmetric cryptography algorithms are based on difficult mathematical problems (i.e. problems that cannot currently be solved using algorithms with polynomial complexity), such as the factorization of an integer into two prime numbers or calculation of the discrete logarithm. However, there is no proof that these problems are truly difficult, and we cannot guarantee that an algorithm of polynomial complexity enabling the solution of these problems will never be found. A discovery of this kind would automatically "break" the cryptographic algorithms using the problem in question (for example RSA and El Gamal, or Elliptic Curve Cryptography (ECC) elliptical curves).

3.1.4.3. *Hash functions*

In addition to cryptographic algorithms that are used to ensure the confidentiality of communications, a specific family of algorithms is used to guarantee the integrity of exchanges. These are known as cryptographic hash functions.

For each message, these functions create a hash value (or simply hash) of a fixed length with a certain number of properties, which will not be discussed formally here. These are "one-way" functions: it is virtually impossible to recreate the input data from the hash alone. Moreover, if a message is modified even slightly, a good hash function will produce a hash very different from that of the original message, and the new hash cannot be predicted based on the modification. Finally, a good hash function should also be resistant to collisions, i.e. it should be very difficult to find two messages M and M' with the same hash.

The hashes produced by widespread hash functions are generally very small in relation to the size of messages. The hashes produced by the MD5 algorithm [RFC 92a], for example, are of 128 bits; SHA-1 [NAT 02] produces 160-bit hashes, and SHA-256 [NAT 02] produces 256-bit hashes. Collisions cannot therefore be avoided completely; the purpose of a hash is therefore not to be "decoded" to obtain the original message, as this will not be possible. The role of the hash is simply to show whether or not a message has been modified in the course of communication.

In order to be effective, a hash function should be combined with other cryptographic primitives in a protocol. It would be easy for an attacker to recalculate a correct hash for a message which he or she had modified; however, if a message and the associated hash are encrypted by the sender, then an attacker would be unable to correctly modify the encrypted value of the message hash.

In the same way, a *digital signature*, whereby the sender of a message encrypts the hash using a private key before attaching it to the message, will ensure integrity, authentication of the sender and non-repudiation of a message. The principle of a digital signature is illustrated in Figure 3.4.

Finally, note that, while they are still widespread, use of the MD5 and SHA-1 hash functions is now strongly discouraged; the first is considered to be broken (it is now easy to create collisions [WAN 05]), and the second is considered to be severely weakened.

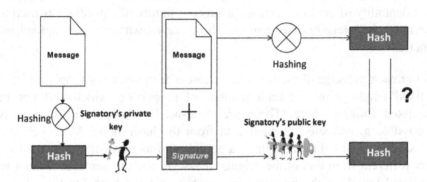

Figure 3.4. *Principle of the digital signature*

3.2. Principal authentication systems

In this section, we will present an overview of authentication systems, grouped by generic operating principle; note, however, that this is not an exhaustive list of all available standardized protocols, which would be of limited interest.

3.2.1. *Static password authentication systems*

As we have already stated in a number of occasions, static password authentication is currently the most widespread method used for the general public, despite its numerous weaknesses. A number of variations are possible, based on the way in which the password is transmitted: unencrypted, encrypted or hashed.

3.2.1.1. *Unencrypted password*

The weaknesses of static password systems with unencrypted transmission are evident; a simple list of some of the most obvious examples is enough to show the ease with which an attacker may be able to obtain a password. These methods include:

– eavesdropping: by "listening" to the network, the attacker obtains a user password and can then take on the identity of the victim by filling in the authentication form;

– dictionary attack: this is used to obtain "weak" passwords. These are passwords which users are able to remember easily, and for this reason, they are widely used. This form of attack takes account for minor variations to dictionary modes, such as the addition of a number or a capital letter in the middle of a word;

– social engineering attack: the attacker attempts to guess the password based on the user's personal information (date of birth, names of children or pets, favorite sports, etc.);

– phishing: this method consists of sending fraudulent e-mails imitating a recognized institution or company, such as a bank, inviting the user to supply login details through the attacker's Website (which also imitates the company Website), ostensibly to reactivate or unblock a personal account.

Minor countermeasures have been adopted by a certain number of Websites in an attempt to limit the impact of some of these attacks. Dictionary attacks are now harder to carry out online due to limitations on the number of authentication attempts that may be made in a given period; however, this is also inconvenient for the victim of an attempted attack, whose account will be blocked for a time.

In addition, many Websites use a more or less precise measurement of user password entropy, i.e. the ease with which the password may be obtained by brute force. Passwords considered to be weak are generally not accepted. However, it is not easy for users to memorize complex passwords. For this reason, users often store passwords in their browser, which is a non-secure environment. This can also generate other problems: when a user changes equipment, for example, they may lose access to one or more accounts for which they have been unable to memorize the password.

Generally speaking, the sole advantage of static password authentication is the supposed ease of implementation. This is only partially true; although it is technically simple to implement, a degree of complexity is passed on to the user, who is responsible for the security of his or her passwords. This presents a real objective difficulty, particularly when managing multiple passwords.

3.2.1.2. Encrypted password

The addition of confidentiality for the transmission of passwords is a superficially attractive idea for counteracting some of the weaknesses of this model. Using encryption, an attacker operating through passive surveillance will not be able to obtain a user password. However, this is the only advantage of this method; taken in isolation, password encryption adds nothing from a security perspective. While an attacker will be unable to obtain a user password directly, they will be able to observe the coded value, and this is sufficient to take on the identity of a victim. This type of attack is known as *replay*, where the attacker records an exchange and replays the obtained values (values which the attacker would be unable to calculate independently).

For password encryption to be effective, an attacker must not be able to replay or predict the encrypted value of a password. A unique and random element must therefore be added to the authentication value. The coded value of the password for a specific authentication session must then depend on this element. This is the principle behind *challenge-response* protocols, which will be described in section 3.2.2.

3.2.1.3. Hashed password

One solution that is widely used by Unix systems is the storage of password hashes, obtained using a hash function such as MD5, on a server. This replaces unencrypted storage of passwords. The advantage of this approach is that it exploits the one-way property of hash functions, meaning that even if an attacker obtained the password hash file, he or she would not be able to retrieve the actual passwords. However, this technique offers no protection against replay attacks, and remains vulnerable to dictionary attacks: an attacker in possession of a hash file will be able to carry out a dictionary attack offline, comparing the hashes of tested words to the hashes contained in the file in order to retrieve simple passwords.

This solution is only truly effective if the password hash file is itself protected, and when system authentication is carried out at local level with no transmission over the network.

3.2.2. Challenge-response authentication systems

Unencrypted transmission in static password authentication systems is clearly not ideal; moreover, the use of encryption or hashing functions alone is not enough to increase the security level of this type of authentication system due to the ease with which an attacker may implement replay attacks.

3.2.2.1. Challenge-response principle

The aim of the challenge-response technique is to provide a simple and efficient defense against replay attacks. The underlying principle may be summarized as follows, in the case of simple client authentication by a server:

– the server sends a challenge to the client, generally a *nonce*, i.e. an arbitrary unique number. This challenge does not need to be encrypted;

– the client calculates a response, based on their secret, typically a password, and the challenge sent by the server. Even with a static password, the response of the client will therefore be different for each authentication procedure;

– the server, which already has the client's secret, carries out the same calculations and compares its results with the response. If the results match, the client is authenticated.

Note that this is simply a generic description of challenge-response-type protocols. A number of variations exist, often much more elaborate. With the exception of the simple examples described in the previous section, most authentication protocols involve this challenge-response mechanism in one form or another. However, the simple implementation of this mechanism is not sufficient to protect against replay attacks: it must also be effectively integrated into the authentication protocol. Notably, the response calculation in step 2 must offer sufficient protection against elementary attacks. This calculation generally involves hashing functions or symmetric or asymmetric encryption.

3.2.2.2. Using hash functions

The calculation carried out by the client in order to respond to the challenge issued by the server often makes use of a hash function. The most typical example of this type is the *Challenge Handshake Authentication*

Protocol (CHAP) [RFC 96], used in layer 2 of the Open Systems Interconnection (OSI) model when establishing point-to-point connections with the *Point to Point Protocol* (PPP). CHAP is an advanced version of the *Password Authentication Protocol* (PAP) [RFC 92a] that is involved in sending the user's password over the network in unencrypted form, and constitutes the simplest challenge-response-type protocol.

The operation of this protocol corresponds precisely to the scenario described before. The CHAP protocol simply stipulates that the client response is equal to H($pw \parallel nonce$), where $\parallel$ is the classic concatenation operator, pw the user password and H a hashing function such as MD5 or SHA-1. The full exchange is shown in Figure 3.5.

While CHAP offers effective protection against replay attacks, it remains vulnerable to the classic dictionary attack. An attacker monitoring a line will be able to access the nonce and the value H($pw \parallel nonce$), and then carry out an offline attack to test dictionary passwords and their derivatives until the value of the client response is obtained. The attacker will then be able to calculate the password. Consequently, CHAP cannot be considered to be a satisfactory authentication protocol, despite the use of the challenge-response mechanism.

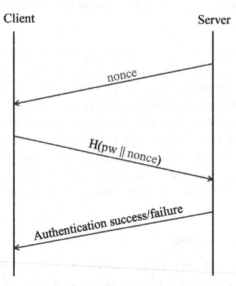

Figure 3.5. *The CHAP protocol*

Another widespread protocol that is similar to CHAP is HTTP Digest [RFC 99], used at application level. HTTP is the leading Internet navigation protocol, and may also be used to authenticate users to control online access to protected resources. However, from a security perspective, HTTP is relatively simple and only offers two user authentication methods: HTTP Basic and HTTP Digest. The first method is equivalent to PAP from an application perspective, and offers no protection against eavesdropping. User names and passwords are transmitted in unencrypted form in the HTTP headers of exchanges following authentication, greatly increasing the risks of surveillance.

The second method, HTTP Digest, is similar to the CHAP protocol, but is somewhat more elaborate, notably because of the additional parameters used in the calculation of a more complex client response. However, it does not allow us to choose a hashing function, imposing the use of MD5, an algorithm that is now considered to be unsafe. Moreover, during an authentication session, the only parameter that remains hidden from an attacker is the client password. Despite using a more complex implementation of the challenge-response principle, HTTP Digest is therefore vulnerable to the same types of attack as CHAP.

Furthermore, HTTP Digest is also vulnerable to man-in-the-middle attacks, where an attacker, placed between the server and the client, is able to intercept the HTTP response of the server requesting an HTTP-Digest-type authentication; the attacker may then transparently replace this request by an HTTP-Basic-type authentication demand. It is then easy for the attacker to retrieve the victim's password and use it for server authentication, following the HTTP Digest method imposed by the server.

3.2.2.3. Using encryption functions

Another form of challenge-response protocols involves using encryption, for example by requiring "correct" encryption of a challenge.

In the case of symmetric encryption, the client and the server must be able to derive the same encryption key using common information, typically the client's secret information and the challenge issued by the server. An attacker would be unable to obtain the challenge encryption key without knowing the client's secret. One significant advantage to this method is that the common secret is not transmitted over the network, even in hash form.

However, weaknesses sometimes remain in the way in which the key is derived, which can lead to information leaks concerning the user's secret or make the method vulnerable to optimized brute force attacks.

As an illustration, let us return to the example of the CHAP protocol. Microsoft has produced two proprietary versions of the protocol: MS-CHAPv1 and MS-CHAPv2. These variations aim to provide a more complex version of CHAP in order to make the type of attack described above harder to carry out (the use of passwords, by definition, means that it will always be possible to crack simple passwords using a dictionary attack). The basic idea used in MS-CHAPv1 was not to send the hash of the password and the nonce, but to use the password to derive symmetric keys used to encrypt the nonce. If the nonce was correctly encrypted, then the client was authenticated. However, these keys were obtained from hashes of the user password using a hashing function that itself possessed significant weaknesses, and the protocol was rapidly broken. MS-CHAPv2 attempted to correct the weaknesses of the previous version and included mutual authentication. However, unfortunate design choices meant that MS-CHAPv2 still contained significant weaknesses in the generation of symmetric keys, and efficient attack methods have been developed for this protocol [SCH 99].

In cases where a challenge-response protocol uses asymmetric encryption, the client is required to encrypt a challenge with a private key which they alone possess. The server can then use the client's public key to decrypt the challenge and check that the value is identical to that sent to the client. In this case, there is no need for a common secret: the client is identified simply by the fact that they possess the private key. However, we cannot be sure that the client is the legitimate holder of the pair of keys, i.e. whether we can trust their certificate, and consequently whether we can trust the principle of PKIs. Moreover, the complexity involved in certificate management means that this type of challenge-response protocol is not suitable for use by the general public.

3.2.2.4. *Conclusion: challenge-response systems*

These considerations show that, while the challenge-response principle presents significant conceptual gains (notably in offering quasi-systematic protection against replay attacks), it is not sufficient to design an authentication protocol free from major security weaknesses. However, this principle is generally a necessary element of secure protocols, and a number of elaborate and robust protocols have been developed based on challenge response. The TLS-PSK protocol (TLS in *Pre-Shared Key* mode), for example, may be considered to be a common-secret authentication protocol (this secret may be a password, although, in practice, pseudorandom values are used), which operates on the challenge-response principle without presenting any significant weaknesses.

Note that other protocols take challenge-response logic even further. These are known as *zero-knowledge* protocols. The verifier sends repeated challenges to the prover, in sufficient number to ensure that an attacker will have a negligible probability of providing the correct response to all of the challenges. No knowledge can be obtained by observing the response to a challenge concerning the prover's secret information, hence the name of the protocol. At the end of the iteration process, the verifier can be certain that the prover has the relevant secret information, but does not possess any other information concerning the secret. However, these protocols are not suitable in cases where the secret is a password, as the random aspect involved is minimum. They are generally based on non-deterministic polynomial-time (NP)-complete problems, for which it is easy to verify a given solution, while it is considered impossible to find a solution, for instances of these problems with a sufficiently large input size.

3.2.3. OTP authentication systems

Many systems have now abandoned static password authentication systems in favor of dynamic OTPs. As the name suggests, the OTP method consists of submitting a password, which is only valid once and at a specified time, for authentication.

The user does not therefore choose his or her own password, which generally consists of a pseudorandom sequence, the length of which varies depending on the implementation. The fact that the password is only valid at a given time and does not allow for errors (if an error occurs, another password is required) constitutes a defense against brute force or dictionary attacks, social engineering attacks and phishing. Consequently, an OTP may often be a simple sequence of four or five characters. In addition to being unique, an OTP must also be unpredictable: knowledge of previous OTPs should not allow an attacker to deduce future OTPs.

A range of approaches have been developed for authentication systems using OTPs. In this section, we shall describe a number of these implementations in order to show the variety of possible techniques.

3.2.3.1. *The S/KEY protocol*

The algorithms used to guarantee the random and unpredictable character of OTPs are somewhat varied. As noted in [ELD 11], the idea of calculating OTPs was first developed by Leslie Lamport in the 1980s, using a one-way function f, for example a hashing function. The basic principle, as used in the S/KEY [RFC 92b] system, for example, is the successive iteration, n times, of function f on a seed s, which constitutes the original secret created by the client and is never transmitted to the server. If an attacker possesses s, the whole protocol will be compromised.

Once the iterations have been carried out, secret s is eliminated, and $f^n(s)$ is transmitted to the server for reference. The list $\{f^{n-1}(s), f^{n-2}(s), ..., f(s)\}$ therefore constitutes an ordered OTP list for the user. Sending $f^{n-1}(s)$ to the server allows client authentication, as the server can apply f to compare the received value to the stored reference value. Following authentication, the server uses $f^{n-1}(s)$ for reference, and the user must then use $f^{n-2}(s)$ for authentication, and so on. The principle of the S/KEY protocol is shown in Figure 3.6.

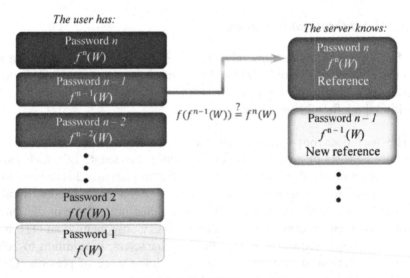

Figure 3.6. *The S/KEY protocol*

The fact that f is a one-way function theoretically makes it impossible for an attacker to retrieve the user's OTP list using passive eavesdropping. However, the S/KEY protocol uses 64-bit hashes, which, nowadays, are too small to prevent space-time trade-off attacks, used to precalculate a set of values in order to speed up the search for $f^{-2}(s)$ based on $f^{-1}(s)$.

3.2.3.2. Hardware OTPs

OTPs a currently most widely used for two-factor authentication, i.e. in addition to another authentication factor. Protocols such as S/KEY, where a user may be identified by simply supplying a correct OTP, are no longer particularly popular.

Two-factor authentication using an OTP can take a number of forms, but the most widely (and almost exclusively) used versions involve a combination of "what the user knows" and "what the user has". Generally, "what the user possesses" is a hardware element, such as an RSA SecurID token, and "what the user knows" is the OTP generated by the token, generally in addition to a token-specific Personal Identification Number (PIN) held by the user.

OTP calculation generally involves a time stamp, deduced from synchronization with the server. The user obtains an OTP that is only valid for a short period, between 30 sec and 1 min. All tokens must be initialized with a different seed in order to prevent multiple tokens producing the same OTP for the same time period.

The use of dedicated equipment with physical and logical countermeasures means that hardware OTPs offer an additional layer of protection during authentication. The limited validity period for an OTP also invalidates phishing or replay attacks. However, this also imposes constraints on the user, first in financial terms, due to the cost of hardware, and in practical terms, as authentication will not be possible if the user forgets or loses their token.

3.2.3.3. Coding tables

Another manner of using two-factor authentication is to reverse the role played by the OTP, which becomes the "possession" element. This implies the possession of an OTP matrix, in material or logical form, used for authentication. Certain banks use systems of this type, sending paper matrices (containing random values) to clients to enable additional authentication for sensitive operations, such as money transfers.

This is a challenge-response-type system: the server requests the OTP stored in a certain place in the matrix, and the client must supply this OTP, which will not be requested again. Clearly, this system is too weak to be used alone; in the case of banks, it is used to supplement a classic password authentication system (using encryption, through a TLS tunnel pre-established by the server).

NTX Research has developed a full solution using this paradigm, which is known as "coding tables". The principle involves creating two OTP matrices for each user, provided to the client and the server, respectively. These matrices are different, but compatible: all OTPs in one matrix must be found somewhere in the other matrix. There is thus a specific shift between the two matrices, deduced using a secret client code and a secret server code. These secret codes may be relatively simple, making them easy to memorize, and are never stored in physical form. Their sole purpose is to initialize the matrices correctly, i.e. with the correct shift.

For example, let us consider a case where a server requests the OTP from square A8. The client enters their secret code. The returned OTP is taken from square B9 (no longer A8) as the secret code has created a (+1, +1) shift for the whole of the matrix. The server has a password that creates a (+2, +2) shift for its matrix, and compares the value sent by the client to that stored in square C10 (and not A8) of its matrix. If the two match, this shows that the client has the correct OTP matrix and knows the secret code required to use the matrix. This constitutes a form of two-factor authentication. The principle of coding tables, implemented for ZigBee sensors, was illustrated by Redjedal et al. [RED 11].

This solution offers a number of advantages, notably the fact that theft of the OTP matrix is not sufficient to enable an attacker to use it correctly, and the that the server does not know secret user codes. Moreover, as the secret code is never stored or transmitted across the network, it is difficult to retrieve. However, a dictionary attack would be possible for short passwords (as the secret codes used are designed to be memorable); this may be blocked at server level by blocking a client account after a given number of unsuccessful authentication attempts. However, this type of countermeasure is never truly satisfactory, as the client loses access to their account for a time and is still therefore a victim of the attack.

Moreover, we need to guarantee that the shift used by the client matrix (generally a transposition algorithm that changes the order of characters in the matrix) cannot be deduced from a sufficient number of passive observations of challenge-response exchanges by an attacker in possession of the matrix. Finally, this solution, like all those discussed above, is entirely vulnerable to MITM attacks.

3.2.3.4. *Vulnerability of OTP methods to man-in-the-middle attacks*

We have not yet touched on the vulnerability of OTPs to MITM attacks, which presents a significant problem. The possibility of MITM attacks represents the main stumbling block for OTP system models, independently of the algorithms or design choices involved.

The principle behind MITM attacks was discussed in section 3.1.3.2. Readers should note that this type of attack is one of the hardest to eliminate from a theoretical perspective, as it is all too easy to neglect a parameter which an attacker may use to mount an MITM attack. This attack type was not discussed in the case of static password protocols, where it can, clearly, be used for the simple reason that the countermeasures implemented in this case can be overcome using far more modest means. This is not the case for OTP methods, where phishing, eavesdropping and dictionary attacks are generally unsuccessful. This represents a considerable achievement in security terms, and should be considered as such. In this context, an attacker must use a password as soon as it is obtained, as the data lose all interest at the end of a brief fixed period of time.

In this case, MITM-type attacks exploit the lack of mutual authentication between the client and the server. The client cannot be certain of sending the OTP to the server, and this information can be intercepted by an attacker, who then relays it to the server in the victim's name. As this type of attack can be carried out in real time, the short validity period of OTPs is of no consequence for the attacker.

One possible countermeasure consists of requiring preliminary authentication of the server by the client, for example using the TLS protocol. However, we should remember that for the purposes of online authentication, the HTTPS protocol is used; this protocol is also vulnerable to MITM attacks, as seen in section 3.2.5.3.

3.2.4. Biometric authentication systems

3.2.4.1. Definition and principles of biometry

Passwords and tokens may be characterized, respectively, as "what the user knows" and "what the user possesses". Biometry represents "what the user is", but also covers "what the user can do". The aim of biometry is to authenticate an individual based on one or more physical or behavioral characteristics.

A variety of biometric methods may be used in authentication protocols: fingerprint or handprint analysis, retina or iris scans, signature analysis, facial recognition, etc. The identity of a person may be verified by comparing the obtained reading with a model stored in a database consulted by the authentication server. Two different approaches may be used:

– *verification* of a nominative reading, i.e. using a single database entry with a known identifier (1:1 comparison);

– *identification* of an anonymous reading, tested for all of the samples in the database (1:N comparison).

In both cases, if the correspondence between the reading and the sample is judged to be sufficient, the identity of the user is considered to be verified. The degree of correspondence is evaluated by a mathematical analysis that defines an acceptance threshold above which the identity is verified. A number of organizations have worked on the standardization of biometric data; in addition to the International Organization for Standardization (ISO) and the International Electrotechnical Commission (IEC), these include the National Institute of Standards and Technology (NIST), which has established the Common Biometric Exchange Formats Framework (CBEFF) standard, defining the digital format used to exchange biometric data [NIS 04].

By construction, biometric authentication can only operate in a symmetric model. The essential difference from the notion of a password lies in the personal, non-secret, and supposedly non-modifiable and non-imitable nature of the data. The fact that biometry is based on individual characteristics means that "authentication" ceases to be the most appropriate term; in reality, biometry is used for *identification*, and the individual declares *who they are* using biometric modalities. This avoids the need to memorize information, something that represents one of the major drawbacks of password authentication. Moreover, the characteristics of biometry guarantee natural association between the supplied information (the modality) and the identity of the user.

There are, however, a number of problems involved in the use of biometric authentication systems. In technical terms, biometric modalities evolve, and in some cases, can be easily imitated. In economic terms, biometric authentication systems require the use of dedicated reading equipment, which comes at a price. Finally, the use of these systems raises ethical concerns: fingerprinting is already considered as an attack on privacy in certain circles, and systems that go even further, such as smart corridors (developed by Thalès in 2008), which analyze people's walking movements in order to detect "suspicious" behavior patterns, are liable to generate considerable opposition.

3.2.4.2. *Limitations of biometric authentication systems*

In this section, we shall concentrate on the technical limitations of biometric systems, which take two forms.

Biometric modalities are an integral part of human bodies or behaviors, meaning that they are necessarily subject to evolution over time and to the hazards of everyday life – in other words, to change. A fingerprint may deteriorate, a voice may be altered by a person's state of health, and faces change over time. This means that the presented modality may be refused, even if the individual is who they claim to be. Moreover, in cases where an individual is the victim of severe physical trauma (loss of a finger or hand, detached retina, damage to the eyeball, damage to vocal cords, etc.), these identification elements cannot be replaced: unlike passwords, which can be changed as often as necessary, the affected biometric modality will need to be substituted for another same type, wherever possible. This is naturally limited, for example, to ten modalities for fingers, two for the eyes, one for the voice, handwriting, face, etc. This is a significant limitation, and certain precautions need to be taken in defining a modality acceptance threshold.

Furthermore, it is generally possible to imitate biometric modalities, although the quality of imitations and their subsequent ability to trick an identification system is variable. Although it is not possible, in practice, to modify one's physiognomy or behavior in order to resemble another person exactly, it is possible to produce an imitation using a sample retrieved by the attacker [MAT 02]. This may be indirect (fingerprint collection, voice recording, photography of a face, etc.) or direct and invasive (amputation of a finger, removal of an eye, etc.).

For this reason, biometric readers use a set of countermeasures. One of the main methods used is *liveness detection*, which aims to guarantee a genuine link between the presented modality and the individual in question. In the case of fingerprints, this method allows the detection of prosthetics or false fingers, and even amputated digits (via a measurement of blood pressure or natural perspiration, for example). A state of the art of *liveness detection* is presented in [SIN 11].

These considerations show that the level of security provided by biometric authentication depends largely on the quality of the biometric reader. The use of individual physical modalities is not sufficient in order to design a faultless authentication system, and should be combined with other authentication factors in order to produce a strong solution.

3.2.5. *The TLS protocol*

Password systems, whether static or dynamic, and biometric systems are fundamentally symmetrical, i.e. based on preliminary sharing of a secret.

TLS [RFC 08] is based on PKIs (see section 3.1.4.2), and therefore uses an asymmetric architecture. This authentication method uses the principles of asymmetric cryptography, i.e. the complementarity between a private key, never transmitted over a network, and a public key, linked to the identity of the user via an X.509 certificate. TLS is therefore different from all of the other authentication systems presented above, and is currently a fundamental protocol for network security.

3.2.5.1. *Definition and principles of the TLS protocol*

The TLS protocol, formerly known as Secure Sockets Layer (SSL), was developed by Netscape in the 1990s. The protocol is situated between the transport layer and the application layer, providing an additional security layer for the protection of application data. This is the manner in which the protocol is generally used: the TLS protocol uses an encrypted channel to add security for all application-level protocols (File Transfer Protocol (FTP), HTTP, Simple Mail Transfer Protocol (SMTP), etc.), with no interoperability constraints. It requires a reliable connection at transport level, such as the TCP protocol. By default, application-level protocols exchange data in unencrypted format, creating a number of risks; the use of a standardized, interoperable protocol offering confidentiality and data integrity is therefore highly recommended, something that goes a long way to explaining the success of TLS.

The TLS protocol allows us to establish the following security services between two entities in a network:

– *data confidentiality*, obtained by creating a secure tunnel between the client and the server, in which data are encrypted using a symmetric cryptography algorithm, such as RC4 or AES.

– *data integrity* via the calculation of a message authentication code (MAC) for each exchanged fragment of application data. This is generally carried out using a HMAC [RFC 97] algorithm, based on classic hash functions such as MD5 or SHA-1.

– *replay protection* by adding a sequence number, used in the calculation of the MAC.

– *simple* or *mutual authentication* using X.509 digital certificates.

The TLS protocol has been subject to a number of security analyses, such as [PAU 99] and [HE 05], which guarantee its robustness. Generally speaking, the only problem with mutual TLS authentication lies in the trustworthiness of PKIs, and TLS cannot be overcome by any classic forms of attack. However, it is not widely used, as it requires users to manage their own certificate. Simple authentication, where the server is authenticated to the client, is generally preferred, as the client is then able to authenticate using another method (the classic "username/password" combination, in most cases), benefitting from the secure tunnel that ensures the confidentiality and integrity of exchanges at application level. This approach remains very different from mutual authentication, where a single protocol is used to authenticate two entities to each other.

To illustrate this difference, let us consider the classic case, used by most banks, where users are authenticated using a password once the server has been authenticated and the TLS tunnel established. Eavesdropping attacks will not be possible in this case, and brute force or dictionary attacks will also be invalid, in terms of identity theft, due to the limited number of authorized authentication attempts. However, phishing attacks work well in this context: unsuspecting users will not think to check whether or not a TLS session has been established, and are therefore susceptible to provide their details to an attacker.

3.2.5.2. *Digital identity in the TLS protocol*

The digital identity model used in TLS is unlike the classic paradigms used in symmetric models and requires more detailed consideration.

Currently, TLS authentication is based almost exclusively on the use of X.509 certificates. This means that the digital identity of an individual or a machine is entirely represented by the certificate. The main (but not the sole) advantage of this approach is that a denomination (the *Common Name*, usually abbreviated to CN, for example the uniform resource locator (URL) of a server or a user name) is linked to an asymmetric public key. The entity holding the certificate therefore also holds the associated private key, which is used, without being transmitted, to prove the entity's status as the legitimate holder of the certificate.

In accordance with the PKI model, certificates are obtained on request from a recognized CA. Certificates generated by these authorities carry a digital signature, preventing third parties from modifying the contents of the certificate, which would invalidate the signature. Security is thus dependent on the solidity of the hashing function used for the signature, and weaknesses in this element may lead to collision problems between certificates, as in the case of the MD5 function [STE 07]. In the case of a server certificate, verification involves the following steps:

– verification of the validity date of the certificate;

– verification of the trustworthiness of the CA. Given that a CA may delegate certificate generation to other organizations, the verification process requires verification of the certificates of the full chain of CAs involved in certification until a recognized CA, predefined by the verifying entity, is found. For a user verifying the certificate of a Web server, for example, the root CA must feature in a list stored by the browser;

– verification of the digital signature of the certificate using the public key of the CA. This involves decrypting the digital signature using the CA's public key, and calculating the hash of the certificate using the same function used by the CA in producing the signature, typically MD5 or SHA-1. If the two values are equal, then the signature is verified.

Once these three stages have been successfully passed, a server certificate will be considered valid. However, an additional step is required to avoid vulnerability to MITM attacks, and it is surprising that this step is not explicitly included in the TLS protocol. This step involves verification of the server domain name, which is compared to the *distinguished name* (DN) of the supplied certificate.

Note that this final verification is impossible in the case of a client certificate. However, clients are required to produce a digital signature for certain data exchanged during the establishment of a TLS session, in order for the server to ensure that the user holds the private key associated with the public key concerned by the certificate.

Other PKI models may be envisaged for more specific contexts, for example limiting the influence of CAs in certificate creation [BOU 11]. However, the reference model, as summarized in this section, is currently unrivaled; the widespread success of TLS naturally leads to the use of X.509 certificates, legitimizing their mode of management.

3.2.5.3. *Limitations of the TLS protocol*

The main limitation of the TLS protocol, as we have stated, is associated with the use of PKIs. In addition to genuine questions concerning the trust placed in CAs [SOG 11], or considerations regarding complexity and the cost of establishing the necessary architecture, a problem has arisen in current Internet use whereby legitimate servers are subject to a relatively high number of authentication failures, due to the use of out-of-date certificates or simple non-recognition by browsers. This is far from ideal, and also generates a certain level of confusion for users who are frequently faced with benign errors, which they can choose to ignore; these users will then be unable to identify a genuine attack.

However, another important weakness makes TLS vulnerable to MITM attacks. This vulnerability does not concern the protocol itself, but its implementation in the HTTPS (HTTP over SSL) protocol. Attackers may prevent the victim from creating HTTPS connections with a server, i.e. by replacing all HTTPS requests with HTTP requests. To do this, the attacker launches an MITM attack, intercepting the first request sent to the secure server, benefitting from the fact that the first request is rarely in HTTPS, and often in simple HTTP, as the victim does not type "https" explicitly into the URL. In other words, the TLS session is not initiated immediately, and the aim of the attacker is to prevent this session from being established. As we see in Figure 3.7, having intercepted an HTTP request, the attacker sends an HTTPS request to the server, and receives an HTML page in response. The attacker then replaces all of the HTTPS links in the HTML, replacing them with HTTP. In this manner, the victim communicates data to the attacker in unencrypted form, while the attacker continues to exchange encrypted information with the server. From the victim's perspective, only subtle indications, for example the color of the URL bar used to show the security of exchanges in certain browsers, will be missing; this will have no impact on non-specialist users. This weakness was identified by Marlinspike [MAR 09]. The author also developed a tool known as *SSLstrip* as proof of the concept involved in this weakness.

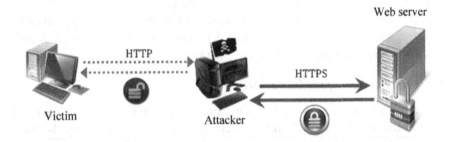

Figure 3.7. *Man-in-the-middle attack on the HTTPS protocol*

Although we need to be aware of these limitations, we should note the considerable significance of this protocol, which plays a key role in network security, notably in securing protocols at application level. When used for mutual authentication, it represents a genuinely strong solution, as long as sufficient precautions are taken to conserve the private key.

3.2.6. *The role of smart cards*

While they do not constitute an authentication system in their own right, it is useful to discuss the specific points of secure microcontrollers, such as smart cards, due to the key role they play in the design of strong authentication procedures.

The storage of secrets, whether passwords, symmetric keys or private asymmetric keys, has been mentioned on several occasions in this chapter. We have implicitly presumed that this storage is secure, without considering the meaning or the way in which this is implemented. These questions, however, are important.

One approach consists of storing these secrets in encrypted form, using a symmetric key derived from a password which the user needs to memorize. This password will be required when the user wishes to use one of their secrets. While this solution does offer secure storage, it is not particularly user-friendly. Moreover, the use of a password, even if it is not stored, is not satisfactory in the long term; malware such as keyloggers may be used to retrieve passwords used for secret encryption, making the information available to an attacker.

Smart cards offer another approach, as they constitute a trusted environment, with physical and logical countermeasures against attacks aiming to read or copy data in a fraudulent manner. If secrets, such as the private asymmetric key, are stored on a smart card, it is almost impossible for an attacker to retrieve them. The use of a PIN protects the card against use by a third party. As a physical object that must be in the possession of the legitimate user, a smart card is an excellent complement to robust authentication systems that require a trusted environment of this type for the storage of private elements. Smart cards may notably be used in addition to the TLS protocol, following the PKCS#15 standard [RSA 00], where they are used to store the private key and, sometimes, the corresponding certificate, in order to facilitate mutual authentication.

A more ambitious approach may also be used, integrating the whole of the protocol and the associated secrets into a card [URI 08]. A smart card is not simply a form of secure storage, but also includes a microprocessor, enabling it to manage state protocols such as TLS. The whole of the TLS session is therefore managed by the trusted environment. In this case, malware cannot be used to disrupt operations or to obtain the master key; the confidentiality and integrity of exchanges for a whole session are dependent on this key, which is generated dynamically, and generally stored in non-secured user terminals. Clearly, this solution, in its non-standardized form, has a limited field of application due to interoperability issues with current Internet servers.

3.3. Authentication in identity management systems

Having considered a large set of authentication systems, highlighting the different types of protocols used and their specific features, we should now give more specific attention to authentication in identity management systems, particularly for controlling access to Web services. For these systems, authentication is just one of the required functions; they must be able to manage specific applicative exchanges involving interservice communications by remote procedure calls (RPCs). These constraints require the use of dedicated protocols and security mechanisms. More generally, in addition to Web service access, identity management systems aim to create solutions that are an extension of classic authentication methods, with the purpose of federating identities at interdomain level, using the principle of trusted circles, as described in Chapter 2.

It is important to note that the integration of an authentication service into an identity management system presents significant advantages in terms of ease of use. Users may be authenticated in exactly the same way for all services connected to the same platform via a single identity server. Otherwise, each online service may offer its own authentication methods, and the user will need to retain several authentication devices and/or, typically, multiple "username/password" combinations (one per service). By simplifying matters from a user perspective in this way, it becomes easier to propose strong authentication methods, even if these are slightly more complex. A user will generally prefer the use of a single high-security key to multiple basic keys. This new configuration therefore offers a higher overall level of security.

3.3.1. *Components of identity management systems*

3.3.1.1. *Abstract description of components*

As stated in the introduction to this chapter, the control of access to a service by an identity management system involves identification, authentication, authorization and access logging functions. For this to be possible, an initiation process must take place, including the following steps:

– user registration with the service;

– creation of user access rights for the service;

– creation of identification and authentication elements for the user;

– communication of identification and authentication elements to the user and the service;

– implementation of client and server authentication components, with the ability to communicate over a network via an appropriate protocol.

In an identity management system, for a given service, the server needs to include the following components:

– an application corresponding to the service;

– an authentication framework, which will be described next;

– an authorization module associated with the service, responsible for managing individual access rights to the service;

– a database of authorized users, with a database of corresponding individual accesses.

We now require a more precise definition of the meaning of an "authentication framework", which concerns both the client and the server, and is not limited to the definition of a simple authentication protocol.

The client authentication framework must include:

– a client identification module, able to give an identity;

– a client authentication module, able to provide proof of identity, and able to support several distinct methods;

– a service identification and authentication module;

– an individual management (creation, modification and deletion) module for the authentication elements used for each method;

– a storage module for client authentication elements.

The server authentication framework is defined in the same way, except that there is no need for a service identification module, as the client initiates connection to the service.

3.3.1.2. *Identity selectors and authenticators*

The form taken by these components, which have been discussed in an abstract manner up to this point, is largely dependent on the identity management system in question. Client identity, for example, can be fully managed by a Web interface specific to the identity management system. However, other options are possible: the InfoCard protocol, for example, used in Windows Cardspace (which is now obsolete), offered an identity selector in the form of a dedicated application, where the user was able to choose which identity to use from a list on their own computer. In systems such as OpenID, identity management is delegated to a third-party server, which the client accesses via a specific URL.

Moreover, the client authentication framework may require the client to use an authenticator, i.e. a hardware element (Universal Serial Bus (USB) key, Secure Digital (SD) card, smart card, etc.) containing, as a minimum requirement, sensitive authentication elements, and possibly make use of available calculation resources to run algorithms or protocols.

We then need to consider the question if interactions between the identity selector, the authenticator and the authentication protocol(s) are responsible for dialog between client and server modules: interoperability should be guaranteed as far as possible in order to avoid the artificial addition of dialog between components.

3.3.1.3. *Security protocols for access to Web services*

Access to Web services, based on identity management systems, involves the use of specific protocols. As these services are online, the HTTP protocol is essential, but other protocols must be added in order to create secure exchanges and to take account of the specific nature of exchanges with Web services.

Exchanges can therefore be secured using HTTPS, which is practical both for authentication (at least simple authentication) and for ensuring the confidentiality and integrity of data. However, Web services sometimes require specific operations, such as RPCs. These are enabled by the *Simple Object Access Protocol* (SOAP) [SOA 01], transported by HTTP, which provides an XML description of the procedure call identified by its URL, alongside the response.

SOAP exchanges may be secured by the use of appropriate mechanisms, such as encryption or signature of certain parts of XML messages (for example to protect a section concerning the authentication of an identity, leaving the rest open to inspection by gateways, load balancers or other intrusion detection tools). This lies outside of the functions of TLS. The *Web Service Security* (WSS) specifications, published by the OASIS consortium, define a security layer for the SOAP protocol, notably through the definition of *XML Encryption* [XML 08a] and *XML Signature* [XML 08b]. For a SOAP message, WSS headers provide:

– identification of the entity or entities involved in the message;

– proof that the entity is from the correct group;

– proof that the entity has the relevant access rights;

– proof that the message has not been modified by third parties.

3.3.2. *Key players in identity management*

3.3.2.1. *Liberty Alliance*

Liberty Alliance is a consortium established by Sun in 2001, currently including more than 150 companies and organizations, with the aim of defining standards for identity management, notably identity federation, interdomain authentication, session management and Web services as a whole. Liberty Alliance technologies are largely based in the *Security Assertion Markup Language* (SAML) standard, which has been presented in section 2.4.1 of Chapter 2.

Significant contributions made by Liberty Alliance include *ID-FF*, the Liberty Identity Federation Framework [WAS 05], which is based on SAML, with complements to enable more complex implementations for companies. The main elements introduced by this standard are:

– control over operated federations;

– true Single Sign On and Single Logout;

– genuine anonymity (no single identifier used between service providers and the identity provider);

– an authentication context (allowing information to be supplied on the form of authentication used, but also on the context, including the registration procedure);

– the exchange of metadata.

The standards defined by Liberty Alliance are in competition with the WS-* standards (such as WSS, discussed in the previous section), which are a product of the association between Microsoft, IBM and Verisign. However, it is important to note that the Identity Web Service Framework (ID-WSF) standard defined by Liberty Alliance, an identity discovery service that allows identity attributes to be common under user control, is fully compatible with WS-* technologies due to the fact that both are based on SAML.

3.3.2.2. Shibboleth

Shibboleth [CAN 05] is the result of an open-source project by the Internet2 consortium, which is directed by American universities in association with industrial partners and the government. It has a number of common points with Liberty Alliance, including its foundations in SAML. The main difference is that the target framework for Shibboleth is much smaller than that of Liberty Alliance, being aimed at universities.

Shibboleth offers a standardized gateway between the existing authentication systems used on university campuses and authorizes interinstitution sharing of Web resources subject to access controls.

3.3.2.3. Higgins

Higgins [HIG 12] is another open-source project, notably including the development of components for the construction of identity management systems. These components are of two types:

– low-level components, which provide an abstraction layer in order to promote the portability of identity data. These components offer identity services, for example attribute services, which provide an identity layer above the data layer.

– high-level components, which provide the user with an identity selector very similar to that used in Windows Cardspace, with which Higgins was compatible. Identities, represented as cards, are obtained either by personal generation (self-signed cards) or via an identity provider. Users may therefore select any identity that meets the requirements of the service provider in terms of authentication.

3.3.2.4. OpenID

From an identity management perspective, OpenID [OPE 07] provides only those functions that are essential for decentralized authentication. This approach is very different from that used by other major players in the domain, essentially due to its simplicity and the fact that it is designed, first and foremost, with end users in mind. OpenID is an open standard; its main aim is to host user identities, with the intention of delegating authentication, rather than providing a real identity management system in the broad sense of the term as covered by the previous examples. The principle used in OpenID is intuitive: any user wishing to authenticate him or herself to a service provider may instead choose to authenticate using an OpenID identity provider for which he or she is already registered. To do this, the service provider – potentially any Website – simply needs to accept the OpenID authentication procedure.

The notion of circles of trust is not part of the OpenID approach. This means that OpenID identity providers and service providers are not engaged in any preliminary trust relationship. In terms of authentication, the protocol used is entirely dependent on the OpenID supplier. While the service provider may have some awareness of these protocols and require a minimum level of security, current implementations generally do not take this into account, and "username/password"-type authentication is used. Certain OpenID providers, however, have taken the leap and use better authentication systems.

3.3.3. Internet trends in identity management

The spectacular success of social networking over the last few years has had a clear and significant impact on the relationship between users and their digital identity. Previously, a certain (generally relatively limited) amount of personal information was required in order to open an account for an online service; now, this information itself represents the key interest of social networks such as Facebook. Users spontaneously share personal information with friends, who may then pass on this information.

This trend raises obvious issues concerning the management of personal data, which can rapidly circulate beyond the circles intended by the user. One solution for identity management, currently at specification stage, has been proposed by World Wide Web Consortium (W3C) using the principle of WebID [SAM 13]. A WebID is a Universal Resource Identifier (URI) identifying an agent (person, group, organization, etc.) and referencing a document that gives a description of this agent. This description is part of the semantic Web and uses the Friend of a Friend (FOAF) vocabulary, allowing identification of the main data associated with an agent (name, connections, blog address, etc.). Some of these data may, moreover, be stored in a protected document in order to restrict access.

Users may be authenticated using a WebID with the addition of the TLS protocol, forming the WebID-TLS [INK 13] authentication protocol. The basic principle is simple, and consists of establishing mutual authentication using an X.509 certificate. WebID-TLS does, however, present certain specificities: the WebID certificate is self-signed, and contains an input corresponding to the URI of the WebID of the agent. Thus, the validity of the agent's public key/private key set is verified by ensuring that the certificate presented by the user is the same as that given in the user profile. The protocol is therefore not based on PKIs, as authentication uses Web of Trust principles, i.e. it is based on rules linked to the content of the agent's profile.

3.4. Conclusion

While authentication is clearly a crucial aspect of computer security, it is extremely difficult to design robust systems suitable for use by the general public. The complexity involved in the implementation of security countermeasures, for example those that require users to possess physical tokens or to manage certificates, generally limits the scale of use. This consideration means that despite the existence of numerous alternatives, the static password model is still the most widely used. The technology and protocols needed for more secure methods exist, but old habits die hard, particularly when dealing with billions of users.

A transition to more elaborate standards giving higher levels of security cannot therefore take place without a significant shift on the part of major Internet players. The standards adapted to identity management systems for Web servers, which are generally complex but relatively successful, only emerged due to the influence on consortiums, i.e. a movement by major organizations concerned by the issues involved in defining specific protocols for managing and securing identities in a network. In all likelihood, a similar move on the part of online companies and organizations, such as that initiated by the W3C, will be needed before we see a general convergence on one or more strong authentication systems, outside of the limited context of identity management systems.

3.5. Bibliography

[BOU 11] BOUZEFRANE S., GARRI K., THONIEL P., "A user-centric PKI based-protocol to manage FC² digital identities", *International Journal of Computer Science Issues*, vol. 8, no. 1, pp. 74–80, 2011.

[CAN 05] CANTOR S., et al., Shibboleth Architecture, Protocols and Profiles, September 2005. Available at http://shibboleth.internet2.edu/docs/internet2-mace-shibboleth-arch-protocols-200509.pdf.

[ELD 11] ELDEFRAWI M.E., ALGHATHBAR K., KHAN M.K., "OTP-based two-factor authentication using mobile phones", *Proceedings of the International Conference on Information Technology – New Generations (ITNG)*, pp. 327–331, 2011.

[HE 05] HE C., SUNDARARAJAN M., DATTA A., et al., "A modular correctness proof of IEEE 802.11i and TLS", *12th ACM Conference on Computer and Communications Security (CCS'05)*, pp. 2–15, 2005.

[HIG 12] HIGGINS 2.0, Personal Data Service, Eclipse project, 2012, Available at http://www.eclipse. org/higgins/.

[INK 13] INKSTER T., STORY H., HARBULOT B., et al., WebID specification, Technical report, 2013. Available at https://dvcs.w3.org/hg/WebID/raw-file/tip/spec/tls-respec.html.

[MAR 09] MARLINSPIKE M., "New tricks for defeating SSL in practice", *Proceedings of Black Hat DC Conference*, 2009.

[MAT 02] MATSUMOTO T., MATSUMOTO H., YAMADA K., *et al.*, "Impact of artificial gummy fingers on fingerprint systems", *Proceedings of SPIE*, vol. 4677, 2002.

[NAT 02] NATIONAL INSTITUTE OF STANDARDS AND TECHNOLOGY, Secure Hash Standard, Federal Information Processing Standard (FIPS) 180-2, 2002.

[NIS 04] NISTIR 6529-A, Common Biometrics Exchange Formats Framework, NIST, April 2004.

[OPE 04] OpenID Authentication 2.0, 2004. Available at http://openid.net/specs/openid-authentication-2_0.html.

[PAU 99] PAULSON L.C., "Inductive analysis of the Internet protocol TLS", *ACM Transactions on Computer and System Security*, vol. 2, no. 3, pp. 332–351, 1999.

[RED 11] REDJEDAL A., GARRI K., BOUZEFRANE S., *et al.*, "A new security architecture for mesh networks: application to sensor networks and ZigBee standard", *Proceedings of the International Conference on Secure Networking and Applications*, pp. 36–39, 2011.

[RFC 92a] RFC 1321, The MD5 message-digest algorithm, IETF, 1992.

[RFC 92b] RFC 1334, Password Authentication Protocol, IETF, 1992.

[RFC 94] RFC 1661, Point to Point Protocol, IETF, 1994.

[RFC 95] RFC 1760, The S/Key One-Time Password System, IETF, 1995.

[RFC 96] RFC 1994, Challenge Handshake Authentication Protocol, IETF, 1996

[RFC 97] RFC 2104, HMAC: Keyed-Hashing for Message Authentication, IETF, 1997.

[RFC 99] RFC 2617, HTTP Authentication: Basic and Digest Access Authentication, IETF, 1999.

[RFC 08] RFC 5246, Transport Layer Security, IETF, 2008.

[RSA 00] RSA Laboratories, Cryptographic Token Information Syntax Standard, PKCS#15 v.1.1, RSA Laboratories, 2000.

[SAM 13] SAMBRA A.V., STORY H., BERNERS-LEE T., WebID specification, Technical report, 2013. Available at https://dvcs.w3.org/hg/WebID/raw-file/tip/spec/identity-respec.html.

[SCH 99] SCHNEIR B., MUDGE, WAGNER D., Cryptanalysis of Microsoft's PPTP Authentication Extensions (MS-CHAPv2). Available at https:// www.schneier.com/paper-pptpv2.pdf.

[SIN 11] SINGH Y.N., SINGH S.K., "Vitality detection from biometrics: state-of-the-art", *Proceedings of the Workshop in Information and Communication Technology*, pp. 106–111, 2011.

[SOA 01] SOAP Version 1.2, 2001. Available at http://www.w3.org/TR/soap/.

[SOG 11] SOGHOIAN C., STAMM S., "Certified lies: detecting and defeating government interception attacks against SSL", *Proceedings of the Financial Cryptography*, pp. 250–259, 2011.

[STE 07] STEVENS M., LENSTRA A.K., DE WEGER B., "Chosen-prefix collisions for MD5 and colliding X.509 certificates for different identities", *Proceedings of the EUROCRYPT*, pp. 1–22, 2007.

[URI 08] URIEN P., PUJOLLE G., "Security and privacy for the next wireless generation", *International Journal of Network Management*, vol. 18, no. 2, pp. 129–145, 2008.

[WAN 05] WANG X., YU Y., "How to break MD5 and other hash functions", *Proceedings of the EUROCRYPT*, pp. 19–35, 2005.

[WAS 05] WASON T., *et al.*, "Liberty ID-FF architecture overview", Liberty Alliance Project. Available at http://www.projectliberty.org/resource_center/ specifications/liberty_alliance_id_ff_1_2_specifications, 2005.

[XML 08a] XML Encryption Workgroup, 2008. Available at http://www.w3.org/ Encryption/2001.

[XML 08b] XML Signature Workgroup, 2008. Available at http://www.w3.org/ Signature/.

Privacy Management and Protection of Personal Data

4.1. Introduction

In Chapter 1, we gave a brief overview of elements involved in the protection of privacy in order to promote basic awareness. In this chapter, we will give detailed consideration to the ways in which the use of technology can infringe on privacy. We will consider technologies that have been around for the last decade revolutionizing the way in which we buy, communicate, contribute and obtain information, and emerging technologies, which use communicating objects (radio frequency identification (RFID), sensors, smartdust, etc.) to provide future solutions for facilitating everyday life. This development creates issues concerning the application of legal provisions, particularly concerning the collection, use and transmission of personal data. The existing rules[1], defined in the late 1970s, serve to defend the privacy of users, alongside other fundamental rights and liberties, including freedom of movement and self-determination. This legal framework is applicable to all technologies, whether they concern direct identification data (names and surnames) or indirect identification elements (biometric elements, DNA).

Researchers concerned with the preservation of privacy are mainly interested in defining solutions to guarantee user anonymity in communications and electronic exchanges, in the broadest sense, on the

---

Chapter written by Maryline LAURENT and Claire LEVALLOIS-BARTH.
1 In France.

Internet. Other main foci include the formalization of user requirements, automatic processing of user requirements in relation to privacy protection, limitation of transmissions by communicating objects, etc. Although some network and software solutions offering anonymity already exist, they are not entirely satisfactory. Research is still needed from both legal and technical perspectives, and there is an increasing need for close collaboration between the two domains. The aim is to offer users a trusted digital environment, where their rights and freedoms, alongside their own personal requirements, are automatically and transparently respected.

In this chapter, we will present the privacy issues to which the user is exposed when using new technologies (see section 4.2). We will then consider the application of the legal framework for the use of personal data (see section 4.3) and the technical solutions currently available for privacy preservation, with their associated limitations (see section 4.4). Finally, we will discuss a number of themes currently under consideration by researchers in the legal and technical domains (see section 4.5).

4.2. Risks in information technology

By their activities, movements and the objects they transport, individuals unwittingly leave traces in a variety of computer systems, which are then accessible by different managing organizations. Using the property of linkability (as explained in Chapter 1, section 1.5.1), these organizations can then create profiles and enrich databases, generally for commercial purposes. The use of multiple identities in no way guarantees the partitioning of traces. Moreover, the combination of multiple traces left by an individual with several different digital identities provides even more information on the natural person.

In this section, we will discuss three technical aspects which raise serious questions concerning the protection of personal data.

4.2.1. Ambient intelligence

Ambient intelligence (AmI) refers to the fact that our environment is increasingly computerized, and the objects which surround us (e.g. key rings, refrigerators, drug packets, clothing, watches, cars, doors, smartphones, switches, passports and so on) have a certain, variable, information processing capacity. This processing capacity lets them to make decisions, communicate and react to individual requirements. Humans interact with these objects, and are able to access a large amount of information anywhere and at any time. This development is known as ubiquitous or pervasive computing, or the Internet of Things [GUI 11].

AmI covers different miniaturized technologies such as smartcards, RFID labels and sensors (reacting to light, temperature, movements, etc.). All communicating objects include these technologies, for example, to control physical access (RFID for company cards, subway user cards, public cycle access cards, electronic passports, etc.), for medical monitoring (e.g. blood pressure and temperature monitors), in domotics, in logistics (tracking packages through a transport system, tracking products) or even for monitoring the cold chain (using temperature sensors).

The danger involved in using these objects lies first in the way in which companies that equip their employees or clients with them may use the created data, for example, to trace the movements of individuals (via public transport) or to gain a clearer picture of buying habits (checkouts, loyalty cards). Moreover, these objects may act as "cookies" or tracers, which can infringe on the user's privacy. RFID labels on objects, for example, are designed to communicate the information stored in their memory to a reader with a range of between 10 cm and several tens of meters. If an unknown person holds an RFID reader near to a victim's bag or pocket, he or she will be able to obtain the data contained in the victim's objects, such as a subway card [CAR 14] with information corresponding to the last three validations of the card[2], and possibly the references of any medication in the bag (if the associated chips have not been deactivated).

Sensors may also constitute sources of personal information regarding a person's state of health, their sporting performance, etc. This trend is promoted by the "quantified self" movement, which offers a wide variety of tools for the measurement, collection, analysis and sharing of data. Moreover, sensors can provide information on the presence or absence of

---

2 For the Navigo system in Paris. For details on the personal data stored in Navigo passes and the associated legal considerations, see [LEV 09].

individuals in their homes (domotic sensors), the presence of certain luxury items in a building, etc.

Great care is required in the use of this miniaturized technology, which provides assistance in everyday life and can carry out certain tasks automatically, but which also has the potential to disclose too much information very easily, revealing personal information concerning the user.

4.2.2. Communications and services

When an individual connects to a network for any reason – e-mail, navigation, chat, etc. – they leaves traces on a variety of levels due to the fact that they generate traffic. This traffic reveals certain information. The Internet Protocol (IP) address shows the country from which the connection is made, and the country hosting the target server. Unencrypted user details also make possible tracing of individuals. Browser cookies, used to communicate user information to Websites in order to personalize the interface, are also a good way of tracing users during navigation over multiple sites[3].

At the Internet access or service provider level, traffic analysis may be used to create profiles of the network and application service consumption of individual users. This profile may be linked to the IP address of the connection, connection times, a list of sites visited, downloaded content, frequently-used keywords, product searches, etc.

These profiles are primarily used for commercial purposes in order to target the tastes and centers of interest of individuals in order to personalize Web advertising and to encourage online purchasing. Other forms of statistical analysis, relating to articles viewed in online shops, may be used to direct users to other articles viewed by clients with a similar navigation profile.

The success of smartphones has provided access to a range of new services based on individual geographic localization. It is now easy to find the closest restaurant, for example, or the local weather forecast for the coming days. However, using client information requests, service providers

---

3 See section 4.3 for a discussion of the legislation concerning the use of cookies.

are able to create profiles including user habits and movements. Certain smartphones (for example, the iPhone) store user movement history locally. If the device is stolen, this constitutes an infringement of privacy; moreover, the history may also be used to supplement profile bases, under cover of maintenance operations.

Finally, the Internet community, World Wide Web Consortium (W3C), has given users the ability to manage their personal attributes, via the concept of WebID [OPE 14], by including identifiers. These identifiers take the form of a uniform resource identifier (URI) [BER 05], used to localize the online profile storage space. The URI may take the form of a uniform resource locator (URL), for example https://my-profile.eu/people/mlaurent/card#me. Thus, when the users need to communicate their personal attributes to a server accepting the WebID concept, they simply need to communicate their personal URI. The server is then freely able to access all of the user's attributes. This solution is currently promoted by the OpenID community and has been adopted by a number of well-known service providers, including Google, Yahoo and Orange. However, it has certain weaknesses, as it does not limit access to attributes according to the intended use.

4.2.3. Social networks

Social networks respond to a demand for sharing and diffusion of information. They may be intended for professional use (LinkedIn, Viadeo, Twitter) or private use (Facebook, Google+), or both (YouTube). Social networks allow users to communicate with a circle of friends, or with an interest group, using multimedia information: photos, videos, recommendations, opinions, announcements, etc. Social networks create a number of issues related to the protection of personal information.

The first problem lies in the difficulty of controlling "friend" lists and mastering the diffusion of personal data. On Twitter, for example, a short message, known as a "tweet", is transmitted to anyone subscribing to the relevant information feed; by default, the subscription operation is not controlled by the user. With LinkedIn, users have a "close" circle, managed by the user, with access to full profile information, and a more distant circle, where only the user's public profile will be visible. Facebook offers a finer level of granularity for information diffusion circles, giving default lists for "Family", "Close friends" and "Acquaintances", and users may define their own lists, with the possibility of grouping contacts based on common characteristics: geographic location, workplace, educational establishment, etc. Facebook also allows users to assign rights to these lists, controlling access to a basic profile and identification privileges for photographs and documents.

The second problem is linked to the way in which social networks operate: information is duplicated in an unmanaged manner throughout the system, through the sharing operations carried out by the user. In this way, it is impossible to know how many copies of the same piece of information are present in a system and where they are stored. More seriously, certain copies are impossible to delete once content has been shared with other users. This is the case for both Facebook and Google.

The traces left in a social network, whether voluntarily or not, allow us to form opinions on an individual, their personality, centers of interest, political opinions, religious beliefs, etc. These traces are rapidly created and easy to access, and are widely used by recruiters for interview preselection. Certain individuals have called for legal recognition of a "right to be forgotten"; in France, companies have begun to adopt an ethical approach which guarantees that only the abilities of candidates will be taken into account, by signing the "*Réseaux sociaux, internet, vie privée et recrutement*" (Social networks, Internet, private life and recruiting) charter [ACO 14].

The third problem lies with the companies managing these social networks, which handle huge amounts of personal data and which are funded by advertising space, and are susceptible to sell all or some of these data. These databases are referred to as "Big Data", which are on a completely different scale to classic databases and thus require sophisticated processing techniques. New economic trends are currently emerging in relation to Big Data. In 2012, Datasift Inc. bought the database of Tweets published over the two previous years by no less than 300 million members, and cross-referenced this data with other sources such as Facebook and Amazon to offer its clients (in commercial, political and financial spheres) a service to improve brand perception, detect trends, improve investments, etc.

4.3. Legal elements relating to the creation, collection, use and sharing of personal data

The use of technologies such as AmI, electronic communications and services, and social networks leads individuals to leave traces.

In France, the creation, collection and use of these traces is subject to Act no. 78-17 of 6th January 1978 on Information Technology, Data Files and Civil Liberties (*loi du 6 janvier 1978 relative à l'informatique, aux fichiers et aux libertés, generally abbreviated as loi Informatique et Libertés*) [CNI 78]. This fundamental text has been modified on a number of occasions, notably in 2004 in order to take account of *European Directive 95/46/EC* of the European Parliament and of the Council of 24 October 1995 on the protection of individuals with regard to the processing of personal data and on the free movement of such data (Data Protection Directive) (see [EUR 95, p. 31]). Note that this directive is currently undergoing revision, following a proposal of regulation by the European Commission on 25 January 2012 [EUR 12].

The aim of the French Data Protection Act is indicated in Article 1, which constitutes the basis of the whole law: "Information technology should be at the service of every citizen. Its development shall take place in a context of international co-operation. It shall not violate human identity, human rights, privacy, individual or public liberties". A framework for the creation and use of personal data is required due to fears that public or private institutions, or even individuals, may use an individual's personal data to infringe upon their capacity for self-determination. The legislation also attempts to provide a framework for a society with a focus on anticipation and prediction. In the United States, Target was implicated in a scandal in which a father discovered that his underage daughter was pregnant when she received advertisements for childcare products, targeted at pregnant women. By giving individuals a certain mastery of their personal data, legislators attempt to regulate the risks associated with the use of technology in a preventive manner. This goal may be attained by limiting data processing activities and by allowing individuals to control the free movement of their personal data.

The French Data Protection Act is designed to ensure a balance between the use of personal data linked to an identity, on the one hand, and the protection of human rights and basic freedoms on the other hand. It aims to provide a framework for the "information" phenomenon; as Professor Yves Poullet writes in reference to George Orwell's 1984: "for those who possess it, information represents power over those concerned by the information. A person who holds information concerning another may adapt his/her decisions based on the knowledge that the collected and processed information gives him/her with regard to this person. They may predict their attitude, and thus respond to, or influence, their demand" [POU 09]. The right to the protection of personal data protects privacy, but also other freedoms, such as the free movement of person, freedom of communication, expression and non-discrimination[4]. These legal questions relate to philosophical notions of autonomy, dignity and free choice, i.e. the capacity of the person to impose their will onto other elements.

The French Data Protection Act is enforced by an independent administrative authority, the *Commission Nationale de l'Informatique et des Libertés* (CNIL, National Commission for Computing and Freedom). The CNIL is a participant in the working party created by article 29 of the Data Protection Directive (*Article 29 Data Protection Working Party* or WP29) which brings together all of the authorities concerned with personal data protection in the European Union (EU). The purpose of the WP29 is to give the European Commission with an opinion in the name of Member States and to promote harmonized application of the Data Protection Directive throughout the EU. The opinions expressed by the WP29 have no bearing from a legal perspective; however, they are recognized as having a certain authority and they constitute a valuable source for analysis and interpretation.

In order to clearly understand the application of rules concerning the use of personal data, we will now consider the example of digital identity

---

4 See Convention for the Protection of Human Rights and Fundamental Freedoms, Rome, 4.XI.1950. Article 8 protects the right to respect for private and family life, home and correspondence. Article 9 protects the right of thought, conscience and religion and Article 10 protects the right of the freedom of expression.

management by social network services (SNS). This approach requires us to define the area of application of the French Data Protection Act (see section 4.3.1) and to understand the key principles (see section 4.3.2) before considering the question of sanctions and brand image (see section 4.3.3).

4.3.1. *Scope of application*

4.3.1.1. *Key notions*

The French Data Protection Act and the Data Protection Directive are applicable if, and only if, "information" relating to a "natural person" is the object of "data processing" by a "data controller".

4.3.1.1.1. Notion of "personal data"

Traces may be qualified as "personal data" when they concern "any information relating to a natural person, who is or can be identified, directly or indirectly, by reference to an identification number or to one or more factors specific to them" (see Art. 2 of the Act [CNI 78]). The Act specifies that "to determine whether a person is identifiable, all the means that the data controller or any other person uses or may have access to should be taken into consideration".

During registration with an SNS, members supply information which is directly nominative: first name and surname, e-mail address, of the type *toto.dupond@abc.fr*, and sometimes a postal address. The user then publishes a detailed profile online, along with information describing his or her actions and interactions with others. In this context, the user's pseudonym[5], telephone number, geographic location, place and date of birth, tastes, preferences, activities and the behavioral segment to which they belong constitute indirectly nominative information. This also applies to the

---

5 This pseudonym may be freely chosen by the social network user, respecting certain conditions (avoiding antisemitic, racist, Holocaust denying or libelous implications, etc.) and the intellectual property rights of others. A name cannot be used if this choice infringes on an established right, notably preventing the use of the name, pseudonym or image already allocated to another user. Once the pseudonym has been selected, it may be involved in legal transactions, and may be rented, sold, or subject to other operations, free or paid.

user's voice, biometric data as a whole, and photo and video representations of the user.

In certain cases, the social network collects the IP address of the user, something which is also considered as personal data by the Court of Justice of the European Union[6]. However, the WP29 draws attention to the particular case of "some sorts of IP addresses which under certain circumstances indeed do not allow identification of the user, for various technical and organizational reasons. One example could be the IP addresses attributed to a computer in an Internet café, where no identification of the customers is requested" (see [WP 07, p. 17]).

Thus, data are considered to be personal as soon as it touches upon the "essence" of a human being [EYN 13]. However, information which has been made anonymous in such a way that a person can no longer be identified is not classified as personal data. The establishment of anonymity constitutes an interesting theme for further reflection.

Anonymization implies the destruction of the connection between information and the identity of a person. This may be achieved using various methods (k-anonymity, aggregation, the addition of noise, deletion, etc.), which may be categorized into two main families: randomization, which consists of transforming data so that it no longer refers to a real person, and generalization, where data values are replaced so that they are no longer specific to a person, but shared by a group.

The WP29 considers a set of data to be "anonymous" if the following three criteria are respected [WP 09]:

– *singling out*: it should not be possible to identify an individual in a data set;

– *linkability*: it should not be possible to link distinct data sets referring to the same data subject;

---

6 European Court of Justice, 3rd Chamber, 24 November 2011, Case C-70/10. Scarlet Extended SA vs. *Société belge des auteurs, compositeurs et éditeurs SCRL* (SABAM), recital 51 according to which: "the injunction requiring installation of the contested filtering system would involve a systematic analysis of all content and the collection and identification of users' IP addresses from which unlawful content on the network is sent. Those addresses are protected personal data because they allow those users to be precisely identified".

– *inference*: it should not be possible to deduce the value of an attribute, with a significant probability, from the values of a set of other attributes.

In order to fulfill these criteria, an SNS must choose a suitable anonymization technique or a combination of techniques. Their analysis must not consider an isolated data element, but all possible cross-referencing of information. With the advent of Big Data and the movement to open up public data using *open data*, the possibilities for cross-referencing, and thus identification of individuals, have increased considerably. One famous example is the collaborative Netflix film evaluations and recommendations site in the United States. As part of a competition aimed at improving their recommendation algorithm, the company published 100 million anonymous evaluations. Researchers cross-referenced this data with other, non-anonymous evaluations: using two evaluations, they were able to identify 68% of users. Faced with the threat of prosecution for infringement of user privacy, Netflix terminated the competition.

In a published opinion concerning advertising billboards using cameras and equipment designed to analyze the behavior of passersby, the CNIL stated that "even if these data are rapidly made anonymous and only statistical data are retained following processing, these data are still obtained using information which allows the identification of individuals". The French Data Protection Act is, therefore, applicable even if images are not recorded, as the anonymization of personal data still constitutes a form of data processing [CNI 10a].

4.3.1.1.2. Notion of the "data subject"

The data subject "is an individual to whom the data covered by the processing relate"[7]. This person may, for example, be the holder of an identification (ID) card or a biometric passport, a professional ID badge or an online bank account.

In the context of social networks, a distinction is made between:

– *members* who provide identity information during registration and communicate personal data of their own will based on their own social networking needs;

---

7 Article 2 of the *French Data Protection Act* [CNI 78]. Working Party 29, Opinion 5/2014 on anonymisation techniques onto the web [WP 14]. p. 5 contains a similar definition.

– *non-members* whose identity or pseudonyms are featured in the profile, wall, news or activities of a user (e.g. "people I've met").

4.3.1.1.3. Notion of "processing of personal data" (data processing)

The "processing of personal data" refers to "any operation or set of operations in relation to such data, whatever the mechanism used, especially the obtaining, recording, organization, storage, adaptation or alteration, retrieval, consultation, use, disclosure by transmission, dissemination or otherwise making available, alignment or combinaison, blocking, deletion or destruction" [CNI 78].

This definition is applicable whatever the technology, data organization and/or service involved. Moreover, "the act of referring, on an internet page, to various persons and identifying them by name or by other means, for instance by giving their telephone number or information regarding their working conditions and hobbies, constitutes the processing of personal data wholly or partly by automatic means..."[8]. By collecting members' personal data, recording and conserving it, transmitting this data to partners and/or providing an electronic messaging service, a social networking service is therefore involved in data processing.

4.3.1.1.4. Notion of data controllers

The data controller is, "unless expressly designated by legislative or regulatory provisions relating to this processing, a person, public authority, department or any other organization who determines the purposes and means of the data processing" (see Art. 3-I [CNI 78]). This entity is therefore the person with the power to define or control the content of a process, with a concrete influence on the process. In practice, this person is responsible for the respect of data protection rules. This person acts as an intermediary when, for example, data subjects exercise their rights.

When a social networking service offers online communications platforms allowing users to publish and exchange information, three distinct categories may be said to constitute data controllers.

The *social network provider* are data controllers, as they define the purposes and the means of processing of users' personal data, along with the

---

8 European Court of Justice, 6 November 2003, Case C-101/01, Bodil Lindqvist.

basic services related to user management (e.g. account registration and deletion) (see [WP 09, p. 5]). They also determine the way in which user data may be used for advertising or marketing purposes, including advertising provided by third parties.

In addition to the basic service, third-party designers may offer additional applications, such as games or a service allowing users to send virtual birthday presents. In this case, the application providers determine the purposes and the way in which personal data are used by the application. They retrieve data via the "programming interface", using logins and passwords supplied by the user. In this way, the application provider constitutes a controller of personal data.

Finally, the users of social networking sites may, under certain circumstances, be considered to be data controllers.

If a member processes the personal data of their "friends" in the context of "exclusively private activities" (see Art. 2 [CNI 78]), the French Data Protection Act is not applicable. This is the case for personal correspondence, or when access to a user's data (profile data, messages, newsfeed, etc.) is limited to their chosen contacts.

However, users' activities can go beyond the exclusively private sphere. For example, a member may use a social network on behalf of a company for the purposes of collaboration and upload the personal data of other users, or for the purposes of a political or social association. In these cases, the WP29 considers that "a high number of contacts could be an indication that the household exception does not apply and therefore that the user would be considered a data controller" (see [WP 09, p. 6]).

The data controller should be distinguished from a *subcontractor*, defined as "any person who processes personal data on behalf of the data controller". In practice, a subcontractor is an external service provider connected with the controller by a contract. The subcontractor acts in accordance with instructions issued by the controller.

When a social network provider uses *cloud computing* services the former is generally considered to be the controller, and the latter a subcontractor [CNI 12a]. However, in the case of certain standardized Cloud offers, the client company may not really provide instructions, and will not be in a position to monitor the effectiveness of the security guarantees offered by the Cloud provider. In these cases, the CNIL considers that the two entities may *a priori* be considered to be jointly responsible. The service provider and the client must share responsibilities and define which entity is responsible for each obligation defined by the French Data Protection Act[9].

4.3.1.2. *Territorial applicability*

The French Data Protection Act is applicable if the data controller is established in France (see Art. 5-I-1 [CNI 78]). If this is not the case, we must distinguish between two situations:

– cases where the data controller is established in an EU Member State;

– cases where the data controller is established outside of the EU.

In the first case, the law of the EU country in which the data controller is established applies. The notion of "establishment" supposes the effective and real exercise of an activity via a stable installation. If a social networking service is established in Ireland, for example, the relevant processing declarations must be made in this country, and personal data must be provided with reference to the Irish Data Protection Act.

In the second case, the French Data Protection Act is applicable to processings carried out by a data controller outside of the EU if the entity uses "processing" located on French territory (see Art. 5-I-2 [CNI 78]). This notion should be taken in a broad sense: for example, it includes collection programs, computer servers, cookies and JavaScript banners. It also covers human or technical intermediaries, as in the case of surveys (see [WP 10a, p. 24]). If a social networking service established outside of the EU is involved in the reading or writing of personal data on a computer located in France, then French law is applicable.

4.3.1.3. *Exclusion of temporary copies*

For reasons relating to the specific nature of different technologies, the provisions of the French Data Protection Act "shall not apply to temporary copies, made in the context of technical operations of transmission and access provision to a digital network for the purpose of automatic,

---

9 Administrative notifications for the client, security obligations for the client and the service provider, etc.

intermediate and transitory storage of data, and with the sole aim of allowing other recipients of the service to benefit from the best access possible to the transmitted information" (see Art. 4 [CNI 78]).

This exception mainly applies to the use of proxy servers by access providers. It is applicable if two conditions are met: first, the objective involved must be to improve the quality of transmission or access services in order to provide better access to transmitted information, and, second, the methods used must be limited to automatic, intermediate and transitory storage of data.

Once personal data has been identified, it must be processed in accordance with the protection principles set down in the relevant legislation.

4.3.2. Key principles

The French Data Protection Act aims to define a balance between personal data protection and the use of data by private or public entities. In practice, its implementation may be complex, and involves legal, technical and organizational aspects.

4.3.2.1. The principle of purpose(s) and the quality of personal data

Personal data must be collected and processed for purposes (i.e. uses or aims) which are "specified, explicit and legitimate" (see Art. 6-2 [CNI 78]); it must not be subject to subsequent processing incompatible with these purposes. Anyone who diverts personal data from its proper purpose is punished by 5 years imprisonment and a fine of €300,000 (see Art. 226-21 of the French Penal Code).

The principle of purpose, which is found throughout the field of personal data protection, lies behind the principle of data quality, according to which personal data must be "adequate, relevant and not excessive in relation to the purposes for which they are obtained and their further processing" (see Art. 6-3 [CNI 78]). In accordance with the principle of proportionality, only that data which are required for the declared purposes should be collected.

According to the intended purpose (registration with a social networking site, uploading and provision of content, establishing contacts between users, user interactions, alerts concerning new content, diffusion of advertising materials, evaluation of site usage by members, treatment of requests sent by users to the administrator, etc.), social networking services collect certain items of identification data, such as a postal address, telephone number, pseudonym or date of birth. This does not, however, mean that the diffusion of this information will be justified by these purposes. The WP29 considers that "SNS providers should justify forcing their users to act under their real identity rather than under a pseudonym". SNSs should "[give] users choice in this respect particularly in the case of SNS with wide membership" (see [WP 09, p. 11]. In a similar manner, the collection of *the date of birth of minors* may be justified by considerations of child protection, the reduction of inappropriate behavior or the provision of appropriate content (notably targeted advertising). Depending on the context, it may be useful to "degrade" the data either by simply indicating whether the person is a minor or an adult, or by creating age groups, in order to avoid publishing the user's age or date of birth.

Finally, data shall be "accurate, complete and, where necessary, kept up-to-date" (see Art. 6-4 [CNI 78]). The data shall not be stored for longer than is necessary for the purposes for which it was obtained and processed (see Art. 6-5 [CNI 78]). After this time, information should be deleted or made anonymous; this creates a "right to be forgotten".

The data retention period may be fixed in a legal text. For example, article L 561-12 of the French Monetary and Financial Code fixes the period of conservation of identity elements for frequent and occasional clients at 5 years after an account is closed or a commercial relationship is terminated.

In the absence of specific legal provisions, analysis by data controllers should take account of all parameters to establish a relevant period of conservation:

– information removed by a user when updating his or her account should be deleted;

– information provided during registration should be deleted as soon as an account is closed. In some specific cases, these data should be retained for longer, for example to prevent malicious operations resulting from identity theft.

If a member does not use an SNS during "*a defined period of time*", his profile should become inactive (i.e. it should no longer be visible to other users or the outside world, see [WP 09, p. 10]). "*After another period of time*", the data linked to the abandoned account should be deleted. The data controller should determine the relevant periods for these different stages based on the specific nature of the service, and inform users of the applicable measures.

4.3.2.2. *Principle of legitimation*

There are six alternative legal criteria relating to the "legitimation" of data processing (see Art. 7 [CNI 78]). Thus, processing can only be carried out if:

– the data subject has given consent;

– the operation is necessary with regard to a legal obligation of the data controller;

– the operation is necessary to protect the data subject's life;

– the operation is necessary for the performance of a public service mission entrusted to the data controller or the data recipient;

– the operation is necessary for the performance of either a contract to which the data subject is a party, or pre-contractual measures carried out at the demand of the data subject;

– the operation is necessary to pursue the legitimate interests of the data controller or the data recipient, provided that this is not incompatible with the interests or the fundamental rights and liberties of the data subject.

Consent is undoubtedly the criterion that offers individuals the power of self-determination, at least in theory. Consent is "any freely given specific and informed indication of his wishes by which the data subject signifies his agreement to personal data relating to him being processed" (see Art. 2-h of [EUR 95]). This manifestation of indication must be "unambiguous" (see Art. 7-a of [EUR 95]). It may be expressed via any type of behavior, if this sign is sufficiently clear for the person to express their will and to be understood by the data controller. In all cases, indication is required, unlike a situation where consent is deduced from an absence of behavior (see

[WP 11, p. 12]). The data subject should be able to withdraw consent at any time.

Social network users enter their personal data themselves, and this constitutes a behavior from which consent may reasonably be deduced. For non-users, the situation is more complex: this involves prior determination of the data controller in order to identify the person or organization responsible for obtaining consent and, more generally, for respecting rights to information, access, rectification, removal and objection (see below). From this perspective, SNSs should advise users not to upload pictures or information about other individuals without their consent (see [WP 09, p. 7]). In all cases, consent should be provided in a specific and determined context; this does not correspond to current usage, notably, according to the CNIL, in Google's confidentiality rules (as of March 2012) [CNI 12b]. Consent may also be biased. Researchers have shown that the creation of a feeling of control encourages users to give their authorization, independently of whether or not they have real control of the personal data in question [BRA 10].

Data controllers may act on bases other than consent, such as the legitimate interests of the data controller or the recipient, "provided this is not incompatible with the interests or the fundamental rights and liberties of the data subject". The application of this criterion is complex, and requires us to study the balance of interests involved, alongside the reasonable expectations of the data subject, while remembering that this individual may exercise their right to object at any time (see [WP 14b]).

Cookies, tracers which are left and/or read when a user consults a Website, for example, to read e-mail, install or use a program, mobile application or tablet, are specifically regulated by the French Data Protection Act:

"Any subscriber or user of an electronic communication service shall be informed in a clear and comprehensive manner by the data controller or its representative, except if already previously informed, regarding:

– the purpose of any action intended to provide access, by means of electronic transmission, to information previously stored in their electronic connection terminal device, or to record data in this device;

– the means available to them to object to such action.

Such access or recording may only be carried out provided that the subscriber or user has explicitly expressed, after receiving said information, their agreement that may result from appropriate parameter settings in their connection device or any other system under their control" (see Art. 32-II [CNI 78]).

The law specifies that this agreement may be obtained from the use of appropriate settings in the connection device, or any other system under the control of the user.

In other words, once the user has been duly informed, the data controller (editors of Websites, operating systems, applications, advertising agencies, SNSs, etc.) must obtain consent before storing cookies on a computer. These cookies may relate to advertising operations, sharing operations on social networks which involve the collection of personal data without the consent of those involved, certain audience measurement cookies, calculation results in the case of "fingerprinting" (calculation of a unique machine identifier based on configuration elements for tracing purposes) or invisible pixels or "web bugs". The CNIL advises that consent should remain valid for a maximum of 13 months [CNI 14].

Certain tracers are free from the need to obtain consent, where these are "strictly necessary for the provision of an online communication service at the user's express request", or when their sole purpose is to enable or facilitate electronic communications. According to the CNIL, this exception is mainly applicable to basket cookies for selling sites, "session ID" cookies for the duration of a session, persistent cookies, limited to a few hours in certain cases, authentication cookies and persistent cookies used to personalize a user interface. The exception also covers certain audience measurement solutions (analytics).

4.3.2.3. *Principles concerning sensitive personal data*

Data revealing racial or ethnic origins, political, philosophical and religious opinions, trade union affiliation of persons, health or sexual life are considered to be sensitive data[10]. French law prohibits the collection of this

---

10 Article 8-I of the *French Data Protection Act* [CNI 78] and the Data Protection Directive [EUR 95]. Data relating to offences, convictions and security measures is also considered to be sensitive information.

information on principle, as the processing of this type of data is considered to present the highest risk to individual rights and freedoms.

However, there are certain exceptions (approximately 10) to this general prohibition. Sensitive personal data may notably be processed if it has been made public, if the processing is justified by the general interest, or if the person concerned gives their consent. If an SNS includes questions concerning sensitive data in registration forms, it should be made clear that these questions are optional.

Expressed consent is also required when personal data collected by electronic certification services, for the delivery and storage of certificates in relation to electronic signatures, are not collected directly from the data subject in question and are used for reasons other than the purposes for which they were collected (see Art. 33 [CNI 78]).

An identification number, or any other generally applicable number which enables identification, such as the French social security number is also considered to be sensitive data. Their use is strictly regulated and requires prior authorization by the CNIL (see Art. 25-I no. 6 [CNI 78]). In this context, the Commission aims to limit the conditions of use of the social security number by systematically requiring the data controller to demonstrate the existence of a legislative or regulatory text which legitimizes their use of the data from a legal perspective. Use of the social security number is therefore limited to health and social services.

4.3.2.4. *Principles of security and confidentiality*

Data security is a key element in the establishment of trust. The data controller "shall take all useful precautions, with regard to the nature of the data and the risks of the processing, to preserve the security of the data" (see Art. 34 [CNI 78]). The data controller must, in particular, prevent data from being altered, damaged or accessed by non-authorized third parties.

The company is required to make its best effort to ensure security by implementing appropriate technical and organizational methods with regard to processing aims, the risk of loss or interception of data, viruses, identity theft, etc. The CNIL has published certain documents on this topic, notably a guide to the security of personal data [CNI 10b] and two "advanced" security guides published in July 2012, including a method [CNI 12c] and a catalog of measures [CNI 12d] for use in managing privacy risks.

Application of the security principle should guarantee that personal data will not be communicated to unauthorized third parties, whether outside of the processing organization or within the organization, where not all employees may be authorized to handle this information. This obligation requires the implementation of access control and authentication mechanisms, notably involving the use of pseudonyms. This obligation also applies to application program interfaces (APIs). In this case, the data controller must ensure that third-party providers of applications are only able to access personal data which is strictly necessary for the functionning of the application, in accordance with purpose and quality principles. As the WP29 has highlighted, in practice, social networks have little control over third-party applications, and, as a general rule, decline all responsibility in relation to these applications.

Security and confidentiality obligations also apply to access to personal data published in a user's profile. This access depends on the settings used for the user's account. If access is unlimited, both members and non-members of an SNS will be able to access the user's private details.

Considering that "only a minority of users signing up to a service will make any changes to default settings", the WP29 considers that: "SNS should offer privacy-friendly default settings which allow users to freely and specifically consent to any access to their profile's content that is beyond their self-selected contacts in order to reduce the risk of unlawful processing by third parties. Restricted access profiles should not be discoverable by internal search engines, including the facility to search by parameters such as age or location. Decisions to extend access may not be implicit, for example with an "opt-out" provided by the controller of the SNS" (see [WP 09, p. 7]).

In cases of subcontracting, the data controller must choose subcontractors who present "adequate guarantees" to ensure the implementation of security and confidentiality measures (see Art. 35 [CNI 78]). They must also sign a contract with subcontractors specifying their obligations and the fact that the subcontractor may only process data "on the instructions of the data controller".

Breaching security and confidentiality obligations may lead to sanctions. The CNIL issued a public warning to DHL following on-site checks on 19 February 2014[11]. The Commission noted that 684,778 client files, requesting the redelivery of parcels, were freely accessible on the Internet. These files included the identity, address, telephone numbers and e-mails of the individuals concerned, along with detailed information intended to facilitate delivery, such as periods of absence for health reasons and access codes for apartment buildings. DHL adopted corrective measures from 28 February 2014 to prevent access to the data in question.

In February 2008, the CNIL issued VPC KHADR a fine of €5,000. Via the order tracking section of their company Website, third parties were able to access a named list of orders, with comments on manufacturing state and client payment details[12].

4.3.2.5. Principle of adequate protection

As to the European Directive 95/46/CE, personal data may circulate freely within the EU. An SNS may import and export data from Spain to France, for example, without needing to undertake any specific administrative proceedings.

Data transfers from the EU to a State outside the Union are only authorized toward countries which ensure "adequate levels of protection"[13]. The "adequacy" characteristic is notably dependent on the dispositions taken in the receiving State, the applicable security measures, specific processing characteristics, etc. Relatively few States respect these criteria: the adequacy decisions taken by the European Commission concern the three additional Member States of the European Economic Area (Norway,

---

11 Deliberation by the Select Committee of the CNIL, no. 2014-238, 12 June 2014, issuing a public warning to the company DHL International Express France.

12 Deliberation by the Select Committee of the CNIL, no. 2008-053, 21 February 2008 imposing sanctions on VPC KHADR.

13 Article 25-1 of Directive 95/46/CE [EUR 95] and Article 68 of the *French Data Protection Act* [CNI 78] which refers to a "sufficient" level of protection.

Liechtenstein and Iceland), Andorra, Israel, Switzerland, Canada, Argentina, Australia, New Zealand, Uruguay, the Faroe Islands, Jersey, Guernsey and the Isle of Man.

However, personal data may be exported to countries without adequate levels of protection in certain cases, where:

– data transfer is carried out by a US company which has voluntarily adhered to the Safe Harbor principles published by the US Department of Commerce[14]. This is notably the case for Facebook and LinkedIn[15];

– the data subject has given their unambiguous consent to the transfer; this exception is interpreted in the strictest possible sense by the CNIL, which considers that its use should be limited to exceptional cases, something which is not generally the case with SNSs;

– the CNIL authorizes processing, as it is able to guarantee an adequate level of protection of privacy and personal data, notably due to the existence of rules within a company, known as Binding Corporate Rules (BCR), or contractual clauses.

In the context of cloud computing, personal data are often hosted in data centers located outside of the EU. If this type of service is used by an SNS, there are two possible solutions which may be envisaged during the creation of a contract with the cloud service provider:

– stipulation that data must only be transferred to countries recognized as providing adequate levels of protection;

– the insertion of standard contractual clauses defined by the European Commission in order to obtain authorization from the CNIL more easily[16].

---

14 Commission decision 2000/520/CE, 26 July 2000, in accordance with European Parliament and Council directive 95/46/CE concerning the relevance of the protection given by the principle of "safe harbors" and associated questions, published by the US Department of Commerce OJEC L 215, 25.8.2000, p. 7.

15 See list of US companies which subscribe to the safe harbor principle: https://www.export.gov/safehrbr/list.aspx.

16 See the models of contractual clauses proposed by the European Commission, or those offered by the CNIL in the document "*Recommandations pour les entreprises qui envisagent de souscrire à des services de Cloud computing*" [CNI 14].

4.3.2.6. *Principle of prior information (or transparency principle)*

The French Data Protection Act establishes the right of users to examine any information held concerning them. This right is essential, and affects the exercise of other personal rights, such as the right to access and the right to object. It targets both the collection and use of information. The data controller must inform the data subject of:

– his identity and of his representative, where applicable;

– the purposes of the processing;

– the compulsory or optional character of responses;

– the possible consequences of an absence of reply for the user;

– the recipients of the data;

– the rights of the user (rights to object to access);

– intended data transfers to a State outside of the EU (see Art 32-I [CNI 78]).

In addition to the information specified by the law, the data controller must provide any other information involved in fair processing of data (see Art. 6-1 [CNI 78]). From this perspective, the WP29 considers that the information provided by an SNS provider should, notably, include the usage of data for direct marketing purposes, the use of sensitive data, and provide an overview of profiles, their creation and chief data sources (see [WP 09, p. 8]). The Working Group also recommends that SNSs should provide adequate warnings to users about the privacy risks to themselves and to others when they upload information on the SNS.

The right to information has certain limits. It is not applicable when the individual in question has already been informed, or when the information is impossible to obtain or would involve disproportionate efforts compared with the interest of the procedure. When collected data are anonymized within a short period of time using a procedure recognized by the CNIL, the required information may be limited to the identity of the data controller and, where applicable, that of his representative, alongside the intended purpose of the processing.

In practice, the right to information can be difficult to implement. For example, how might non-users of an SNS be informed that information concerning them, notably photos in which they are shown and/or tagged, is available online, given that the SNS site will not have their contact details? How can all of this information be shown on a cell phone screen? Despite this, the principle of transparency is an essential condition for the exercise of other rights by the data subjects.

4.3.2.7. *Principle of the right to access and the right to resale*

Any data subject has the *right to question the data controller* in order to obtain "confirmation as to whether the personal data relating to him forms part of the processing" (see Art. 39 [CNI 78]) along with "information relating to the purposes of processing, the categories of processed data, the recipients to whom the data are disclosed and information relating to intended transfers of personal data toward a State that is not a Member State of the European Union". The individual also has the *right to obtain a copy of* their *data* "in an accessible form", along with all available information concerning the origins of the data. If the request cannot immediately be fulfilled, the data controller must provide a signed, dated acknowledgment of receipt, and provide a full response within 2 months[17].

Continuing in the same manner as the right to query, the *right of rectification* allows a person to demand that data which are inaccurate or outdated, or which has been collected illegally, be rectified, updated, blocked or deleted (see Art. 40 [CNI 78]). The data controller must notify third parties about the required modifications in cases where they hold copies of the personal data in question. This is the case, for example, if a social networking site has shared data with a third-party application provider.

In all cases, the data subjects must provide proof of their administrative identity (name, surname, address, etc.). If the demand is expressed in writing, it must be "signed and accompanied by a photocopy of a proof of identity carrying the holder's signature"[18]. However, on the

---

17 Article 94 of decree no. 2005-1309, 20 October 2005, enacted for the application of Act no. 78-17 of 6 January 1978 on Data Processing, Files and Individual Liberties (Amended by Decree 2007-451 of 25 March 2007), JORF no. 247, 22 October 2005.
18 Article 92 of decree no. 2005-1309, cited above.

Internet, and particularly in the context of SNS, most users do not communicate their administrative identity using a pseudonym and a password. "The absence of a legal framework for the definition and protection of digital identity prevents individuals from exercising their rights, and notably from requiring search engines to reveal the data they hold concerning these individuals" (see [DES 12, p. 168]).

Certain SNS have identified a solution, where users are invited to provide their administrative identity when filling out the registration form. This subverts the objective of the law, as in order to exercise their rights, individuals must give up their anonymity and supply personal data. One possibility suggested by the WP29, but which does not solve the problem of administrative identification, involves the creation of a "complaint handling office", accessible from the SNS homepage, to deal with data protection and privacy issues, along with complaints from both members and non-members (see [WP 09, p. 11]).

4.3.2.8. *Principle of objection*

All data subjects have two distinct rights to object:

1) Individuals should be able to register their objection on "legitimate grounds" to the processing of their data (see Art. 38 [CNI 78]). While the French Data Protection Act does not define these legitimate grounds, the Data Protection Directive states that these must be "compelling legitimate grounds relating to his particular situation and to the processing of data relating to him" (see Art. 14-a [EUR 95]). These motives are therefore subjective. Taken on a case-by-case basis by data controllers, they must allow a person to exercise their right to objection in order to control the collection of their data for their own reasons.

These reasons were assessed by the CNIL in the Juriscom affair. The association manages an online directory which allows users to access the contact details of members of regulated legal professions. In this case, the Commission considered that complainants fulfilled the condition of "legitimate grounds" for the deletion of their data. Certain legal professionals are barred from advertising, which is punishable by disciplinary action. Moreover, Juriscom was held to be responsible for damage to professional reputations "*by the replacement of real telephone numbers by premium-rate numbers*". The CNIL also considered that "the fact that the complainants' data was freely accessible online does not constitute an obstacle to their right to demand rectification or deletion and that "this right remains applicable whatever the nature of the source(s)". For these reasons, the CNIL imposed a €10,000 fine for non-respect of the right to object[19];

2) In the case of canvassing, notably for commercial ends, the right to object may be exercised free of charge and on request, without requiring individuals to provide a reason. The persons in question must be informed before their details are communicated to third parties for marketing reasons, and must be able to object this communication.

4.3.2.9. *Principle of notification to the CNIL*

Certain processings do not need to be notified to the CNIL, generally because they pose no risk in terms of privacy and freedoms. However, in most cases, data controllers must complete certain administrative formalities before processing begins (see Art. 22-I [CNI 78]). Failure to meet this obligation is sanctioned by law (see Art. 226-16 and 226-16-1 of the French Penal Code). Moreover, failure to notify prevents later disposal of personal data [DEL 13].

The notification obligation requires data controllers to determine the appropriate notification status depending on their purposes and the personal data which they process:

– standard declaration (this is the case for a Clients and Prospects file);

– normal declaration;

– opinion request (this is notably the case for online administration services);

– request for authorization (required when processing biometric data for identity checks).

Processing of personal data carried out on behalf of the State, using biometric data to authenticate or check the identity of individuals, shall be authorized by a State Council decree, taken after a reasoned and published opinion of the CNIL (see Art. 27-I-2 [CNI 78]). This is the case of decree

---

19 Deliberation by the Select Committee of the CNIL no. 2014-041, 29 January 2014, imposing a fine on the Juriscom & Associés association.

no. 2005-1726, the current version of the decree relating to electronic passports[20].

The normal declaration procedure generally applies. This declaration can be made either on paper or electronically, sent directly via the CNIL Website. Once the declaration file is complete, the Commission must immediately deliver an acknowledgment of receipt. The declarant can begin data processing as soon as acknowledgment is received, although this does not constitute acknowledgment of conformity.

The notification may be avoided by designating a Personal Data Protection Officer (or *Informatique et Libertés* correspondent)[21]. This possibility is currently optional, and does not apply in cases where personal data may be transferred to a State outside of the EU.

4.3.3. Sanctions and prejudice to brand image

Data controllers are subject to several types of sanctions in cases of infringement of the personal data protection principles.

Criminal sanctions: failure to meet any of the obligations incumbent on the data controller is subject to penal sanctions (see Art. 226-16 of the French Penal Code). In principle, this responsibility lies with the legal representative of the judicial entity considered to be the data controller. It may be transferred to another natural person via delegation of powers. For example, the non-respect of notified purposes or the fact of carrying out processing for marketing purposes despite the data subject's objection is punishable by 5 years imprisonment and a fine of €300,000 (see Art. 226-21 and 226-18-1 of the penal code). The same sanction applies for the collection of personal data by fraudulent or unfair means (see Art. 226-18 of the penal code).

In a ruling by the Paris Court of Appeal on 18 May 2005, judges upheld this infraction, considering that the implementation of two programs by a

20 Deliberation by the CNIL no. 2007-368, 11 December 2007, giving an opinion on a projected decree by the State Council modifying decree no. 2005-1726 of 30 December 2005 regarding electronic passports.
21 Article 22-III [CNI 78]. See the *Association Française des Correspondants à la protection des Données Personnelles* (AFCDP), Website: www.afcdp.net.

company intending to harvest the e-mail addresses of individuals online constituted illicit and unfair collection of data. The defendant was ordered to pay a fine[22] of €3,000.

Civil sanctions: based on article 1382 of the French Civil Code, which stipulates that "any act whatever of man, which causes damage to another, obliges the one by whose fault it occurred, to compensate it": several companies have been obliged to pay damages and interests, in addition to their criminal liability, for direct personal prejudice resulting from an infringement of the terms of the French Data Protection Act.

Administrative and financial sanctions: the CNIL is able to issue warnings, formal notice or injunctions to cease processing, and fines not more than €150,000 for a first offense (see Art. 45 [CNI 78]). The Commission also has the power to make spot checks and inspections.

In practice, criminal sanctions are rare, but sanctions by the CNIL are more widespread[23]. In February 2009, the Commission issued DirectAnnonces with a €40,000 fine: the company harvested person-to-person real estate advertisements online in order to compile and sell them[24]. The sale of these results to banks and real estate professionals was carried out without the knowledge of the data subjects, who were thus unable to object to marketing activities by the "partners" of DirectAnnonces.

Pages Jaunes (the French site of the Yellow Pages company) was issued with a public warning in March 2010 for adding personal data taken from six social networks to the more traditional directory information on its site www.pagesblanches.fr[25]. The information on the Pages Blanches Website included names, surnames, photos, pseudonyms, educational establishments, employers, professions and geographic localization. Users with profiles on

---

22 Paris Court of Appeal, 11th chamber, section B, 18 May 2005, Prosecutor vs. Fabrice H. confirmed by the Court of Cassation, Criminal Chamber, 14 March 2006, Fabrice H. vs. Prosecutor.

23 In 2013, the CNIL issued 57 notices, 4 of which were made public, 5 warnings and 14 sanctions, of which 7 were of a financial nature. In 2012, the Commission issued 43 notices, 9 warnings and 4 financial sanctions.

24 Deliberation by the Select Committee of the CNIL no. 2009-148, 26 February 2009, imposing a financial sanction on the DirectAnnonces company.

25 Deliberation by the Select Committee of the CNIL no. 2011-203, 21 September 2011, issuing a warning to the Yellow Pages company.

Facebook, Copains d'Avant, Viadeo, LinkedIn, Twitter and Trombi were not informed that their personal data are subject to being "harvested" and published online by Pages Blanches. Moreover, the processed information included details of minors and individuals on the red list (telephone preference service). This made it difficult for users to exercise their right to object, and the modification or deletion of a profile on a social networking site did not immediately lead to the removal of the relevant information from the Pages Blanches Website.

Consideration should also be given to the *risk of prejudice to the company image*. Given the weakness of criminal, civil and administrative sanctions, this constitutes the highest risk for companies. The inclusion of sanctions issued by the CNIL in publications, including newspapers, is no longer subject to the condition that the organization acted in bad faith[26]. The fact that failings are now published can cause significant damage to the image of an organization: when the Acadomia company was issued with a public notice by the CNIL in May 2010[27], its stock price fell dramatically, from 15.23 on 31 May 2010 to 10.78 at the end of December 2010.

The risks posed by the French Data Protection Act, therefore, need to be taken into account as early as possible with the establishment of a conformity program. This law and the CNIL tenets provide a legal framework, but do not offer a ready-made solution. In order to avoid sanctions and ensure reasonable use of personal data, global reflection is required on a case-by-case basis. This analysis must take account of ethical and societal parameters, notably the way in which users perceive the protection of their personal data and privacy, in association with the context of use of this personal data. The processing of medical data of SNS users, for example, would be considered differently if used to prevent an epidemic than if it was used for targeted marketing of hunger-suppression products.

It may also be useful to consult the CNIL in order to establish a climate of confidence. This approach should not be considered as a constraint, but as an opportunity for dialog. This development, toward a reduction in

---

26 In application of the law of 29 March 2011 relating to the defense of rights, the Select Committee of the CNIL is permitted to publish the fines imposed. Article 8-3 of the law of 29 March 2011, relating to the defense of rights, modifying article 46 of the *French Data Protection Act*.

27 Deliberation by the Select Committee of the CNIL no. 2010-113, 22 April 2010, issuing a warning to the company AIS 2, operating as Acadomia.

administrative procedures and increased accountability, is clearly visible in the proposed Personal Data Protection regulations of 2012 (see below).

4.4. Technical solutions for privacy and personal data protection

4.4.1. *Increasing control over ambient intelligence*

The difficulty in securing environments including communicating objects lies in the implementation of complex operations to control access in low-cost equipment with very limited resources in terms of CPU, memory, energy and bandwidth (emission capacity). Development of a solution with high enough levels of security to resist any and all hacking attempts is not realistic, as the associated costs would severely limit the sale of objects on a large scale. Instead, we need to design methods with a sufficient level of difficulty/complexity to prevent the majority of attempts to "scan" an individual's personal details.

From an object perspective, control of access to generated data consists of deciding whether or not to release the stored information. In computer systems, this type of access control generally requires the request issuer to communicate a credential (see Chapter 1, section 1.5.1) to prove knowledge of the correct secret. The authentication system then carries out verification using a secure database of secrets (such as passwords or cryptographic keys) and certain cryptographic operations. These operations cannot be carried out at object level as they are too costly in terms of resources. Traditional security solutions involve a minimum of 20,000 logic gates, well above the capacity of a passive RFID tag used in commercial settings (with a maximum of 15,000 gates). One solution consists of using simplified cryptographic algorithms, such as the ECC encryption algorithm, which is based on elliptical curves [FOU 03] and has already been integrated into sensors. Currently, only the solution patented by Télécom SudParis [EL 13] offers a satisfactory response in terms of cost for the RFID, resistance to attacks and scalability factors.

In addition to the limited capacity of objects, there are other fundamental problems associated with AmI. The integration of access control mechanisms means that secrets must be configured and administrated within the objects themselves; this raises questions about which entity is responsible for configuration – should this be the sensor or RFID producer, the industrial entity providing the application (logistics or domotics), or the individual user? Should the same secret be configured for all objects in order to simplify access control procedures, thus leading to a lower level of security? Does a secret update procedure need to be included? What should happen if the secret is cracked by hackers? Is an update mechanism required? If several generations of communicating objects are launched over years, how can we guarantee that they will still be able to communicate? These questions are not currently being considered from a global perspective, but only in a partial manner and in relation to the specific functions of applications using these objects, in cases where security measures are included.

Individual wireless technology enthusiasts have already begun to implement peering procedures via their domestic Wireless Fidelity (Wi-Fi) networks, connecting computers and Internet access routers. In this context, peering is carried out over Bluetooth connections. This may soon be possible for other household and domotic equipment so that televisions may be able to interact with games consoles or refrigerators, while avoiding interaction with the neighbors' equipment. Industrial actors are currently working on the creation of simple, reliable peering solutions which will be accessible to all (adolescents, homemakers, etc.). Several conditions need to be taken into account in order to respect user privacy. A device should not be able to initiate dialog with another piece of equipment, for example, unless the user has physical access to the second device and triggers the peering order by a physical action proving proximity (e.g. by pressing a button). Once a peering connection has been established, shared information flows should be encrypted in order to prevent access by third parties in the vicinity, for example to intercept vacation photos transmitted from the family computer to the television.

While no global security solution has yet been found for communications between any communicating objects – known as "Machine to Machine" (M2M) – some progress has been made in various specific economic sectors (automobile, logistics, health, etc.). Sensors will play an increasingly significant role in day-to-day life for certain niche applications. However, this impact will be minimal compared to the takeoff of RFID technology, which will revolutionize logistics within the next few years, from use on luggage in airports to shopping carts and consumer goods. Certain companies are already using these methods, including Metro and DHL, and more recently Adler (a German distribution company), Scarmor (the purchasing department of the Leclerc supermarket chain in Brittany) and Macys. These companies expect to make significant gains in terms of logistics and new uses (inventory management, pallet flow control with alerts in case of errors or forgeries, etc.) [LEF 09].

RFID [EL 12] is a contactless technology used to scan and identify ticketed products without requiring physical or visual contact. Three types of RFID tags are available. Passive tags are used in logistics due to their low cost (a few Euro cents). These tags do not possess their own energy source and are made up of a chip and an antenna. The memory is used to store an electronic product code (EPC) [EPC 14] and a small amount of additional information. The data contained in the tag may be read by an RFID reader from a reasonable distance (a few meters); the reader provides the energy required by the tag to carry out a certain process (e.g. integrity checks) and produce a response, generally containing the product's EPC.

Several improvements have been made for tag reading, particularly in facilitating quasi-simultaneous error-free readings of several thousand tags. This is important in the field of logistics, where it may be necessary to scan the contents of a truck carrying tens of pallets of products. Other progress has been made concerning privacy protection via the integration of access control.

The EPC Class-1 Generation-2 standard (EPC Gen-2) was approved in 2004 and ratified by the International Organization for Standardization (ISO) as an amendment to 18000-6 in 2006 and 2013 [EPC 13]. The standard is intended for use in logistics, with a UHF frequency band of 860–960 MHz. It defines reading/writing functions and controlled access zones for tags, and introduces a function for permanent deactivation of tags. In technical terms, this is achieved by sending a command including a 32-bit PIN via the reader antenna. The process is generally carried out when checking out goods. While this function presents the advantage of deactivating the tag, it also prevents later reuse, for example when a product is returned to the store.

The version of the EPCGen2 standard approved in 2013 [EPC 13] also specifies an access control protocol by which the tag authenticates the reader before supplying information. This protocol, which limits data accessibility, has not been widely used for commercial products. It requires the reader and the tag to share a 32-bit APWD (Axis Password) and include 16 bits of simple basic functions, such as XOR gates and cyclic redundancy checks

(CRCs) in order to detect transmission errors. It also requires the inclusion of a pseudo-random number generator (PRNG). Pseudo-random numbers help tags making the electronic exchanges be unique per authentication session.

The protocol shown in Figure 4.1 includes two phases, which follow an identical path: the reader begins by emitting a request, waits for the emission of a random number by the tag (RT1 and RT2) and responds with a CCPWdM or CCPWdL message. Messages are generated by applying the XOR function to the first (and, respectively, last) 16 bits of the APWDM (respectively, APWDL) to the random number RT1 (respectively, RT2). Thereby, message 3 in Figure 4.1 enables the tag to verify that the reader knows half of the APWD, and message 4 the other half. Presuming that the numbers are genuinely selected in a pseudo-random manner, messages 2, 3, 5 and 6 will be different for each authentication session. This means that the authentication phase of the exchange will be unique.

However, this standard is subject to several security issues; (i) the reader does not authenticate the tag and can, therefore, receive erroneous information from the wrong tag; (ii) by monitoring exchanges in cases of successful authentication, it is possible to reconstruct a shared 32-bit password. This can be done by applying the XOR (reversible) function as follows: $CCPWd_M$ XOR R_{T1} = $APWD_M$ and $CCPWd_L$ XOR R_{T2} = $APWD_L$. Thereby, a tag may be cloned via initialization using the same password.

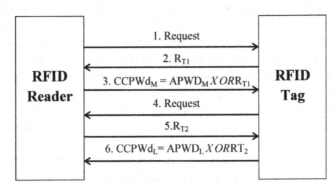

Figure 4.1. *Authentication protocol in the EPC Gen2v2 standard*

4.4.2. Communication anonymization solutions

Several technical solutions have been suggested in order to satisfy user anonymity requirements. These solutions require a clear understanding of IP addresses and web routing, and also use certain cryptographic notions. These basic elements are described in section 4.4.2.1. The technical solutions are discussed in section 4.4.2.2, and section 4.4.2.3 gives a more detailed analysis of solutions that have been implemented and are available online.

4.4.2.1. Fundamental elements of IP networks

As a simplification, we may consider that Internet traffic is structured as variable-size IP packets, each made up of an IP header and a payload [TOU 03]. Among other things, the header contains the source and destination IP addresses for the packet. The payload contains the information that are wished to be transmitted by the source equipment to the destinator. Generally, these devices are terminals which send and receive packets upon user's request; however, some network equipments (e.g. routers) may also generate IP packets for ensuring efficient networking operations. That is, they exchange information about their connectivity with other networks, so they are able to establish routes. Several routing protocols exist, such as BGP, RIP and OSPF, used to enable routers to maintain routing tables.

When a router receives an IP packet, it must analyze the destination IP address, consult the routing table and decide which router the packet should be transmitted to, if the router is not itself connected to the destination terminal. Packets are thus transmitted hop-by-hop until the destination is reached. The number of hops corresponds to the number of intermediate routers the packet travels through between the source and the destination.

A proxy is a program on a server in a private company network which applies a particular process to a specific type of traffic for all terminals in the private network. This may involve filtering the flows emitted by terminals to verify their authorization to access the Internet, for example to check whether the site an employee wishes to consult from their work computer is included in the list of sites authorized by the employer. The principle of the proxy is to relay traffic between a terminal and a server. It is transparent for both the terminal and the server during traffic exchanges. In other words, the terminal feels like it is communicating directly with the server, and *vice versa.* This raises an interesting point regarding the use of proxies in relation to privacy concerns. A proxy hides equipment located on either side. An analysis of the traffic exchanged between a terminal and a proxy allows us to observe packets which have the IP addresses of the terminal and the proxy, while analysis of the traffic exchanged between the proxy and the server only gives us the IP addresses of the proxy and the server. It is therefore not possible to obtain both the origin and destination points of the traffic on either side of the proxy. This property may contribute to user privacy in the objective of anonymity preservation.

When an IP packet is encrypted, only the payload or part of the payload is affected. The header remains in cleartext so that routers can pass the packet through the network. The protocols used for encryption include IPsec, SSL and SSH [LAU 11]. The advantage of encryption is that the content remains ununderstandable to unauthorized individuals, As such it can help anonymizing communications.

4.4.2.2. *Traffic anonymity techniques*

As discussed in section 4.4.2.1, simple analysis of traffic and IP addresses may be used to trace the communications of an individual. Two groups of solutions may be used to anonymize communications.

The first group of techniques consists of modifying the traditional packet routing methods. Like proxies, it involves indirect routing between the source and the destination of traffic. Several intermediate proxies may be used. Thus, wherever eavesdropping occurs in the network, it is impossible to discover the identity of the communicating terminals through simple analysis of the IP addresses of packets.

This group includes the Crowds [REI 98], Buses [BEI 08], and Mixes solutions [CHA 81]. Crowds requires devices to subscribe to the service and to work together. When a terminal wishes to connect to a Website, it randomly selects a Crowds member, who then decides randomly whether to transmit the message directly to the recipient or to another member of the Crowds group. It is therefore impossible for a third party, or even a member, to know from where a message originates. Buses operates using an analogy with public transport, where a user is harder to trace if they change buses frequently. Buses terminals are the equivalent of bus stops, and regular lines are established between certain terminals. Thus, the terminals route messages until the destination is reached. A terminal needing to send a message waits for a "bus" to pass by or to leave from its "stop" to add a message. Mixes operates in a similar way to Crowds in that "Mix" nodes participate in an anonymization service. However, Mixes goes a step further, providing cryptographic protection of exchanges between Mix nodes and "mixing" flows so that it is impossible to distinguish the flows exiting a Mix. A Mix receives a message from a source node, then stores the message for a certain period of time, during which it receives other messages from other nodes. It then transmits all of the collected messages simultaneously to other Mix nodes, or to the recipients. This mixing procedure creates a property of unlinkability between the source and destination (see Chapter 1, section 1.5.1) in addition to anonymity for both source and destination. An attacker, with a high capacity for monitoring all of the connections between mixes, would even not be able to connect a message emitted by a Mix to another message previously received by the same Mix. Note that messages are not transmitted in real time, and this system was initially designed for electronic messaging systems.

The second group of solutions operates in a similar way to single-use aliases for social networks (see Chapter 1), and aims to make IP addresses, or even MAC addresses[28], ephemeral. The basic principle involves frequently changing IP address, thus preventing any linkability between these addresses or any association to a particular source terminal. However, the use of ephemeral IP addresses is meaningless within the local network of the terminal in question. Within this perimeter (and only within this perimeter), it is very easy to identify a communicating terminal using its static MAC address. To extend terminal anonymity to the local network, ephemeral IP addresses should be paired with ephemeral MAC addresses; distinct sets of MAC and IP addresses should be used to avoid the possibility of connecting these addresses, destroying anonymity. This solution is offered by FLASCHE [ZUG 05] for an IPv6 network environment [CIZ 05]. FLASCHE requires the terminal to generate and use a different set of IPv6 and MAC addresses for each access to a service. Several MAC/IPv6 address sets may be used simultaneously by the same terminal (same network

---

28 A Media Access Control (MAC) address is assigned to the network card of a device to enable communication with other equipment connected to the same local link.

interface). The identifier, made up of the IPv6 and MAC addresses, is therefore heteronymous.

This idea has been taken further for IPv6 networks with protection against IPv6 address spoofing, via the use of cryptographically generated addresses (CGAs) [CHE 11]. A CGA address associated with a terminal is a specific IPv6 address which makes possible any node in the neighborhood of the terminal to verify that the sending terminal genuinely holds the announced cryptographic material (the private key). CGA addresses were created in order to protect the Neighbor Discovery mechanism [NAR 07] and are included in the secure version of the mechanism, Secure Neighbor Discovery (SEND) [ARK 05]. CGAs must verify a certain number of properties and are not generated immediately. In T. Cheneau's doctoral thesis [CHE 11], performance tests showed that seven CGAs can be generated per second, and it is thus possible to establish seven connections per second, which is entirely realistic.

Another solution [GRU 05] considers the 802.11b wireless environment. It proposes periodic changes of MAC addresses only in order to reduce linkability between connections. However, this solution only partially responds to anonymity problems, as linkability is always possible when static IP addresses are used.

Finally, note that the level of anonymity offered by the heteronymous property of IP/MAC addresses is not perfect. If the data carried in IP packets contain important information (allowing identification of the source or linkability between two or more connection flows), then an attacker will simply need to carry out a more detailed analysis of exchanges in order to breach flow anonymity, as shown in [ECK 10] for web applications.

4.4.2.3. *Software solutions*

The Onion Router (TOR) and Anonymity.Online (AN.ON) are two software solutions currently available to Internet users. The Tarzan and Freedom Network projects, which are presented briefly below, are no longer maintained. Other poorly documented solutions, such as Anonymizer (http://www.anonymizer.com), are commercialized. The aim of these projects is to provide Internet users with the ability to anonymize their connections.

The AN.ON research project (http://anon.inf.tu-dresden.de/index_en. html) aims to allow anonymous and unobservable use of the Internet. It is based on the Mix solution [CHA 81] described in section 4.4.2.2. Users must download a free program, "JonDonym Anonymous Proxy" (JAP). Mix nodes are provided by independent institutions (universities and public infrastructures) which have officially declared that they do not store traffic traces (log files).

The Tarzan solution [FRE 02] is no longer maintained. It offered an anonymous peer-to-peer network, also based on Mix [CHA 81], where each Mix corresponded to a peer-to-peer node.

Freedom Network (http://freedomnetwork.info/) [BOU 00] provided a set of private proxies administrated by the Freedom operator. The service ceased to be available in 2010. The service was based on two key ideas: first, to guarantee user anonymity during access to web services (e-mail, Websites, etc.) and, second, to allow them to bypass the filtering policies of their access provider (company, school, etc.). To do this, users were required to register with Freedom in order to receive periodic e-mails with new proxy addresses. In this way, users simply needed to configure their applications using suitable proxy addresses in order to access web services, and to change their address if flows are blocked.

The TOR project (https://www.torproject.org/) [DIN 04] is the most significant project currently in use. It responds to the anonymization problem for web flows (TCP type[29]) and is actively maintained by the open source community. In 2010, the TOR project was awarded an open-source program award in the social interest category.

The TOR network is based on several hundred relay nodes, known as TOR servers. When a user wishes to send a message to a recipient, they construct a random path among TOR servers, where each node only knows the previous and subsequent nodes in the path. Before sending the message, the user must encrypt the information as many times as there are TOR servers on the path. This process starts by using the cryptographic material which will be used for decryption by the final server in the path. The result is then encrypted with the material used for the penultimate node, and so on,

---

29 TCP: Transmission Control Protocol. This corresponds to an application flow exchange protocol in connected mode (with signaling for the beginning and end of connections). TCP flows include e-mail, peer-to-peer, web, etc., applications.

until the message is encrypted using the cryptographic material for the first node. In this way, the first node receiving the message is able to decrypt the information needed to identify the next node on the pathway. The second server is then able to decrypt the message from the first server, and so on, until the destination is reached. This is known as the "onion" procedure, as with each passage through a TOR server, a layer of encryption is removed. Clearly, this procedure means that each node is only aware of one server either side of them on the pathway. The source and destination of the message therefore remain anonymous. Note that in this case, routing is applicative. To improve efficiency, it is recommended that the same pathway should be used for a maximum duration of 10 min for transmission of all the messages sent from the same source.

TOR is used by a wide range of users, including government agencies, but also members of the general public, military figures, journalists, the police and political activists. However, TOR presents certain weaknesses for a number of specific applications, which reveal the IP address of the user, particularly in the case of the P2P BitTorrent application [MAN 10].

The Invisible Internet Project (I2P) (http://geti2p.net/en/) offers a decentralized solution, which is an alternative to TOR project. It is based on cryptographic identifiers defined for I2P sources and destinations, thus guaranteeing anonymity to both the communicating entity and third parties. The path from the source to the destination is constructed by interconnecting two one-way partial paths associated with each terminal. A partial path is characterized by the two I2P routers through which connection is made, and is associated with an I2P node. The inbound path is used to get in touch with a node, and the outbound path allows nodes to emit traffic. Each node has several inbound and outbound paths. An inbound path must simply be connected with an outbound path to enable communications between two I2P nodes. This path may change in the course of communications to offer a higher level of anonymity. The I2P project offers several possible configurations depending on anonymity, reliability and performance (bandwidth, latency) requirements.

4.4.3. *Personal data protection tools for transactions*

Personal information often needs to be collected and retained in the course of electronic transactions in order to ensure correct operation of the service. The first difficulty in this case lies in the distinction between data which needs to be collected for running the service and additional, optional data used to enrich profiles with various intentions (targeted advertising, profile merchandizing). The second difficulty lies in the interpretation and evaluation of the personal data protection practices used by service providers. A provider collecting data with the only purpose of performing the requested service must store this data for the duration of the transaction, with the sole objective of offering the requested service, and with no data disclosure to third parties.

Current work enables the definition of languages for the expression of privacy, allowing different programs involved (navigators and servers) to establish a common understanding of the practices involved in protecting user privacy. Multiple software solutions, some of which require a particular network architecture, can then be brought together to evaluate practices and automatically decide on their acceptability by the navigator.

4.4.3.1. Languages for privacy support

The Platform for Privacy Preferences language, known as P3P, was standardized by the World Wide Web Consortium (W3C) [CNI 14] in 2002. A second version was standardized in 2006 [WOR 06]. P3P considers that the protection of privacy and personal data should be covered by an agreement between the Website collecting the data and the individual concerned. The system is based on the principle that users give consent to the sites collecting their personal data, providing that the published site's privacy practices are compliant to the users' wishes. Site practices and user preferences are expressed using a common vocabulary, expressed in a format which can be understood by a machine (for example, a web browser). P3P is implemented in Internet Explorer, but its success was qualified as adoption was limited to few Websites.

P3P [WOR 06] is based on eXtensible Markup *Language* (XML). It defines its own XML tags, allowing a Website to specify a number of fundamental elements, directly extracted from the European Data Protection Directive 95/46/EC [EUR 95]. These fundamental elements consist of responding to the following questions:

– which entity wishes to collect the data (ENTITY tag)? The XML ENTITY tag gives a precise description of the web service provider wishing to collect data;

– what type of data will be collected (DATA tag)? This tag expresses the nature of the collected data;

– why, and for what purpose, is data to be collected (PURPOSE tag)? A relatively large number of reasons exist, from the simple need to complete a transaction (PURPOSE=<current />) to an unspecified purpose (PURPOSE=<other-purpose />) via the web browsing personalization for an identified user (PURPOSE=<individual-decision />);

– how long will data be stored by the service provider (RETENTION tag)? Among other things, the service may specify that data will be destroyed once a service has been provided (RETENTION=<no-retention />) or retain the information indefinitely (RETENTION=<indefinitely />). Note that indefinite data retention is not permitted under European legislation and does not conform to data quality principles (see section 4.3.2);

– whom, if anybody, will the data be shared with (RECIPIENT tag)? In other words, who will receive the data? For example, a service provider may specify their intention to share data with other close business entities having the same privacy practices (RECIPIENT=<ours />), or with product delivery entities (RECIPIENT=<delivery />), or even to make the data public (RECIPIENT=<public />).

Service providers use P3P to publish their privacy practices in the form of a set of rules indicating the contents of the PURPOSE, RETENTION and RECIPIENT tag for each piece of data requested by the provider.

Other languages have also been developed which are complementary to P3P, such as APPEL [CRA 02] or XPref [AGR 03], permitting users to express their privacy preferences, i.e. the manner in which they will allow their personal data to be handled. These languages, based on XML and P3P, define additional elements specific to the needs of users. For example, the RULE element specifies the behavior (BEHAVIOR) attribute, i.e.:

– if data may be disclosed in the mentioned conditions (BEHAVIOR=Request);

– if data should not be disclosed (BEHAVIOR=Block);

– if data disclosure should be limited to the data specified as obligatory by the service provider (BEHAVIOR=Limited).

In practice, this vocabulary may not be suitable for the requirements and regulatory framework of specific geographic zones. It is not based on the most stringent privacy and personal data protection standards, i.e. those adopted by the EU, but uses less strict shared standards [WP 98]. Moreover, we should remember that access to a technical platform is not, on its own, sufficient to ensure protection of user privacy, and involves risks which have not yet been fully mastered. From an individual perspective, the risk is that responsibility of privacy protection lies with the users. This responsibility presumes that users have a clear understanding of the privacy risks involved in data processing, but this is not the case for the majority of individuals. From the operators' perspective, there is a risk that these groups may consider themselves free of certain legal obligations by simply collecting user consent in the context of online negotiations.

4.4.3.2. *Personal data use for transactions*

According to the right of concerned individuals to access information (see the Data Protection Directive and its equivalent in the French Data Protection Act) [EUR 95], service providers have the obligation to disclose their privacy practices to clients. The W3C standard recommends several different methods for the communication of provider practices (see section 4.4.3.1). Several programs enable user's browsers to automaticaly handle provider practices: these are presented in section 4.3.3.2.1. Finally, other solutions implemented by the identity provider (see Chapter 1, section 1.5.3) ensure personal data handling along with data transmission to service providers.

With modern browsers, users now have the option to communicate their preferences to users. The "Do-Not-Track" option, activated via a browser window, allows users to avoid the creation of a profile during navigation. This option is available in Internet Explorer, Safari, Firefox and Google Chrome; however, few sites respect this function due to the absence of effective legal provisions. Finally, for clarification purpose, note that private navigation modes such as "Incognito" in Google Chrome, "Private Browsing" in Firefox and "In Private Browsing" in Internet Explorer have very different objectives. These modes guarantee that when a navigation window is closed, the browser will not retain information concerning the session (e.g. site history, temporary files, cookies, names and passwords). As such, these options do not prevent service providers from using the information created during the session.

4.4.3.2.1. Provider–user communication of privacy policies

The privacy policies of service providers can be accessed by web (browser) clients via a unique URI reference[30]. Using the URI, in the form http://www.URLsite/P3P/PolicyReferences.xml, clients are able to download the corresponding XML document. The service provider may define the same practices for each web page making up the service, or use distinct practices for each individual page.

The URI reference of privacy policies can be communicated to web clients in one of the following four ways, depending on the language used by the service provider: in a specific HTML tag, a specific XHTML tag, an HTTP header or via a URI reference easily deducible from the visited page, i.e. http://www.URLsite/w3c/p3p.xml.

Once the client has obtained the URI of the site, they may then download policies, as shown in Figure 4.2. In the case shown in the figure, the client requests the URI from the Website, then downloads the content. Before retrieving the webpage, the client evaluates and accepts the policies of the provider. The process carried out in step 5 of Figure 4.2 assumes that a specific client program is used; this is described in greater detail in the following section.

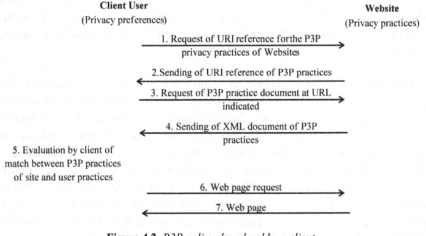

Figure 4.2. *P3P policy download by a client*

---

30 Uniform Resource Identifier (URI) used to localize an online web resource.

4.4.3.3. *Automated policy processing by client terminals*

Several software modules may be integrated into browsers in the form of plug-ins. These modules work closely with the browser to enable automatic interpretation of the privacy policies of Websites, compare them with user preferences and interact directly with the user, for example by highlighting practices which may not conform to the user's preferences. These agent modules mean that users do not need to read site policies themselves, and allow them to ensure respect of their privacy requirements in the course of navigation.

Privacy Bird [PRI 02] is the best-known P3P plug-in available for Internet Explorer from version 6 onward. It was developed in the United States in 2002 by the operator AT&T, and then was taken on by Carnegie Mellon University. It offers a preference configuration interface which allows users to either manually define the data they are willing to disclose or to select one of the three predefined default confidentiality settings (low/medium/high). During web exchanges, Privacy Bird offers the possibility to display site policies, to compare policies to user preferences and to assist the user in deciding whether or not to disclose data. During navigation, users are informed of the adequacy of site policies in relation to their preferences by the color of a bird icon. A green icon shows full adequacy, while a red bird shows, at least, the presence of an incompatible element. In this case, the plug-in is able to show the list of incompatibilities; however, it does not block user access to these sites, and thus does not respect user wishes.

4.4.3.4. *Remote data management*

In certain technical approaches, personal data is not managed in the client terminal, but by another entity in the network. One advantage of this approach is that users can access their data, profiles or identities from any terminal. Another advantage is that access to personal data does not require the user to be online, meaning that certain applications requiring continuous access to data will be able to continue processing. The main drawback of this approach is often the loss of user control over the diffusion and processing of their personal data, as users are rarely informed of the use of their data.

For the open source community, discussed in section 4.2.2, the preferred approach requires users to possess a storage space with a URI reference, used to manage data. This approach does not currently allow users to monitor whom their data is disclosed to, nor for what purposes. This issue is currently under consideration by several research groups (see section 4.5.3).

In the commercial sphere, Identity Providers (IdPs) manage clients' personal data. This approach corresponds to the federated or centralized identity approach described in Chapter 1, sections 1.5.3.2 and 1.5.3.3. One of the main advantages of IdPs, in addition to maintaining up-to-date client databases, is that they profit financially from the base, maintain controls of transaction exchanges and have sufficient economic weight to oppose service providers (SPs). The management of these personal databases requires careful attention, as the sale of this type of data can be particularly lucrative.

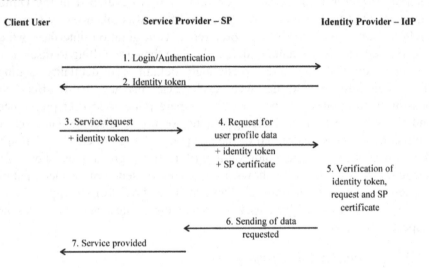

Figure 4.3. *Flow diagram for an identity federation method, where the IdP provides data to the SP*

A variety of flow diagrams, relatively complex in terms of the volume of generated exchanges, have been defined between IdPs, SPs and web clients, as described in Chapter 2. These are based on the Security Assertion Markup Language (SAML) 2.0[31] protocol [MIS 05] and Simple Object Access Protocol (SOAP) [SOA 14]. They result in the disclosure of data to SPs after verifying the request is justified. All flow diagrams, such as that presented in a simplified manner in Figure 4.3, are based on prior authentication of the

31 See the description of SAML 2.0 in Chapter 1, section 1.5.5.

user with the IdP, which then supplies an identity token. The token is then communicated by the user (via their web client) to the SP. The SP sends the token to the IdP to prove that the user temporarily consents to the use of their profile; simultaneously, it requests some of the user's profile data from the IdP and sends its own token, justifying its identity and the legitimacy of the request. After verifying the identity token, the IdP verifies the conformity of the SP request to the token. The IdP then supplies the SP with the required data.

4.4.3.5. Post-transaction processing of personal data

The European Directive 95/46/CE [EUR 95], implemented in France via the French Data Protection Act, establishes a certain number of key principles structuring the use of personal data. Online service providers are notably obliged to implement technical and organizational measures to guarantee a certain level of protection for stored data, tailored according to the sensitivity of the data in question and the risks associated with its destruction, alteration or disclosure. Service providers must also declare their data processing activities to the relevant national monitoring body (the CNIL, in France) which has the power to carry out inspections of the provider's data processing activities, and impose sanctions where necessary (see section 4.3).

Independently of regulations, the scientific community has considered two main approaches to limit illicit use of personal data, once this data has been released to a service provider.

The first approach consists of linking each piece of sensitive personal data with metadata describing the rules for data processing as authorized by the owner. This principle, known as "sticky policies", was introduced in 2002 [KAR 02] and is based on two strong hypotheses. First, metadata should not be altered or removed from the associated personal data. The association must therefore be secured by cryptographic operations [TAN 08]. Second, all personal data treatment activities must respect the rules defined by the metadata. In the case of an electronic transaction, this means that the service provider is not authorized to delete metadata, and should respect the usage restrictions determined by the individual concerned.

The second approach focuses on the issues involved in managing large bases of anonymized data. The aim of this research is to prevent the use of anonymized data to collect other data referring to the same individual, eventually leading to identification of the person. This problem relates to the notion of indistinguishability, i.e. the inability to pick out an individual in a group [YAO 06]. A report produced by the WP29[32] [WP 14a] describing anonymization techniques gives a clear overview of the state of the art of existing approaches. It makes a distinction between the "Randomization" approach, which aims to randomly alter the veracity of data elements in order to weaken the link between a person and their data, and the generalization approach, which consists of generalizing or "diluting" data to give a rougher level of granularity and prevent identification. The best-known solution currently in use for personal data protection is k-Anonymity [SAM 98, ASH 09], which belongs to the generalization family. The original idea behind the solution is based on a model of a database, containing a given set of attributes for each entry. A database is k-Anonymous if, for any and all combinations of these attributes, there are at least k entries in the database with the same attribute values. This means that a single person will not be identifiable among a group of (k-1) individuals. The higher the value of k, the better the level of indistinguishability.

4.5. Research themes

In this section, we will describe some of the research activities currently underway concerning the protection of personal data. Note that the developed techniques do not always conform to regulations for a number of reasons. First, scientists are not always fully aware of legal texts, or do not fully understand how to implement them in practice (on this point, it may be useful to consult the CNIL, as stated in section 4.3). The time scales involved in technological and legal developments are also different: sometimes, years may pass before a law is adopted to regulate the use of new techniques. For implementing newly developed techniques, it is important to take into account both the current legal framework and the regulation for data protection under definition for later adoption.

---

32 The WP29 is a European work group focused on the protection of physical individuals in relation to the processing of their personal data. It was created in response to article 29 of Directive 95/46/CE.

Note that the research themes presented below must take into account current technological trends, including miniaturization, but also green computing. These approaches must ensure that their proposed solutions are as efficient as possible in energy, memory, calculation and communication terms. Moreover, in order to be widely accessible, these solutions must be simple in terms of configuration, administration and maintenance, be easy to update and offer robust resistance to security threats.

4.5.1. Development of simple, evolutive "construction block" tools

In this section, we will present a number of elementary technical "blocks", both hardware and software, whose inclusion might help to bring personal data protection into account when designing new technical solutions. These blocks interface with a number of actors, including companies, the general public and regulatory bodies, and aim to offer simple and evolutive tools to assist in administration, decision-making, operational control, etc.

4.5.1.1. Limitations of the P3P and APPEL languages and ontological requirements

The P3P and APPEL languages presented in section 4.4.3.1 have certain limitations. For example, P3P does not allow service providers to specify whether or not they intend to modify collected data, or whether they subscribe to the regulatory principle of user consent, in their privacy policies [EUR 95].

The drawbacks of P3P and APPEL are particularly visible when identifying the service providers to which sets of rules apply. In P3P, the ENTITY XML tag, which is intended to describe the service provider, does not permit to identify the category of services of the service provider. The key principles of personal data protection are applied on a case-by-case basis and, as we have seen, this depends on the intended purposes of the processing entity. The privacy rules for definition in P3P are extremely variable depending on the nature of the online service, from Internet shopping (3 Suisses, La Redoute, etc.) to car rental services. According to the principle of proportionality, for example, an online clothes retailer would struggle to justify collecting the number of a client's drivers' license, something which would be entirely justified for vehicle rental. To facilitate the move toward automation, privacy rules need to stipulate the types of services to which they apply; service providers would then need to specify a service category in their policies, and users would need to specify the service(s) and/or purpose(s) concerned by preference configurations. The need to differentiate between types of services and purposes is highlighted by the use of different regulations for different domains: for example, specific regulations are applicable to the healthcare sector.

Service types or purposes may be differentiated by the use of an additional XML tag in P3P and APPEL, perhaps "SERVICE-TYPE". However, to use this tag, a set of values would need to be predefined to provide service providers and users with a clear and shared interpretation, enabling dialog. Ontologies may be used for this purpose, although they may also be used in a number of other ways.

Ontologies present a number of advantages in the classification of personal data, service types, purposes and usage rules, allowing the creation of a common understanding of ontological objects for all entities in a network (clients, service providers, etc.). Above all, they allow different entities to carry out in-depth reasoning concerning the management of these objects. This reasoning is particularly useful for two entities needing to agree on the terms of privacy policies before carrying out a transaction (see section 4.5.3). Moreover, ontologies offer the possibility of hierarchical classification of service types, data types, etc. For example, the service/purpose types "SellingDigitalItems" and "SellingMaterialItems" are naturally included in the "OnlineShop" type, which itself belongs to the "RetailServices" service type. Data types can also be classified: the "AgeRange" type, for example, is included in the "AgeValue" type, which itself is included in the "Age" type. Moving beyond this simple classification, it is possible to define relations between types, and this constitutes the principal attraction of ontologies. For example, independently of hierarchical classification, we may specify that the "AgeRange" type provides less detailed information than the "AgeValue" type, and that "AddressCity" provides less specific address information than "AddressStreet". Data precision levels can thus be reduced in accordance with the principle of proportionality, and certain personal data processing rules can be considered to be less invasive than others in privacy terms, while still allowing services to be provided.

The configuration of default user privacy preferences has a considerable influence on the level of protection. Most users do not modify the default parameters used by their browser software. In cases where data is expected to leave the EU, it is also important to inform users of the rules applicable in the destination country, the sanctions in place for non-respect of these rules and the available methods of redress in case of infraction.

4.5.1.2. *Facilitating administration and control*

Service providers must respect legal rules concerning privacy and data protection [EUR 95] or face sanctions and damage to their brand image. Certain tools have been developed to assist in ensuring conformity. These solutions follow three main approaches:

– an ergonomic user interface for the definition of personal data processing rules in accordance with the applicable regulations, with sufficient documentation to provide users with appropriate information, or for step-by-step learning of the correct application of legal rules for service providers;

– the creation of minimalist and maximalist regulatory ontologies, where the relevant authorities publish a definition of a first (strict) and second (permissive) category of data protection policies (see section 4.5.1.1). The first definition corresponds to a service provider requiring a set of personal data simply to provide a service, using default parameters. The second definition corresponds to a service provider collecting data not only for service purposes but also with the aim of profiting from the obtained data;

– a comparison engine for personal data management policies (preferences and practices), allowing entities to identify whether or not a policy corresponds to the expectations of the person concerned.

Note that the sole objective of the user interface is to assist in the definition of practices and preferences. It may usefully exploit regulatory ontologies (defined above) to ensure that service providers correspond to legal regulations and to allow users to define their preferences. It does not guarantee conformity to all legal obligations for service providers, particularly in terms of personal data confidentiality and security aspects. However, the interface enables independent monitoring bodies to automatically check the conformity of personal data processing practices [EUR 95], either on-site or remotely. This may be useful for the CNIL in implementing their new investigative powers, enabling remote detection of infringement of the French Data Protection Act over the Internet[33].

From a technical perspective, the use of regulatory ontologies in a user interface requires the capacity to compare rules concerning the processing of personal data. This is not currently possible with respect to the existing standards (P3P). P3P defines a set of values for the PURPOSE, RETENTION and RECIPIENT criteria, but these values are not ordered on a scale, from "most permissive" to "strictest", for example. Moreover, these criteria are not intercomparable for any given rule. Finally, privacy policies generally correspond to a set of distinct rules with the same weightings.

Dari-Bekara's doctoral thesis [DAR 12b] offers several responses to these issues, including a scale of P3P values and a preference definition interface based on this scale (see Figure 4.4). Note that this scale may differ from one service type to another.

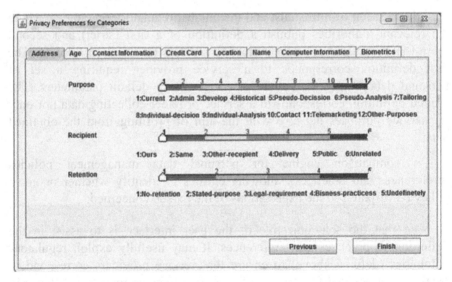

Figure 4.4. *Interface with ordered classification of P3P values [DAR 12a, BEK 11]*

---

33 Article 105 of law no. 2014-344 of 17 March 2014 regarding consumption, modifying article 44-II of the French Data Protection Act, JORF no. 65, 18 March 2014.

4.5.1.3. *Certification and respect of a "code of conduct"*

As [EUR 11] highlights, Internet users do not feel sufficiently protected in legal terms and feel the risks involved in accessing online services. One way of (re-)establishing trust would be to implement a certification system for service providers. This would provide an almost instant indication of the level of personal data protection on offer. The audit and certification process could be carried out by personal data monitoring authorities (the CNIL already labels certain audit procedures, and has recently begun granting labels for digital safes [WEB 14]) or by certification companies acting with the authorization of monitoring authorities or the European Commission. A methodology could be developed to evaluate certification levels, similar to the methodologies currently used to evaluate the security levels of information systems within companies (e.g. MEHARI). Different levels of certification could be awarded based on the levels of rigor demonstrated by service providers. This method would offer security guarantees to users visiting sites with the appropriate certification, raising trust and thus, hopefully, consumption. It would also give service providers the motivation to fulfill their regulatory obligations, with the aim of achieving a high level of certification and, potentially, improving sales as a consequence.

Another option for protection against fraudulent service providers and for raising user trust in the certification system would be to implement automatic cross-verification of the certification level shown by the site and an official, secure database of certified providers.

Finally, all of these developments (certification levels and evaluation methodologies) could be implemented in a wider context by industrial actors wishing to preserve their brand image from both a client and an employee perspective. These companies all manage databases, and could use this certification to provide additional proof of their commitment to data protection within the organization.

4.5.1.4. *Anonymity services under control*

While a considerable amount of work has been done on anonymization techniques, few projects have considered the creation of a framework of trust for both users, wishing to remain anonymous during transactions, and service providers, requiring access to competent authorities in case of disputes (fraud, hosting of illicit content, etc.). Note that this framework would make possible the removal of anonymity, even in the case of anonymous communications (see section 4.4.2).

These approaches aim to achieve a delicate balance between user anonymity and the following:

– removal of anonymity if required, for example, for legal proceedings. The aim is to provide a technical solution with a number of key properties. First, the service provider offers services to a customer, who will remain anonymous. The customer then provides proof that they are associated with a natural person, using a different proof for each session. This proof can be verified by the service provider, but does not make possible the removal of anonymity; however, competent authorities are able to identify the user;

– proof of user consent to the processing of personal data, while maintaining user anonymity, based on opt-in mode[34] (localization or anonymized data[35]). The proof must be verified by the service provider, and must guarantee the existence of a link to the natural person who initialized the session. It must be different every time in order to prevent users from being traced between sessions, and the service provider should not be able to remove anonymity. In case of disputes, only the appropriate authorities would be able to identify the natural person responsible for the proof and verify its validity.

The two mechanisms described above are very similar. However, the "consent" proof presents an additional difficulty in that it needs to be correlated with the proof supplied when initializing a session.

4.5.2. Management of personal attributes

Research activity concerning the management of personal data, with increasingly fine approaches and improved user control, currently centers around three broad areas. The first area concerns the user interface, which

---

34 The service provider requests prior authorization from the user for the collection and processing of their personal data.
35 Anonymized data may, for example, come from an intermediate proxy (as described in section 4.4.2.1). As several research groups have suggested, a proxy of this type could be used for a group of users, and ensure that the data transmitted to the service provider cannot be used to distinguish individual user profiles.

must both allow definition of user preferences and create a space for communications with the service provider in the course of transactions. Each user should be able to define their own preferences, independently of their skill level; beginners might choose one of the proposed default configurations (such as those offered by Privacy Bird, see section 4.4.3.3), while experts would be able to modify advanced configuration details. This configuration might be based on the two regulatory ontologies described in section 4.5.1.2, in which case the interface would offer a limited number of choices corresponding to these ontologies.

When using the Internet, users should be kept informed of the policies applied by the sites they visit (in cases using adequate certification, see section 4.5.1.3) and points which may be in conflict with their preferences. If authorization is required, then sufficient data must be provided in order for the user's consent to be given freely, specifically and knowingly, in accordance with the Data Protection Directive. The interface should be easy to use, with relevant and explicit visual indicators. Moreover, the dialog space should be developed in such a way that experts will be able to understand problems which arise and offer simple explanations suitable for all users. The possibility for dialog should be richer than that offered by Privacy Bird, and the method should block access to sites in case of severe regulatory infringements or insufficiencies in relation to user preferences.

Another area of research concerns the management of personal data in a remote context, essentially for social networks. Work on this subject has been carried out by the SAMOVAR laboratory [SAM 13] at Télécom SudParis, based on a number of key ideas. This work, partially connected with the MyProfile project (https://my-profile.eu/) launched in collaboration with the W3C, concerns user management of interest groups (in the social networking sense). Human relationships evolve, and users may need to manage a significant number of interest groups. Users could therefore benefit from software tools for dynamic relationship management [SAM 12]. Based on this consideration, a connection was established with human relationships as they exist in the real world; the results of this parallel are shown in Figure 4.5. The illustration shows different contexts (collaborators, colleagues, boss, spouse, children, parents, etc.), which are then classified into categories (professional, family, friends, etc.) and by proximity (e.g. intimate, close, social and public). Using this representation, each contact may be given a label (e.g. "close friends"). The underlying aim is to allow contacts access to certain data (images, texts, documents, etc.) as a function of their label. Based on this representation, tools may be designed for dynamic management of relationships based on the frequency of interactions between individuals and the contents of exchanges. Thus, a simple "acquaintance" could evolve to become a "close friend" following intense interaction over a short period of time. Inversely, the relationship distance might increase following a long period with no interactions.

Another area addressed in [SAM 13] concerns control of the disclosure of personal data (images, text, etc.) within interest groups. The project considers tools and concepts for use in guaranteeing that data will not be passed from person to person into other groups or to third parties without the consent of the individual in question.

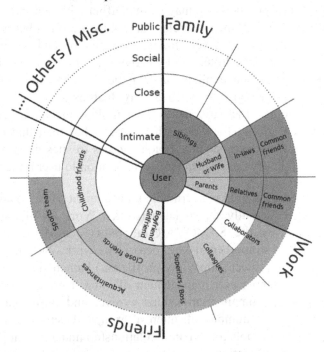

Figure 4.5. *Representation of contextualized levels of proximity [SAM 13]*

4.5.3. *Negotiation of contract terms regarding privacy*

In future exchanges associated with electronic transactions or other requirements which have yet to be identified, multiple entities (providers, users, subcontractors, authorities, etc.) may interact, each with their own requirements in terms of privacy (preferences, practices and regulatory ontologies, etc.).

In this context, it is useful to create policy comparison tools in order to determine the requirement levels of each party (from strict to permissive) and policy negotiation tools for the creation (or otherwise) of a common privacy policy to serve as a basis for interactions. As shown in section 4.5.1.2, certain approaches envisage comparison of P3P/APPEL policies. However, these approaches are generally based on strict correspondence. This is the case of Privacy Bird, where the rules specified in provider policies must be identical to those set out in user preferences. This type of comparison process leads either to transactions being blocked, as the provider's requirements are too high, or to the user accepting the provider's policies. [DAR 12a] provides an ordered classification of P3P values (see Figure 4.4), enabling measurement of the differences between policies and practices, potentially enabling the creation of a tolerance margin. In all cases, personal data is only collected if provider practices have been accepted by the user. There is, therefore, a significant risk that users will configure minimal requirements, which do not fully correspond to their initial desires, in order to prevent transactions from being blocked.

A number of research activities focus on establishing contractual privacy terms which truly reflect the wishes of all parties through the use of multi-exchange negotiation protocols. On provision of an initial request, solicited entities should respond with a counter-proposition, and so on until entities converge on a shared policy. The difficulty of this approach lies in balancing negotiations from the perspective of both entities and in attaining rapid convergence, with the aim of avoiding excessive delays and use of resources (calculations, communications, etc.). A number of responses have been offered to the negotiation issue, but most are not realistic (for example, including a potentially infinite number of exchanges) and are not sufficiently detailed to envisage implementation [BEN 03].

Two main approaches for negotiations between users and service providers have been described in [DAR 12b]. However, these ideas are still at an early stage of development. They assume the following forms:

– negotiation of the P3P terms of a contract concerning each type of personal data, based on the ordered classification of P3P values (see section 4.5.1.2). The user must define two thresholds: the first corresponding to a strict, non-negotiable policy and the second corresponding to the most permissive authorized policy. For each category of personal data, the provider must define two data lists: one containing data which must absolutely be collected and processed for a transaction to take place and the other containing optional data, i.e. personal data which is desirable but not essential for the service to operate. The basis of a shared policy would then be negotiated via a maximum of four exchanges [DAR 12a];

– negotiation around the data itself, based on the ontology described in section 4.5.1.2, the notion of private concepts and game theory. The ontology would be used to establish connections between certain categories of data, helping the user and provider in constructing their reasoning with the aim of converging on a shared policy [DAR 12b]. This reasoning is specifically concerned with the levels of degradation which the tool considers to be useful for a given type of data, making disclosure less risky for the user (disclosure of an age bracket instead of a date of birth, for example). A private concept is a set of data types which may reveal global identity in case of disclosure (such as an ID card) and constitute a risk for the user. These concepts may be defined using the ontology and an associated disclosure risk function. Finally, game theory may be used to define utility functions and to predict convergence of the negotiation procedure.

4.5.4. Reforms to the European data protection rules

European data protection legislation is currently undergoing revision. This process started with wide-ranging consultation activities, notably in the form of a high-level conference in May 2009 and two public consultation phases, one from July to December 2009[36] and the second from November 2010 to January 15, 2011[37].

---

36 The first consultation concerned the legal framework applicable to the fundamental right to protection of personal data. The European Commission received 168 responses. Contributions may be found at http://ec.europa.eu/justice/newsroom/data-protection/events/090519_en.htm.

37 The second consultation concerned the Commission's global approach with regard to the protection of personal data within the EU. The European Commission received 305 responses. Contributions may be found at http://ec.europa.eu/justice/newsroom/data-protection/events/101104_en.htm.

In January 2012, the European Commission proposed to replace the 1995 Data Protection Directive by a regulation[38]. The Commission considers that: "the current framework remains sound as far as its objectives and principles are concerned, but it has not prevented fragmentation in the way personal data protection is implemented across the Union, legal uncertainty and a widespread public perception that there are significant risks associated notably with online activity" [EUR 11]. The Commission also evokes the necessity for "strong enforcement which will put individuals in control of their own data and reinforce legal and practical certainty for economic operators and public authorities" [EUR 12].

Once adopted, the regulation will be directly applicable and will not need to be transposed into national laws. The French Data Protection Act will be revoked and the CNIL will operate directly using the new text. Reinforced harmonization of the rules applicable in the EU should improve the current situation of fragmentation, created by different national laws, which puts companies on a certain uneven legal footing. Thus, a company may currently be punished for certain actions in Germany which would go unpunished in the United Kingdom, as the British data protection regime is more relaxed than in France, Germany and Spain, for example, on a number of points.

The Commission's draft proposition is extremely complex (covering 120 pages); it retains the protection principles discussed in section 4.3 (concerning purposes, data quality, legitimization, reinforced protection of sensitive data and an adequate level of protection), while adding new elements.

One of the main modifications concerns the obligations of the data controller. This includes *reinforcement of rules regarding consent*: consent can no longer be considered to be tacit or implicit. It is only valid if the data subject has the effective power to revoke their consent and oppose the processing of their data at a later date. Consent must also be given in response to clear, precise and complete prior information. The data controller is responsible for proving that the person in question has authorized processing. *Specific obligations* have also been defined regarding processing of data belonging to children under 13 years of age. This type of processing is only permitted if consent has been obtained from a parent or custodian; the data controller must make "reasonable efforts to obtain

---

38 For the way in which the procedure was carried out and the proposed modifications (see [NAF 12, pp. 67–72]).

verifiable consent, taking into consideration available technology". The framework for *international data transfers* has also been rationalized. The authorization of the CNIL will no longer be necessary if the transfer is based on standard contractual clauses and Binding Corporate Rules (BCRs). The obligation to *report data breaches* to the supervisory authority (the CNIL, in France) has been generalized to all data controllers.

The rights of individuals concerned by data have also been extended. *Information* must be provided concerning the period for which the personal data will be stored, the right to lodge a complaint with the CNIL, with provision of the details of the data controller and all other information required for processing to take place in good faith. In cases of indirect collection, information must be given regarding the data source. Moreover, the proposal obliges data controllers to allow the data subject to exercise their rights electronically, ending the requirement to lodge complaints in writing. The data controller must issue a response within a month, renewable once. If the demand is sent electronically, the data controller must respond in the same way, unless the individual concerned has stipulated a preference for another method.

The right to access has been extended to a new notion of "right to data portability", i.e. the right to obtain a copy of data in a standardized, computerized form, and the right to transmit data from an automated processing system to another system if the processing is based on consent or on a contract.

The proposition also includes *the right to be forgotten,* in the form of a right to erase personal data and prevent further dissemination, particularly concerning data which the data subject in question made available during their minority.

The text specifies that data controllers must respond to requests to erase personal data made public by taking all reasonable steps to transmit these request to all third parties which are processing such data. The "right to be forgotten" should, however, be exercised with consideration for the right to information and freedom of expression.

Measures based on profiling have also been established: "Every natural person shall have the right not to be subject to a measure which produces legal effects concerning this natural person or significantly affects this natural person, and which is based solely on automated processing intended to evaluate certain personal aspects relating to this natural person or to analyze or predict in particular the natural person's performance at work, economic situation, location, health, personal preferences, reliability or behavior"[39].

Finally, if the data processed by a controller does not permit identification of a natural person, the controller shall not be obliged to acquire additional information in order to identify the data subject simply to respect the regulation.

New concepts have also emerged in the English-speaking world. The principle of "Privacy by design", which is strongly based on the technological dimension, aims to integrate data and privacy protection from the earliest stages of service or product design. In this case, the goal is to limit the nature of collected data, the duration of conservation and the conditions under which it may be accessed.

The principle of accountability concerns the internal measures taken by controllers in order to demonstrate the level of conformity of their processing operations [WP 10b]. This demonstration may take different forms: the creation of transparent internal rules which are easy to access for the data subjects, the implementation of data security obligations, the establishment of a complaints procedure, retention of documents used to give instructions to the processor, designation of a data protection officer (compulsory for companies with more than 250 employees), internal and external audits, and impact assessments. Concerning the last point, controllers may use the new AFNOR EN 16571 standard from July 2014, "Information Technology – RIFD Privacy Impact Assessment Process"[40].

---

39 This article takes account of the European Council recommendations concerning profiling. CM/Rec (2010) 13.

40 The EN 16571 standard defines a common European method for privacy impact assessments (PIA) for RFID applications. It identifies the conditions for revision or replacement of an existing PIA. In doing this, it implements a recommendation issued by the European Commission in 2009, and makes use of the Impact assessment framework for RFID applications with regard to privacy and data protection, from 11 February 2011 (available at www.centrenational-rfid.com/docs/users/file/pia-fr.pdf). This document was established by companies in January 2011, approved by the WP29 in February 2011 then signed by the main interested parties.

In any and all cases, the controllers shall maintain documentation of all processing carried out under their responsibility. This obligation also applies to processors, who may be held directly responsible. A processor will be held jointly responsible for processing if data is processed in a manner other than that specified in instructions received from the controller. With the introduction of stricter security and confidentiality measures, processors must also maintain the documentation concerning processing carried out under their responsibility, and cooperate with the CNIL.

Accountability forms part of a co-regulation approach, inviting companies to accept responsibility and to define their own conformity measures in accordance with their specific situation. Working on this basis, the controller is accountable to both data protection authorities and the data subjects. Member States and the Commission should encourage the creation of certification mechanisms, marks and seals allowing data subjects to quickly assess the level of data protection. In parallel, current administrative aspects judged to be redundant have been reduced, while the CNIL has retained considerable power to monitor implemented measures. The available sanctions have also been reinforced (with fines of up to 1 million euros and 2% of the worldwide turnover).

Another significant change is that the regulation is also applicable to controllers established outside of the EU, in cases where their processing activities relate to the offering of goods or services to data subjects residing in the EU or the monitoring of their behaviors.

One of the main points for negotiation concerns the applicability of laws, particularly the question of a "one-stop shop". In the case of a data controller established in several Member States, the data controller would be answerable to *a single national data protection authority* in the EU country of their main establishment[41]. This new criterion has been criticized by the CNIL [FAL 12], as an SNS collecting personal data from EU users may decide to install its main establishment in Ireland, for example; in this case,

---

41 This is either the location of the company's European headquarters, or the place where the main decisions are taken regarding data protection issues. If the controller is not established within the EU, the regulation is applicable to the data belonging to data subjects with their residence in EU territory, in cases where processing is linked to the provision of goods and services to these individuals or to the observation of their behavior.

the processing of data pertaining to French citizens would no longer come under the primary control of the CNIL, but of the Irish authority.

The draft regulation was discussed and amended via a first reading by the European Parliament on 12 March 2014[42]. The most significant modifications include reinforcement of rules concerning consent, profiling and data transfers outside of the EU, and the replacement of the right to be forgotten by the right to erasure of data. Data controllers are now obliged to designate a data protection officer in cases where processing relates to more than 5,000 individuals within 12 months. Financial sanctions have also been strengthened, with the authorization of fines of up to 5% of the global annual turnover of a company.

This project is now awaiting approval from the Council of Ministers. Once the text has been adopted, a transition period will be established over 2 years to allow data controllers to adapt. This means that new data protection rules will not be implemented before 2017 at the earliest. Those companies involved in handling of personal data would do well to anticipate these new obligations, which are likely to be imposed in the near future.

4.6. Conclusions

This chapter provides a broad overview of the technical and legal concerns associated with the protection of privacy and personal data. It does not claim to be exhaustive. It is important to understand that research concerning the protection of privacy and research concerning security currently produce virtually equivalent results, following a spectacular boom in the 2000s.

In this context, it is essential for actors in the legal and technical domains to work together in order to create a digital environment including higher levels of respect for privacy and personal data. This work includes the design of basic building-block programs which can easily be integrated into new products, programs, services, etc., so that equipment and software may

---

42 European Parliament legislative resolution of 12 March 2014 on the proposal for a regulation of the European Parliament and of the Council on the protection of individuals with regard to the processing of their personal data and on the free movement of such data (General Data Protection Regulation) (COM(2012)0011 – C7-0025/2012 – 2012/0011(COD)) (Ordinary legislative procedure: first reading), A7-0402/2013.

progressively and naturally take account of privacy concerns, in accordance with legal provisions. This development must also aim to provide configuration and control tools which may be easily understood by all those involved: individual users, who need assurance that their rights and freedoms will be respected, service providers, who must feel supported in their administrative choices and who must ensure that their data processing activities are legally acceptable, and data protection authorities, who require automated tools to simplify checks and, where necessary, target specific providers.

4.7. Bibliography

[ACO 14] A COMPÉTENCE ÉGALE, http://www.acompetenceegale.com/association/ signer-la-charte-reseaux-sociaux-internet-vie-privee-et-recrutement, 2014.

[AGR 03] AGRAWAL R., KIERNAN J., SRIKANT R., et al., An XPath-based Preference Language for P3P, May 2003.

[ARK 05] ARKKO J., KEMPF J., ZILL B., et al., Secure Neighbor Discovery (SEND), RFC 3971, Internet Engineering Task Force, March 2005. Available at http://www.rfc-editor.org/rfc/rfc3971.txt.

[ASH 09] ASHOURI M., TALOUKI S., NEMATBAKHSH M., et al., "k-Anonymity privacy protection using ontology", 14th International CSI Conference, 2009.

[BEI 08] BEIMEL A., DOLEV S., "Buses for anonymous message delivery", Journal of Cryptology, vol. 16, no. 1, pp. 25–39, 2008.

[BEK 11] BEKARA K., LAURENT M., MILLET R., "Privacy policy negotiation at user's side based on P3P tag value classification", Proceedings of the International Conference on e-Learning, e-Business, Enterprise Information Systems, and e-Government (EEE'11), Las Vegas, NV, pp. 559–564, July 2011.

[BEN 03] BENNICKE M., LANGENDORFE P., "Towards automatic negotiation of privacy contracts for internet services", 11th IEEE International Conference on, pp. 319–324, 2003.

[BER 05] BERNERS-LEE T., MASINTER L., BERNERS-LEE R., Uniform Resource Identifier (URI): Generic Syntax, Standards Track, RFC 3986, January 2005.

[BOU 00] BOUCHER P., SHOSTACK A., GOLDBERG I., Freedom Systems 2.0 Architecture, December 2000. Available at http://www.freedom.net/info/white papers/Freedom_System_2_Architecture.pdf?Session=fbf49f6af59aaba0fb88219 fd1e09dae.

[BRA 10] BRANDIMARTE L., ACQUISTI A., LOEWENSTEIN G., "Misplaced confidences: privacy and the control paradox", *9th Annual Workshop on the Economics of Information Security (WEIS)*, Harvard University, Cambridge, Massachusetts, 7–8 June 2010.

[CAR 14] CARDPEEK, http://code.google.com/p/cardpeek/wiki/Navigo_FR, 2014.

[CHA 81] CHAUM D., "Unfootprintable electronic mail, return addresses, and digital pseudonyms", *Communications of the ACM*, vol. 24, no. 2, pp. 84–90, 1981.

[CHE 11] CHENEAU T., Amélioration des adresses CGA et du protocole SEND pour un meilleur support de la mobilité et de nouveaux services de sécurité, PhD Thesis, Paris 6, January 2011.

[CIZ 05] CIZAULT G., *IPv6: Théorie et pratique*, 4th ed., O'Reilly, Paris, 2005.

[CNI 04] CNIL, Act of 6 August 2004 relative to the protection of individuals with regard to the processing of personal data OJ, 7 August 2004.

[CNI 10a] CNIL, *Dispositifs analyse du comportement des consommateurs: souriez, vous êtes comptés!*, 19 April 2010. Available at http://www.cnil.fr/ linstitution/ actualite/article/article/dispositifs-danalyse-du-comportement-des-consommateurs-souriez-vous-etes-comptes-2/.

[CNI 10b] CNIL, *GUIDE La sécurité des données personnelles*, 2010 ed., 2010. Available at http://www.cnil.fr/fileadmin/documents/Guides_pratiques/Guide_securite-D.pdf.

[CNI 12a] CNIL, *Recommandations pour les entreprises qui envisagent de souscrire à des services de Cloud computing*, 25 June 2012.

[CNI 12b] CNIL, *Règles de confidentialité de Google: une information incomplète et une combinaison de données incontrôlée*, 16 October 2012.

[CNI 12c] CNIL, *GUIDE Gérer les risques sur les libertés et la vie privée*, June 2012. Available at http://www.cnil.fr/fileadmin/documents/Guidespratiques/CNIL-Guide_Securite_avance_Methode.pdf.

[CNI 12d] CNIL, *GUIDE Mesures pour traiter les risques sur les libertés et la vie privée*, June 2012. Available at http://www.cnil.fr/fileadmin/documents/Guidespratiques/CNIL-Guide_securite_avance_Mesures.pdf.

[CNI 14] CNIL, *Cookies & traceurs: que dit la loi?*, 2014. Available at http://www.cnil.fr/vos-obligations/sites-web-cookies-et-autres-traceurs/que-dit-la-loi/.

[CNI 14] Un nouveau label pour les services coffre-fort numérique, Article, 2014.

[CNI 78] CNIL, Act no. 78-17 of 6 January 1978 on information technology, data files and civil liberties (*French Data Protection Act*), OJ 7, January 1978.

[CON 14] CONSTITUTIONAL COUNCIL, *Loi relative à la consommation*, decision no. 2014-690 DC 13 March 2014. Available at http://www.conseil-constitutionnel.fr/ conseil-constitutionnel/francais/les-decisions/acces-par-date/decisions-depuis-1959/2014/2014-690-dc/decision-n-2014-690-dc-du-13-mars-2014.140273.html.

[CRA 02] CRANOR L., ANGEHEINRICH M., CARCHIORI M., A P3P Preference Exchange Language 1.0, http://www. w3.org/TR/P3P-preferences/, 2002.

[DAR 12a] DARI-BEKARA K., LAURENT M., MILLET R., "Privacy policy negotiation at user's side based on P3P tag value classification", *Proceedings of the International Conference on e-Learning, e-Business, Enterprise Information Systems, and e-Government (EEE'11)*, pp. 559–564, Las Vegas, Nevada, 18–21 July 2011.

[DAR 12b] DARI-BEKARA K., Protection des données personnelles côté utilisateur dans le E-Commerce, PhD Thesis, University of Paris 6, 2012.

[DEL 13] DELEPORTE B., Annulation du contrat de cession d'un fichier d'adresses clients non déclaré à la CNIL, 2013. Available at http://www.journaldunet.com/ ebusiness/expert/ 54995/annulation-du-contrat-de-cession-d-un-fichier-d-adresses-clients-non-declare-a-la-cnil.shtml, 2013.

[DES 12] DESGENS-PASANAU G., *La protection des données à caractère personnel, La loi Informatique et Libertés*, LexisNexis, 2012.

[DIN 04] DINGLEDINE R., MATHEWSON N., SYVERSON P., "Tor: the second-generation onion router", *Usenix Security 2004*, August 2004.

[ECK 10] ECKERSLEY P., *A Primer on Information Theory and Privacy*, January 2010. Available at https://www.eff.org/deeplinks/2010/01/primer-information-theory-and-privacy.

[EL 12] EL MOUSTAINE E., LAURENT M., "Les systèmes RFID: la technologie, les risques et les solutions de sécurité", *Techniques de l'Ingénieur, Sécurité des systèmes information*, 2012.

[EL 13] EL MOUSTAINE E., LAURENT M., Procédé pour crypter des données dans un cryptosystème NTRU (N,p,q), Patent no., PCT/IB2013/055122, June 2013.

[EPC 13] EPCGlobal, *EPC Radio Frequency Identity Protocols Generation-2 UHF RFID Specification for RFID Air Interface Protocol for Communications at 860 MHz - 960 MHz*, Version 2.0.0 Ratified, November 2013.

[EPC 14] EPCGlobal, *EPC Tag Data Standard Version 1.8*, February 2014.

[EUR 11] EUROPEAN COMMISSION, Special Eurobarometer 359, *Data Protection and Electronic Identity in the EU*, 2011. Available at http://ec.europa.eu/public_ opinion/archives/ebs/ ebs_359_en.pdf.

[EUR 12] EUROPEAN COMISSION, Proposal for a regulation of the European Parliament and of the Council on the protection of individuals with regard to the processing of personal data and on the free movement of such data (General Data Protection Regulation), 25 January 2012.

[EUR 95] EUROPEAN PARLIAMENT, COUNCIL OF THE EUROPEAN UNION, Directive 95/46/EC of the European Parliament and of the Council of 24 October 1995 on the protection of individuals with regard to the processing of personal data and on the free movement of such data, Official Journal of the European Community, pp. 31–50, 23 November 1995.

[EYN 13] EYNARD J., *Les données personnelles: quelle définition pour un régime de protection efficace?*, Michalon, 2013.

[FAL 12] FALQUE-PIERROTIN I., Présidente de la CNIL, "Quelle protection européenne pour les données personnelles *?*", *Question Europe*, no. 250, 3 September 2012, Fondation Robert Schuman. Available at http://www.robert-schuman.eu/question_europe.php?num=qe-250.

[FOU 03] FOUQUE P.-A., "Cryptographie appliquée", *Techniques de l'Ingénieur,* Sécurité des systèmes information, H5210, 2003.

[FRE 02] FREEDMAN M., MORRIS E., "Tarzan: a peer-to-peer anonymizing network layer", *Proceedings of the 9th ACM Conference on Computer and Communications Security (CCS '02)*, pp. 193–206, 2002.

[GRU 05] GRUTESER M., GRUNWALD D., "Enhancing location privacy in wireless LAN through disposable interface identifiers: a quantitative analysis", *Mobile Networks and Applications*, vol. 10, no. 3, pp. 315–325, 2005.

[GUI 11] GUILLEMIN P., "Etat de l'art en recherche européenne sur l'Internet des Objets et la RFID", *Techniques de l'Ingénieur,* Sécurité des systèmes d'information, RE165, 2011.

[KAR 02] KARJOTH G., SCHUNTER M., "A privacy policy model for enterprises", *IEEE Computer Security Foundations Workshop*, 2002.

[LAU 11] LAURENT M., "Introduction à la Sécurité des Systèmes d'Information", *Techniques de l'Ingénieur,* Sécurité des systèmes d'information, H5000, 2011.

[LEF 09] LEFEBVRE J.N., "Traçabilité des bagages dans le transport aérien – Déploiement de la technologie RFID", TR670, *Techniques de l'Ingénieur*, Traçabilité section, May 2009.

[LEV 09] LEVALLOIS-BARTH C., "Navigo: simplification ou traçabilité absolue?", Chapter 5 in LICOPPE C., *L'évolution des cultures numériques*, Fyp Editions, pp. 173–181, 2009.

[MAN 10] MANILS P., ABDELBERI C., LE BLOND S., *et al.*, Compromising Tor anonymity exploiting P2P information leakage, Technical Report, Inria-00471556 Version 1, 2010.

[MIS 05] MISHRA P., MALER E., *et al.*, "Conformance Requirements for the OASIS Security Assertion Markup Language (SAML) V2.0 – Language (SAML)", *OASIS Standard*, vol. 2, p. 1, 2005.

[NAF 12] NAFTALSKI F., DESGENS-PASANAU G., "Projet de règlement européen sur la protection des données: ce qui va changer pour les professionnels", *Revue Lamy Droit de l'Immatériel*, March 2012.

[NAR 07] NARTEN T., NORDMARK E., SIMPSON W., *et al.*, Neighbor Discovery for IP version 6 (IPv6), RFC 4861, Internet Engineering Task Force, September 2007. Available at http://www.rfc-editor.org/rfc/rfc4861.txt.

[OPE 14] OPENAM, http://www.forgerock.com/openam.html, 2014.

[POU 09] POULLET Y., HENROTTE J.F., "La protection des données (à caractère personnel) à l'heure de l'Internet", Chapter 5 in LAFFINEUR J., *Protection du consommateur, pratiques commerciales et T.I.C.*, pp. 197–245, 2009.

[PR 02] PRIVACY BIRD, http://www.privacybird.org/, 2002.

[REI 98] REITER M., RUBIN A., "Crowds: Anonymity for web transactions", *ACM Transactions on Information and System Security (TISSEC)*, vol. 1, no. 1, pp. 66–92, 1998.

[SAM 98] SAMARATI P., SWEENEY L., Protecting privacy when disclosing information: k-anonymity and its enforcement through generalization and suppression, Technical report SRE-CSL-98-04, SRI Computer Science Laboratory, 1998.

[SAM 12] SAMBRA A., LAURENT M., "Context-aware decentralized approach for web services", *The 2012 IEEE 19th International Conference on Web Services (ICWS '12)*, IEEE Computer Society, Honolulu, HI 24–29 June 2012.

[SAM 13] SAMBRA A., Data ownership and interoperability for a decentralized social semantic web, Joint TSP-UPMC PhD Thesis, November 2013.

[SOA 14] SOAP, http://www.w3.org/TR/soap/, 2014.

[TAN 08] TANG Q., On using encryption techniques to enhance sticky policies enforcement, TR-CTIT-08-64, Centre for Telematics and Information Technology, University of Twente, 2008.

[TOU 03] TOUTAIN L., *Réseaux locaux et Internet: Des protocoles à l'interconnexion*, 3rd ed., Hermes-Lavoisier, pp. 844, 2003.

[WOR 06] WORLD WIDE WEB CONSORTIUM, *Platform for Privacy Preferences specification 1.1.*, 2006. Available at http://www.w3.org/P3P/.

[WP 07] Working Party 29, Opinion No. 4/2007 on the concept of personal data, WP 136, 2007.

[WP 09] Working Party 29, Opinion 5/2009 on online social networking, WP 163, 2009.

[WP 10a] Working Party 29, Opinion 8/2010 on applicable law, WP 179, 2010.

[WP 10b] Working Party 29, Opinion 3/2010 on the principle of accountability, WP 173, 2010.

[WP 11] Working Party 29, Opinion 15/2011 on consent, WP 187, 2011.

[WP 14a] Working Party 29, Opinion 05/2014 on anonymisation techniques onto the web, WP216, 2014.

[WP 14b] Working Party 29, Opinion 06/2014 on the notion of legitimate interests of the data controller under Article 7 of Directive 95/46/EC, WP217, 2014.

[WP 98] Working Party 29, Opinion 1/98: Platform for Privacy Preferences (P3P) and the Open Profiling Standard (OPS), WP 11, 1998.

[YAO 06] YAO C., WANG L., WANG S.X., *et al.*, "Indistinguishability: the other aspect of privacy", *Proceedings of the 3rd VLDB International Conference on Secure Data Management (SDM'06)*, Springer-Verlag Berlin, Heidelberg, pp. 1–17, 2006.

[ZUG 05] ZUGENMAIER A., *FLASCHE – A Mechanism Providing Anonymity for Mobile Users*, Privacy Enhancing Technologies, Springer, pp. 121–141, 2005.

5

Digital Identity in Cloud Computing

5.1. Introduction

The concept of cloud computing has become increasingly present since the early 2000s, and is now a key aspect of the evolution of the Internet. Cloud computing is highly attractive to companies, as it eliminates the need for advanced allocation of resources; supply adapts to demand, according to the "pay-as-you-use" concept. However, although cloud computing offers significant possibilities in terms of service sharing and financial savings, it also involves a number of risks, notably in relation to the security of user data. After presenting the main concepts and actors involved in cloud computing, our aim in this chapter is to highlight the importance of digital identity management in the cloud, and to present the solutions currently available.

5.2. Concepts of cloud computing

5.2.1. *Definition of cloud computing*

The term "cloud" has been used in a variety of contexts, such as the description of large-scale Asynchronous Transfer Mode (ATM) networks in the 1990s. However, the term only really became popular in 2006 when Eric Schmidt, the executive chairman of Google, used it to describe the economic model associated with the provision of Web services [ZHA 10]. In this

---

Chapter written by Christophe KIENNERT, Samia BOUZEFRANE and Amira Faiza BENKARA MOSTEFA.

chapter, we shall use the definition supplied by the NIST[1] [MEL 11], which describes cloud computing as a model enabling on-demand access to calculation and storage resources (such as network infrastructures, servers, storage space, applications and services) accessible with minimal effort in terms of service management and maintenance.

5.2.2. *Principles of cloud computing*

Despite the spectacular upsurge in interest in cloud computing over the last few years, alongside increased media interest, turning a real architectural model into an indefinable abstraction, the basic concept of the cloud itself is relatively old. This basic concept simply involves using third parties to store data and carry out computer processing. In other words, cloud computing consists of renting the equipment of a third party, which is known as a *cloud service provider*, for hosting and management, and thus outsourcing, of given services. These services can take varying and almost unlimited forms, and the computing community invents new service types on a regular basis.

Cloud computing is therefore not a new idea in and of itself. X terminals, popular in the 1990s, already used the principle of *software as a service* (SaaS). The main development over the last few years is, in fact, the remarkable increase in the scale of the adoption of cloud computing. Cloud service providers (CSPs) now manage such large quantities of data, software and platforms that special data centers have had to be built. This has also led to considerable reliance on virtualization techniques.

Forrester Research predicts that the global cloud computing market will grow from 40.7 billion USD in 2011 to 241 billion USD in 2020, as shown in Figure 5.1.

5.2.3. *Deployment models for cloud computing*

Data may be externalized in different ways. Several different types of cloud exist, whether private, public or hybrid [ZHA 10], as shown in Figure 5.2.

---

1 National Institute of Standards and Technology: http://www.nist.gov/.

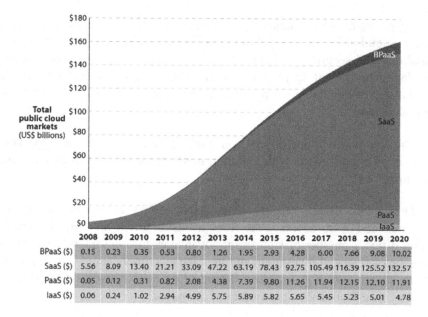

	2008	2009	2010	2011	2012	2013	2014	2015	2016	2017	2018	2019	2020
BPaaS ($)	0.15	0.23	0.35	0.53	0.80	1.26	1.95	2.93	4.28	6.00	7.66	9.08	10.02
SaaS ($)	5.56	8.09	13.40	21.21	33.09	47.22	63.19	78.43	92.75	105.49	116.39	125.52	132.57
PaaS ($)	0.05	0.12	0.31	0.82	2.08	4.38	7.39	9.80	11.26	11.94	12.15	12.10	11.91
IaaS ($)	0.06	0.24	1.02	2.94	4.99	5.75	5.89	5.82	5.65	5.45	5.23	5.01	4.78

Figure 5.1. *Cloud market forecast according to Forrester Research*

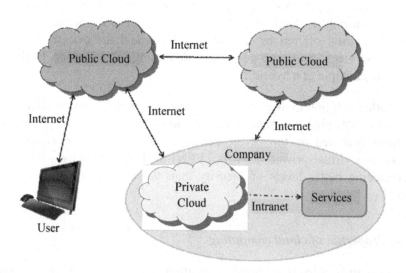

Figure 5.2. *A hybrid cloud*

The private cloud, considered as an internal cloud, is designed for use by a single organization, and can only be accessed by this organization. The infrastructure may be managed by the company itself or by a third party. The private cloud offers full control of the infrastructure in terms of performance, reliability and security. However, this cloud type is often criticized as being similar to traditional proprietary server farms; it does not offer all of the advantages of cloud computing, such as the absence of financial investment or maintenance.

The community cloud differs from the private cloud in that it is extended to a set of organizations with common missions or aims (such as insurance organizations).

The public cloud, on the other hand, offers resources via service providers and opens access to the cloud infrastructure to all users. The public cloud offers a number of significant advantages for consumers, such as the absence of financial investment and maintenance implications. However, the public cloud cannot guarantee full control of data, networks and security, limiting its effectiveness in a variety of scenarios.

Finally, the hybrid cloud uses an architecture that combines at least two different cloud types. For a company, this may combine the use of a private cloud and a public cloud, in order to achieve a balance between data and service security, offered by the private cloud, and the availability of on-demand services, using the public cloud. Figure 5.2, based on [AHR 10], shows an example of a hybrid cloud.

Another solution to overcome the limitations of public and private clouds consists of defining a virtual private cloud (VPC). A VPC is essentially a platform executed on top of the public cloud. It gives service providers access to a virtual private network (VPN) to design their own topologies, guaranteeing better levels of security than those encountered in a public cloud.

5.2.4. Properties of cloud computing

To be truly attractive, cloud computing needs to satisfy five essential characteristics, set out by the NIST [MEL 11]:

1) On-demand self-service: the client of a cloud supplier should be able to obtain an extension of resources: processing capacity, storage capacity,

network infrastructure, a virtual machine, etc., on demand, and without the need for human interaction with the service provider.

2) Resource pooling: a given cloud service should be able to serve multiple users simultaneously, using a multitenant model, with physical and virtual resources dynamically assigned and reassigned according to customer demand. The customer has no idea of the location of the requested resource, but may be able to specify a rough location (such as a country or state) in their requests.

3) Rapid elasticity: the capabilities of the cloud should appear unlimited to the user. These capabilities should be elastically scalable both outward and inward in accordance with demand, whatever the quantity of resources required, and at any time.

4) Broad network access: capabilities should be accessible over the network through standard mechanisms for any type of thin or thick client terminal (desktop or laptop computer, smartphone, tablet, etc.).

5) Measured services: resource usage is metered independently for each cloud user, which notably allows pay-as-you-use billing.

5.2.5. *Advantages of cloud computing*

The properties of cloud computing set out above present a number of specific advantages, including [SAL 14, REN 14]:

– flexibility: a company that suddenly finds itself in need of added bandwidth can access this resource instantaneously due to the elasticity of the cloud;

– cost reduction: as we saw in section 5.1, cloud services are offered to customers on a "pay-as-you-use" basis. In other terms, a company only pays for access to the cloud supplier, leading to significant savings through the absence of investment and maintenance fees;

– data availability: data stored in the cloud are available via any Internet-enabled platform. Moreover, data retrieval procedures are greatly simplified, as they are managed by the cloud supplier;

– mobility: any user with Internet access may use any terminal (personal computer (PC), cell phone, tablet, etc.) to access cloud data. This adds flexibility and removes the need to maintain data consistency (i.e. via synchronization);

– extension of resources: the cloud can be used to extend the capacities of an individual platform (PC, smartphone, tablet, etc.). This capability is extremely useful in the context of resource-hungry services, using large amounts of processing power, storage or energy. Voice-recognition, image recognition, video sharing and online gaming applications fall into this category. When the client is a mobile device, we generally speak about mobile cloud computing; for video game applications, the term *cloud gaming* is used.

5.3. Other key characteristics of cloud computing

5.3.1. *Cloud computing services*

The provision of equipment for service externalization by CSPs raises questions concerning which types of service are externalized, and the way in which CSP resources will be used by the client. In other terms, we wish to know whether the CSP or the client will be responsible for the management of different specific resources (software, hardware, network, etc.).

There are three main models of cloud service [MEL 11]:

– Software as a Service (SaaS): The CSP gives the client access to a software application. This application is accessible to all authorized users via a simple interface, such as that provided by a Web browser. In this model, the CSP controls all of the underlying architecture, including the software application, with the exception of certain configuration options determined by individual users. The advantage of this service type is that nothing needs to be installed on the user's local machine; there is no license fee and no updates will be required. The client is simply billed for on-demand services;

– Platform as a Service (PaaS): The CSP provides a platform, i.e. a set of tools, such as development environments, used by authorized users to develop their own applications. The CSP is not responsible for managing the developed applications, but retains control of the underlying infrastructure. The user avoids the need to install development software or to obtain material. For the moment, however, the development types offered by PaaS are limited to Web applications, and the range of supported languages is also limited. For example, Google allows development using Python and Java, while Microsoft Azure proposes development using .NET;

– Infrastructure as a Service (IaaS): The CSP provides all elementary computing resources, such as processing power, network interfaces and storage capacity, allowing authorized users to develop programs of any type, from operating systems to high-level applications. The CSP manages the equipment and resources provided to users, but the users are responsible for all of the developments carried out using the cloud infrastructure. The advantage of IaaS lies in the fact that users may access programs of any type, without needing to consider the management, maintenance or control of servers. However, this model requires users to have a strong Internet connection, without which it will be difficult to access the infrastructure.

Figure 5.3 shows which entity, i.e. the company or the cloud, is responsible for different architectural elements depending on the chosen model.

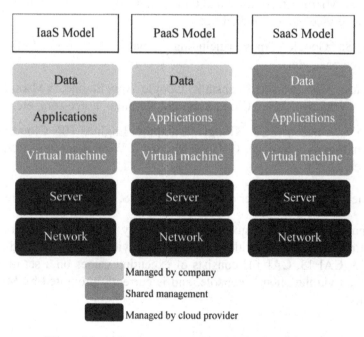

Figure 5.3. *Architecture management by cloud model type*

In addition to cloud providers, other intermediary cloud suppliers, known as cloud brokers, attempt to profit from the cloud market; these include services such as DropBox. These brokers may notably offer more specific models if actors consider this to be useful. One of these models will be considered in more detail later in this chapter:

– IDentity as a service (IDaaS) is an authentication infrastructure [IDA 14] that is built, hosted and managed by a cloud provider or a cloud broker. IDaaS is based on single sign-on (SSO) authentication and user authorization for access to the cloud.

5.3.2. *Actors in cloud computing*

A number of actors in the computing world have been involved in the development of cloud computing offers over the last decade. Salesforce.com was one of the pioneers in the genre, launching their public cloud offer in 2003. Subsequently, numerous companies, including computing leaders such as Google, Microsoft, Amazon and Oracle, developed their own solutions for different service models, including:

– SaaS: Google Apps (including Gmail), Microsoft Office 365, Salesforce.com, etc.

– PaaS: AWS Elastic Beanstalk, Google App Engine, VMware Cloud Foundry, Windows Azure Cloud Services, NetSuite, Force.com, etc.

– IaaS: Amazon EC2, Google Compute Engine, HP Cloud, Oracle Infrastructure as a Service, GoGrid, Microsoft Windows Azure, Rackspace Cloud, etc.

Table 5.1 gives a number of examples of IaaS, PaaS and SaaS offers.

In parallel to these major developments by a variety of actors, cloud computing has also been widely developed for video gaming. Cloud gaming [SHE 13, CAI 13, CAI 14] consists of executing games on a set of servers rather than via the client's console, and is currently promoted by Microsoft and Sony.

Offers	Provider	Product	Notes
IaaS	Amazon Web services	Amazon EC2	
	IBM	IBM Smart Business Cloud	
	EMC/Vmware	Hypervisor vSphere	
	Microsoft	Microsoft System Center	
	GoGrid	Cloud Hosting	
	Eucalyptus Systems	Eucalyptus (open source)	
	RackSpace	OpenStack (open source)	
	Citrix	CloudStack	
	Numergy	OpenStack	
	CloudWatt	OpenStack	
	HP	OpenStack	
	DataPipe	CloudStack	
PaaS	Microsoft	Microsoft Azure	Supported languages: Java, PHP, RUBY, ASP.NET
	Google	Google App Engine	Supported languages: Python, Java, JEE, PHP
	Salesforce	Force.com, Heroku	Supported languages: Java, Apex, Flex
	Rackspace	Cloud sites	Supported languages: PHP, Perl, Python, MySQL, ASP.NET
	Redhat	OpenShift	Supported languages: Ruby, Java, JEE, PHP, MongoDB, node.js
	Vmware	Cloud Foundry (open source)	Groovy, Java, Java script, Ruby, etc.
SaaS	Google	Google Apps	Office applications
	Microsoft	Microsoft online services	Office applications
	Salesforce	Sales cloud 2, Service cloud 2, Chatter collaboration cloud	Trade applications
	Netsuite	Netsuite CRM+, Netsuite Financials, etc.	Trade applications

Table 5.1. *Examples of Cloud Computing services*

Finally, cloud computing is currently a key focus in mobile networks (Mobile Cloud Computing). The aim of this approach is to externalize local data and applications from the mobile terminal to dedicated servers. This notably reduces the resource consumption of mobile platforms, something that is necessarily limited; it also reduces their energy consumption, prolonging battery life. Operators including Vodafone, Orange and Verizon are currently heading in this direction. However, the recent development of mobile cloud computing [HUA 10, DIN 13, NIR 13, PAT 13] goes beyond the externalization of data and processing to the cloud, proposing models that consider mobile devices as service providers. In this case, the so-called "virtual cloud" [MAR 09] can collect data from different mobile devices via their sensors, or via mobile applications for the management of user data. The analysis of collected data and their processing via statistical methods or data mining may be valuable for the cloud, enabling it to offer new services based on data collected in real time. Another model that is increasingly used in the mobile cloud domain is that of *Cloudlets* [SAT 09, SIM 12], which aim to bring the cloud closer to the mobile terminal. In this model, cloudlets may be hosted in wireless fidelity (WiFi) terminals, offering users better connectivity. The cloudlet would then act as a service provider to the mobile terminal, and only the cloudlet would be able to access the cloud servers.

5.3.3. *Key issues*

The context of the cloud, as described earlier, raises certain issues concerning the risk of data loss and unauthorized third-party access to data, and the location and duration of data storage. These questions are crucial in the context of cloud computing and present a number of problems needing to be solved.

Data security: one major problem associated with cloud computing is data security. According to Gartner, in 2012, more than 50% of companies had adopted the bring your own device (BYOD) solution. This consists of virtualizing a workspace in the cloud, generating an increasing demand in security terms. In a private cloud, data are managed by the company following its own security rules. In a hybrid cloud, the company may choose to store sensitive data in a private cloud and less critical data in a public cloud. However, for public cloud use, users must choose a provider whom they trust, although this is not sufficient.

Lack of interoperability: if a cloud provider is bought out by another CSP or collapses, it is currently difficult for users to retrieve their data and platform in order to change supplier. There are currently no established tools and procedures for data portability; users are therefore strongly advised to pay special attention to data output or export clauses in supplier contracts. Using Amazon, for example, data are not deleted if a contract is terminated; however, it is only possible to retrieve this data if a chargeable option is selected in the initial contract [HEL 14].

Service quality: service quality is an important parameter in the choice of a cloud provider, and is based on permanent access to the network. If this access is not reliable, work within the company may be interrupted.

Breakdowns or attacks on data centers: in April 2011, Amazon data centers in Virginia went offline for several days. This demonstrates the vulnerability of dematerialized computing, which is based on the reliability of immense servers[2]. This example should help to raise company awareness of the need to save data in a private or public cloud, where possible and according to capabilities.

Legal problems: certain problems still need to be solved from a legal perspective. Data are often distributed across multiple territories, and the applicable laws differ from one country to another. A French company, for example with data hosted in a different country, is subject to the laws of this second country.

5.3.4. *Intercloud interactions*

The nature of the cloud computing architecture needs interactions between CSPs. Data from one client may be spread between multiple providers, a fact that may lead providers to work together to enable the client to access all of their information. In the same way, the access to a cloud service may depend on the specific usage of an application hosted in another cloud.

Furthermore, the elasticity of the cloud, described above, means that suppliers must always be in a position to respond to high resource

---

2 http://geeko.lesoir.be/2011/04/30/la-panne-chez-amazon-illustre-les-risques-de-linformatique-dematerialisee/.

consumption; this may be achieved by mobilizing the resources of other cloud providers.

Two types of intercloud interactions exist:

– between clouds of the same level: both cloud providers are visible by the client. When a client wishes to access their data, they may authenticate to both clouds, typically using identity federation;

– nested clouds: the client is only aware of one cloud provider, but when he or she wishes to access the cloud, this first provider calls up resources from a second cloud which the client is not aware of. This second cloud may itself call up resources from a third cloud, and so on.

The digital identity of clients is managed differently depending on the case in question. These management approaches will be considered next.

5.3.5. *Cloud computing and digital identity*

Generally speaking, the question of digital identity is fundamental in cloud computing, particularly with the recent upsurge and the consequent scale on which the architecture is used. We have already considered the importance of digital identity in terms of managing access to personal data or Web services. Cloud computing, which centers on the storage and network accessibility of sensitive and personal data, is strongly concerned by these considerations.

The trend to encourage users to take advantage of the cloud, notably in terms of the offered processing power and network data storage, has created increasing dependency on cloud providers. This dependency must go hand in hand with a relationship of trust, which is only possible with guarantees of security relating to access to data and to processes using this data (this is very similar to the banking principle, where clients entrust their money to third parties on condition that their security guarantees are considered to be satisfactory).

The security of access in complex architectures, such as those used in cloud computing, is strongly linked to the quality of digital identity management, notably via authentication, authorization and privacy protection. Thus, a user should be the only person able to access all of their data from different cloud providers, and should be able to exploit cloud resources for a variety of operations without, for example, interfering with another user's data. Moreover, users need to know that the personal information provided to the cloud during authentication will not be retransmitted to other cloud providers without their explicit consent. In this chapter, we will provide a detailed discussion of the different methods used to manage digital identity in the context of cloud computing.

5.3.6. *Beyond digital identity in the cloud*

It is important to notice that digital identity does not solve all of the problems associated with cloud computing. Other guarantees are needed, but these are outside the scope of this book. For example, guarantees are needed regarding the confidentiality of data stored by a cloud provider, i.e. to ensure that the provider will never have access to the contents of the data. Means are also needed to guarantee effective deletion of data.

Legal constraints also exist. In the United States, the Patriot Act [PAT 01] allows authorities to access data stored in a cloud located anywhere in the world, as long as the cloud providers are American companies or have economic interests in the United States. This contravenes the confidentiality and privacy properties expected of cloud providers.

Moving beyond security concerns, cloud computing also raises questions concerning data ownership. By externalizing data to a third party, a user implicitly accepts the loss of exclusive control over his data, as they no longer have a local copy. The user is the only person with the right to access the data, but no longer physically possesses it. The phenomenal success of cloud computing has thus created radical changes in the relationship between users and their data.

5.4. Classic solutions for digital identity management in the cloud

By nature, cloud computing involves the use of service architectures that are distributed among different cloud providers. A given company may make use of several suppliers, according to the services they wish to implement. For example, a company may use two different SaaS providers, with an additional supplier for IaaS. Consequently, users wishing to consume these services will generally need to authenticate themselves to each cloud provider, even though the services are supplied by a single company. This implies that user accounts will be managed by each provider, although these providers are simply intermediaries hosting one or more given services.

This example shows that digital identity management in the cloud is necessarily based on identity federation, which allows users to access a set of services following a single authentication procedure, while maintaining a specific identity for each of these services. However, it is important to consider the different types of interaction that may exist in the cloud. The simplest case is that of a client wishing to consume a service in the cloud; more complex cases involve intercloud interactions, as discussed in section 5.1.4. Moreover, we must distinguish between identity management in a private cloud and in a public cloud, as the issues involved are very different.

In this section, we will present the basic principles of identity management in cloud computing, which are explained and illustrated in a very clear manner in [BER 12]. These principles are involved in almost all of the existing solutions; each brings innovations or variations suited to particular contexts. A general overview of several of these solutions, focusing on the specific points of each, may be found in [GUN 12].

5.4.1. Client–cloud interactions

5.4.1.1. Private clouds

By definition, a private cloud can only be accessed by a single company, made up of a certain number of individuals who may be able to access the cloud. In this specific case, digital identity management is simplified, as the company already has a list of the users authorized to access the services in the cloud. As the company will already have a system for managing the digital identities of its staff, typically using a database and access federation, this database may be reused. The company must use a security token service (STS, see Chapter 2, section 2.2.2.3) that generates identity tokens for identity federation purposes. This federation may already exist for all other intranet services, and may easily be extended to the private cloud.

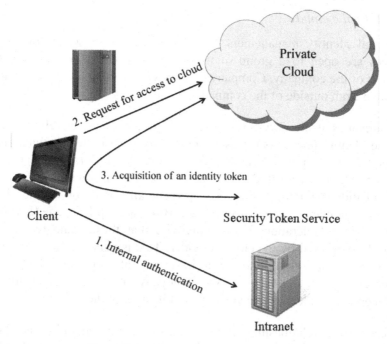

Figure 5.4. *Authentication in a private cloud*

A private cloud authentication scenario, as illustrated in Figure 5.4, may be described as follows:

– the user, a member of the company, is authenticated internally, typically to allow access to the intranet;

– when the user wishes to use a service from the private cloud, the cloud requests an identity token from the STS;

– an identity token is generated using the user's attributes, as contained in the company database. This token is transmitted to the private cloud;

– the private cloud checks the validity of the token and, if successful, allows the user to access the service.

In this way, the user can access the private cloud in a simple and entirely transparent way. In this case, there is no recourse to identity providers; this avoids the need to establish a trust relationship, as access is only possible within the company.

5.4.1.2. *Public clouds*

Digital identity management for a public cloud is more complex, as services are open to a group of users that may considerably exceed the confines of the company. Company employees may also, in this case, access the cloud from outside of the company.

Companies using services delocalized to the cloud therefore need to become identity providers (or use a third party to provide this function, see section 5.3.1). A public cloud uses Application Programming Interface (APIs) designed to accept identity tokens rather than passwords (or any other authentication method). These APIs are generally based on classic identity federation standards, such as security assertion markup language (SAML) or Web Services Federation. Note, moreover, that these standards must be explicitly supported by the cloud provider. This is generally the case for all current SaaS providers, and, to a lesser extent, for PaaS. IaaS is not concerned by this issue, as the company itself is responsible for implementing an identity management architecture in the cloud.

Finally, trust relationships (in the sense of identity federation) need to be established between the company and the different cloud suppliers providing infrastructure services. Trust relationships are also needed between different cloud providers in order to ensure digital identity management in intercloud interactions.

5.4.1.2.1. Cloud access by a company member

When a company member wishes to access the public cloud, his authentication, and more generally the management of his digital identity, follows the identity federation principle as set out in Chapter 2.

The cloud provider is therefore the service provider, and the company is the identity provider. The user accesses a cloud service in the following manner, as illustrated in Figure 5.5:

– the user attempts to connect to the cloud provider in order to access a service;

– the cloud redirects the user to the identity provider, in this case the company, for authentication;

– the user inputs his authentication data;

– the identity provider verifies the authentication data and generates an authentication token, containing a number of details regarding the identity of the user;

– the identity token is sent to the cloud provider, which checks its validity;

– if this is successful, the user is permitted to access the cloud service.

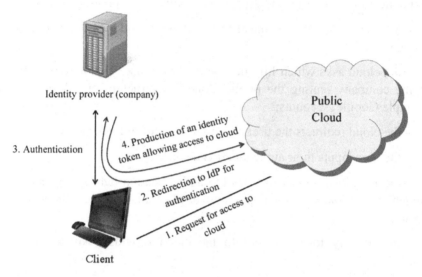

Figure 5.5. *Authentication in a public cloud*

This is thus a classic scenario. The cloud provider does not manage authentication or digital identity management; however, they may request certain elements of personal information relating to the user's identity, raising questions of privacy, which will be discussed in section 5.4.

5.4.1.2.2. Cloud access by a user outside of the company

A company that externalizes services to a public cloud necessarily becomes an identity provider. However, other actors may also be legitimate Identity Provider (IdPs), i.e. share a trust relationship with the cloud. This is the case, for example, when cloud services are opened up to partners of the company, where each partner will act as an IdP for its own members. The situation also occurs when services are offered to final users, typically in a business to consumer (B2C) model, where the company develops products for public consumption.

Web IdP identities are used to authenticate users with no affiliation to the company; examples include Google Accounts, Windows Live ID, OpenID, etc. The set of IdPs trusted by the cloud is predefined. Thus, the user will be able to select an IdP for authentication in order to access the cloud. The authentication scenario is therefore very similar to the previous example:

– the user attempts to connect to the cloud provider in order to access a service;

– the cloud asks which IdP the user wishes to use. This may be a partner of the company renting the public cloud infrastructure or a Web IdP, for example Google Accounts;

– the cloud redirects the user to the selected IdP for authentication;

– the user inputs their authentication data;

– the identity provider verifies the authentication data and generates an authentication token, containing a number of details regarding the identity of the user;

– the identity token is sent to the cloud provider, which checks its validity;

– if this is successful, the user is permitted to access the cloud service.

User authentication to a public cloud can therefore always be carried out simply using identity federation. The company externalizing services to the public cloud needs to define which IdPs it will accept.

5.4.2. Intercloud interactions

As we highlighted in section 5.1.4, digital identity management in cloud computing is not limited to studying the interactions between clients and cloud providers. We also need to take account of the interactions between different clouds.

A distinction should be made between cases where the interacting clouds are all visible to the client, which we will refer to as "clouds of the same level", and cases where a cloud consumes services from another cloud without the client's knowledge, known as "nested clouds".

5.4.2.1. *Clouds of the same level*

The interaction between two clouds of the same level allows a client to access both clouds while only being identified to one of the two. Once again, identity federation provides the necessary architecture for digital identity management.

Several cases are possible depending on the trust relationships in question. If the two clouds, CSP 1 and CSP 2, belong to the same circle of trust, then the same identity token will allow the client to access both cloud providers. If the client authenticates to CSP 1, for example, they will obtain access following one of the scenarios presented in the previous section. To access CSP 2, the necessary identity token is provided immediately by the IdP, avoiding the user to repeat the authentication process.

Access to CSP 2 may also be envisaged via CSP 1, for example if CSP 1 offers services that have been delegated to other clouds, while belonging to the same company. In this case, the identity token used for client authentication and authorization with CSP 1 is directly transmitted to CSP 2 to enable identity federation in a manner that is completely transparent for the client. Note that this mechanism does not require the use of a common identity federation standard by all of the cloud providers involved. For instance, it is entirely possible for CSP 1 to use SAML, while CSP 2 uses WS-Federation. If the standards used are the same, then the identity token may be transmitted directly with no particular treatment. If the standards are different, however, then CSP 1 will require access to a module enabling "translation" of the identity token from one standard to another before transmission.

5.4.2.2. *Nested clouds*

Let us now consider another situation, in which CSP 1 is a customer of CSP 2, without the client's knowledge (the second provider is therefore "nested" inside the first). In this case, the client does not have direct access to CSP 2. In this case, the client's digital identity may be managed in two different ways.

The first method consists of transferring the client's identity directly from CSP 1 to CSP 2. The identity token transmission method described above may easily be applied in these cases. However, we must ensure that CSP 1 and CSP 2 share a trust relationship, without which the identity token supplied by CSP 1 will not be considered valid by CSP 2.

Using the second method, we consider that all users of CSP 1 are aggregated into a single identity, that of CSP 1 itself. In this case, CSP 2 will not be able to differentiate between users of CSP 1, as CSP 1 will always be seen as the customer. If, for example, CSP 1 uses CSP 2 to increase its resources in carrying out costly calculations, then it will not be necessary, or even justified, to transmit the client's identity to CSP 2.

In this case, CSP 1 becomes a client of CSP 2, and will need to authenticate to CSP 2 via an identity federation architecture. A trust relationship is therefore not required between CSP 1 and CSP 2. As Celesti *et al.* [CEL 10] suggest, the simplest solution in this case is for CSP 1 to create an account with an identity provider involved in a trust relationship with CSP 2. CSP 1 then authenticates to CSP 2 using this identity, according to the following scenario:

– CSP 1 attempts to connect to CSP 2;

– CSP 2 asks CSP 1 to authenticate via a trusted IdP;

– CSP 1 authenticates to the IdP;

– the IdP verifies the authentication data and generates an identity token containing information relating to the identity of CSP 1;

– the identity token is sent to CSP 2, which verifies its validity;

– if this is successful, CSP 1 is permitted to consume the resources of CSP 2.

Once again, this authentication scenario is very ordinary, and is simply an adaptation of the identity federation principle for intercloud relationships. The scenario is illustrated in Figure 5.6, with numbers 1–5 corresponding to the steps of the scenario described above.

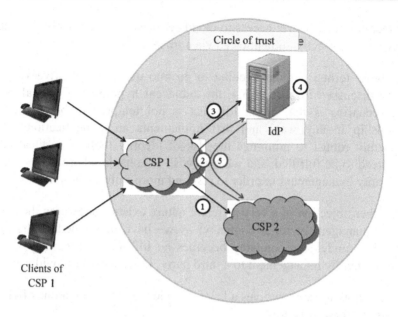

Figure 5.6. *Authentication in a nested cloud with aggregated client identities*

Irrespective of the way in which CSP 1 accesses resources from CSP 2, CSP 2 may call up resources from a third CSP, CSP 3, and so on, in the same manner. The elastic nature of cloud computing means that cloud providers must be able to provide the requested quantity of resources very rapidly; a sudden, significant increase in demand can generally only be dealt with by using resources from other cloud providers.

5.4.3. *Limitations of classic identity management solutions in the cloud*

In this section, we have shown how digital identity management in the cloud is based on classic identity federation standards. These standards may easily be adapted to the context of cloud computing, both in the case of client–cloud interactions and for intercloud interactions.

Identity federation is therefore clearly an essential element of cloud computing. However, it does not provide a response to all issues involved in digital identity management, notably with regards to security. The scenarios described in this section simply ensure correct identity management from an architectural perspective: access to cloud services or resources is guaranteed to any client correctly authenticated via a trusted IdP.

In other terms, without needing to go into questions of privacy, which will be discussed in section 5.4, the subjacent hypothesis for ideal use of these scenarios is that of an IdP that is not tempted to break the trust relationship in any way, and that implements an authentication system sufficiently robust to minimize the risk of identity theft. This ideal is not guaranteed to be fulfilled, and we may wish to consider alternative solutions for identity management in order to respond more fully to these issues.

Another objection of a very different nature exists, concerning the cost of identity management for a company; as we have mentioned in the cloud computing model, the company becomes an IdP. Companies may wish to delegate identity management to a third party, i.e. to a cloud provider.

The following section gives a brief overview of some solutions offered in response to these concerns.

5.5. Alternative solutions for digital identity management in the cloud

No digital identity management solution can exist without identity federation. However, as we have seen, the field is open to the possibility of alternative or complementary solutions, focusing on different possibilities for the implementation of identity federation.

5.5.1. *Identity as a Service*

Identity management may itself be delegated to a cloud provider. It thus becomes an on-demand service, following the same principle as SaaS, PaaS or IaaS. This is known as IDaaS. In this case, the company externalizing services to the cloud is no longer the identity provider. This approach can lead to a reduction in costs and in the complexity of implementation and maintenance of identity federation technologies; however, it also raises a number of significant issues.

The management of user identities is a critical element for a company, so the externalization of this management should only be envisaged if it poses no major security or trust problems, something that is not always evident.

The first point for consideration is the question of access to users' personal data. In the IDaaS model, the company must submit all (or at least a large part) of the personal information stored in its database to the third-party IdP. This naturally raises questions concerning the trust placed in this third party. The questions raised by identity federation are clearly repeated here, but the notion of trust is also extended to cover the capability of the third party to access and exploit users' personal data, which would usually remain within the perimeter of the company.

The second point is an extension of the first point. If a third-party provider is supplied with users' personal data, should they also receive their sensitive authentication data, for example passwords? This pushes the notion of trust to its limits, and the dangers involved in the disclosure of highly sensitive information are generally considered to be too great for this to be a serious possibility.

One possible solution, described in [DEU 11], consists of retaining sensitive information such as passwords within the company, typically in a directory. User authentication requests would therefore be relayed to the company via an intermediary module, the *IDaaS Agent*, maintained by the company, behind their firewall. This module would implement the necessary Lightweight Directory Access Protocol (LDAP) requests to obtain the user and user group database. In parallel, the module would communicate with the IDaaS provider over a secure connection (LDAP over SSL), partly to duplicate the database for the IDaaS provider and maintain synchronization, and partly to transmit user authentication data to the company.

The user authentication scenario thus proceeds as follows:

– the user attempts to access a cloud provider hosting a service provided by his company. The user is redirected to the IDaaS provider for authentication;

– the user inputs his identification data, which is transmitted to the IDaaS Agent located within the company network;

– authentication data are verified locally; if this is successful, an authentication token is generated and retransmitted to the IDaaS provider;

– the user is able to access the desired service from the cloud provider.

The architecture of the IDaaS model is shown in Figure 5.7, where the authentication data transmitted from the client to the IDaaS provider are then retransmitted within the company via the IDaaS, providing "indirect" authentication of the client to the company directory. A simpler architecture might be envisaged, with the IDaaS in possession of all the information needed to authenticate users on its own, including passwords, but this poses certain problems in terms of trust, as we have seen. The approach described in section 5.3.2 removes the issue of trust in cases where authentication is delegated to a third party.

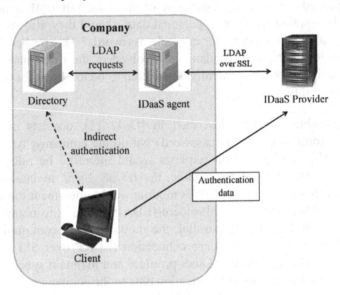

Figure 5.7. *Architecture of the IDaaS model*

The main advantage of IDaaS, as we have seen, is that it simplifiers management of user access to company services. Evidently, this needs to be weighed against the main drawback of this architecture, where an external service provider is responsible for enabling access to all company applications hosted by the cloud.

5.5.2. *Authentication as a Service*

Another approach to authentication management in the cloud involves offering solutions to the trust issues that arise when third parties, notably

IdPs, are involved in authentication. This approach may be suitable for companies requiring a robust authentication system without wishing to manage the system internally, while totally avoiding the question of trust placed in an IdP.

In this approach, it is not identity management that is delegated, but rather authentication. This is *authentication as a service* (AaaS). In this approach, the cloud provider has access to the most sensitive user data; for the method to be meaningful and unaffected by questions of trust in the cloud provider, mechanisms are needed to guarantee that attempts by the provider to access further information will not succeed. In other terms, while the cloud may access all of the sensitive data involved in user authentication (passwords, private keys, etc.), the provider should not be able to actually *obtain* this data.

A key element in solutions of this type is the use of secure microcontrollers, such as smart cards, which constitute both physical and logical countermeasures. The information stored in these components cannot be fraudulently read, deleted or rewritten. Moreover, each component also contains a processor that is able to execute code. Components may therefore contain not only the data needed for authentication (passwords, X.509 certificates and the associated private keys, etc.), but also the authentication protocol itself. The solution proposed in [URI 10] implements mutual authentication using a TLS protocol contained within smart cards, which act as authentication servers. Once authentication is complete, an authentication token, for example in SAML format, may be produced to demonstrate the success of the authentication process to the service provider. Other solutions exist, such as that proposed by Choudhury *et al.* [CHO 11], offering strong user authentication within the cloud using a smart card for each user; Marx *et al.* [MAR 10] offer a digital identity management solution based on the use of a smart card, which is known as an IDdentity Management (IDM) card, which stores user profile information such as pseudonyms, security keys and attributes.

Figure 5.8 shows an authentication scenario using an AaaS provider, aiming to obtain a SAML token in order to access a SaaS provider.

We clearly see how these secure components may justify the implementation of AaaS: the third party simply becomes an intermediary, supplying the calculating power needed for user authentication, and avoiding the need to establish a trust relationship. However, tempted an AaaS provider may be to carry out fraudulent activities, they will not be able to access any items of data used in authentication, as long as authentication exchanges do not involve sending sensitive elements in cleartext across the network (in this case, spying would evidently still be possible).

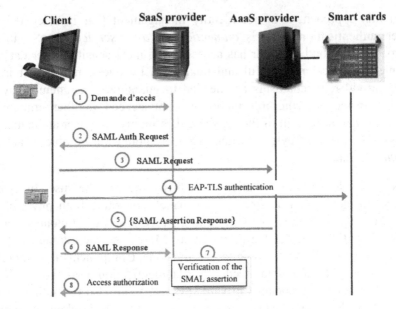

Figure 5.8. *Authentication to an AaaS provider to obtain an SAML token*

To respond to scalability issues, large numbers of these components should be available from the AaaS provider. Each component may be prepersonalized by the company, and freely updated by the company whenever necessary. Personalization typically consists of integrating the company identity. In [URI 10], this is an identity allowing mutual TLS authentication; this requires loading of an X.509 certificate corresponding to the identity of the company, along with the certificate of the certification authority. Each smart card is therefore a representative of an authentication server belonging to a given company. Several different companies, with no particular connection, may therefore be hosted by the same AaaS provider.

The quality of an AaaS provider is determined by the performance offered by his architecture. While smart cards belong to the company, and so the authentication carried out by the smart card itself does not depend on the AaaS provider, the correct and efficient management of parallel entries, distributed to different smart cards, is the entire responsibility of the provider.

Despite offering clear advantages in terms of security, there are two major drawbacks to the use of AaaS. The first drawback is the cost, notably for the company. The use of components such as smart cards for robust authentication comes at a cost, linked to the acquisition, prepersonalization and updating of cards, for example to optimize the application code managing user authentication.

The other drawback of AaaS concerns scalability, and is directly linked to the fact that user authentication is dependent on the availability of server cards from the AaaS provider. Companies need to obtain sufficient quantities of components before attempting to scale up the approach. In cases of unexpected high demand, the AaaS provider will be unable to provide each client with satisfactory service, even by requesting assistance from other AaaS providers; in reality, the performance issue is dependent on the total number of cards available for client authentication. If this number is not sufficient, it will not be possible to meet cloud elasticity requirements, as new cards would need to be added in real time; evidently, this is impossible.

AaaS is thus only meaningful when the number of cloud clients is both relatively stable and known in advance, allowing satisfactory dimensioning of the number of smart cards to manage.

5.6. Management of privacy and personal data in cloud computing

The question of privacy and personal data protection was covered in Chapter 4, which gave a broad overview of the topic. However, it is interesting to look at this question again in the specific context of cloud computing.

Our personal data, such as information regarding our personal relationships or sensitive details such as a credit card number, are already at risk of being disclosed or sold whenever it is accessible to service providers. This issue is even more important in cloud computing, where data are spread across the network avoiding the user to know where his data are located.

Cloud computing uses identity federation mechanisms, and IdPs need to transmit certain elements of personal data to the cloud provider with which a client wishes to interact. However, mechanisms specific to the cloud, such as intercloud interactions (for example in the case of nested clouds, aiming to respond to high demand for resources) may lead to personal data exchange with no control by the user.

The issue of managing the privacy and personal data of an entity in cloud computing may be summarized using the following questions:

– what data are transmitted?

– to whom are the data transmitted?

– who will be able to access this data, once it has been transmitted?

We do not currently have a set of tested technical standards to provide a satisfactory response to these questions once and for all; however, a legal framework concerning the management of personal data online requires certain limitations on the behavior of service providers. This framework is of a general nature, and is therefore particularly applicable to cloud providers, as specified in a document produced by the World Privacy Forum [GEL 09].

5.6.1. *Identity federation and management of personal data*

Cloud computing uses identity federation technologies, and the mechanisms involved in personal data management are naturally inherited from these technologies. However, as we have seen, the cloud is more sensitive to data dispersion across the network, meaning that these mechanisms are insufficient to provide satisfactory privacy protection. This observation is the motivation for a number of research projects that attempt to provide a response to these issues, some of which will be presented below.

By default, a user has an account with an identity provider, which is contacted by the cloud provider when the user wishes to access a service. The IdP possesses a set of personal information that, by definition, reveals aspects of the user's private life. A certain amount of this information must be disclosed to service providers – in this case, cloud providers – on demand. Cloud providers may demand more or less information in order to precisely identify a client, determine whether or not they are authorized to access the service, and potentially in order to put this information to somewhat less honorable use at a later date.

Moreover, the personal data transmitted to different cloud providers, if pooled, may allow CSPs to trace a given user. Identity providers are generally able to monitor users' navigation based on the origins of authentication requests, or the domain of validity of the generated identity tokens. Finally, using default settings, the personal data are transmitted in clear-text, further adding to the probability that the information will end up in an unauthorized database.

Identity federation technologies include more or less effective security methods for use in the transmission of these data, using different approaches according to different standards. We will briefly consider the cases of Open ID and SAML.

5.6.1.1. *The OpenID approach*

A standard such as OpenID [OPE 07], which aims to be open and simple, uses a graphic interface to allow users to identify what specific personal information is required by a service provider. This information is generally divided into two categories: compulsory information and optional information. If the user refuses to supply some or all of the first category, they will not be able to access the service provider, even if authentication is successful. However, the user remains free to refuse to communicate all pieces of optional data.

This approach presents the advantage of placing the user at the center of the decision whether or not to transmit certain elements of their personal data. However, it does not solve all of the associated problems. For example, the question of who will be able to access data once transmitted is not considered. Moreover, the graphical interface may lead to excessive trust by users, offering the option to always share personal information with a given service provider. This information will therefore be retransmitted automatically for each connection to the specified service provider, without a request for explicit consent by the user. This may be problematic, as it allows service providers to monitor all updates made to the personal data held by the identity provider, leading, for example, to collection of several different e-mail addresses belonging to the same user.

5.6.1.2. *The SAML approach*

SAML (see Chapter 2, section 4.1) technology is based on a different logic to that of OpenID. Its primary characteristic is a certain level of complexity, resulting from the ambition to adapt to as many situations as possible (hence the definition of a very large number of profiles). SAML therefore offers numerous functions, notably in terms of security; the appropriate implementation of these functions is essentially dependent on the IdP.

It is notably possible to encrypt all or part of an SAML token, using the *XML Encryption* standard defined by the W3C [XML 08]. SAML is therefore able to implement confidentiality in the transmission of personal data to a service provider very simply. However, as SAML aims to be as transparent as possible for the user, it is not particularly easy for the user to monitor whether the personal data are transmitted in the identity token.

These two examples demonstrate the difficulty of implementing satisfactory management of personal data, offering true privacy protection. While identity federation technologies include specific tools to overcome this issue, individual IdPs are responsible for satisfactory implementation. Generally speaking, the guarantees concerning the future of information transmitted to service – or cloud – providers are, in all cases, very weak.

5.6.1.3. *Current solutions*

A considerable amount of research has been carried out over the last few years on the way to manage digital identities in cloud computing. Bhandari *et al.* [BHA 13] provide an overview of different digital identity systems, such as SAML, Liberty Alliance, CardSpace, OpenID, PRIME, OAuth and OneLogin, and compare these systems in the context of the cloud. The authors of [CHE 12] propose a decentralized approach to digital identity management in the cloud. Their solution is based on identity federation using SSOs, introducing trust circles (known as contexts). The authors of [ELU 11] recall the specificities of cloud computing and offer a general solution based on authentication, authorization and accounting (AAA) for better management of digital identity systems. They illustrate this principle by highlighting the different cloud services that would be involved in a banking transaction. Sanchez *et al.* [SAN 12] consider federated management of digital identities, based on SAML, for the cloud and propose implementation of an infrastructure. Stihler *et al.* [STI 12] propose a cloud architecture based on different domains (IaaS, PaaS, SaaS, etc.) and show how these domains work together to achieve efficient digital identity management. Celesti *et al.* [CEL 10] propose intercloud infrastructure management identity (ICIMI), a solution for intercloud identity federation, where each cloud is considered as a circle of trust. Similarly, Dreo *et al.* [DRE 13] have developed the intercloud identity management (ICEMAN) platform, which implements technical and organizational solutions for secure management of federated clouds. Casola *et al.* [CAS 10] present a *PerfCloud* architecture, which uses a calculation gate as IaaS; the authors demonstrate how this architecture may be used to manage digital identities. Gopalakrishnan [GOP 09] proposes and compares three digital identity models: the first is a trust model for use in private clouds, the second is an external model for public clouds and the third is an interoperable module to enable cooperation between different digital identity systems, such as OAuth and OpenID. Finally, Kon *et al.* [KON 10] suggest a distribution of authentication functions to calculation nodes in the cloud in order to reduce the number of authentication requests sent to the identity provider; this is obtained by distributing the authentication process within the federated environment of the cloud, due to an algorithm dedicated to healthcare. Users or patients would thus be able to authenticate via different nodes in the cloud.

5.6.2. Solutions for privacy protection in the cloud

The improvement of privacy protection, particularly in a sensitive context such as the cloud, is a particularly active field of research. The current solutions are still at draft stage, and have therefore yet to become standards. In this section, we will describe the bases of a number of solutions, as described in a number of recent publications, notably [ANG 10] and [RAN 10].

These solutions are based on components known as *active bundles* [OTH 09], which are middleware components made up of three distinct elements:

– personal data;

– metadata;

– a virtual machine.

Personal data are the data that are specific to a user and are of a sensitive nature. These data will therefore be encrypted (using a symmetric key obtained from a dedicated security server), and third-party access should be controlled as precisely as possible. Access control depends on the definition and implementation of specific management policies to the personal data carried in the active bundle. These policies are presented in the form of metadata, describing not only access control for the transported personal data, but also the provenance of the active bundle, the algorithm used for integrity validation, the lifetime of the personal data (which will be destroyed at the end of this period) and disclosure policies, which notably specify which entities have the right to retransmit the active bundle, and under what conditions. Finally, a virtual machine carries out random integrity verification on the active bundle, and verifies that access to personal data respects the policies described in the metadata. The basic structure of an active bundle is shown in Figure 5.9.

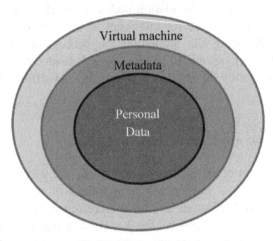

Figure 5.9. *Structure of an active bundle*

This structure gives high levels of flexibility in controlling the release of personal data to third parties, as the metadata contained in an active bundle allow the definition of accurate policies. It is notably possible to define trust thresholds for each data element; these are compared to the (estimated) trust level of the entity receiving the active bundle. This entity, whether acting as the final recipient of the data or as an intermediary, may only be able to access certain data elements, and not all of the information contained in the active bundle. The trust level of a host is estimated using a "trust server", which may use reputation analysis techniques, for example.

A number of defensive mechanisms may be used for true data protection. When the security of an active bundle is threatened, for example in case of an integrity verification failure, the bundle may self-destruct (*apoptosis*). Moreover, if a host does not have a sufficient trust level for access to all of the personal data, excessively sensitive data are subject to an evaporation operation. This consists either of deleting the data entirely, or of replacing it with less sensitive data (such as less accurate or less recent data). This has the effect of lowering the associated trust threshold.

The principle of active bundles allows genuine consideration of privacy issues. Work on promoting the use of active bundles in digital identity management, notably in cloud computing, has focused on a variety of implementation scenarios in order to validate the relevance of these solutions.

However, the architectural complexity required in order to use active bundles presents clear limitations. Unless all hosts are interoperable with active bundles (which are exchanged via a dedicated protocol, and therefore not natively supported), we require both a security server, responsible for generating an encryption key for personal data and metadata, and a "trust server" used to evaluate the trust levels of the host (which is naturally disputable as the metric involved is eminently subjective). Moreover, there are no real guarantees concerning the future use of information revealed to a host, notably regarding fraudulent disclosure of this information to other, less worthy, parties.

This example clearly shows the difficulty of designing a satisfactory solution for the management of privacy and personal data, i.e. a solution allowing precise control of the disclosure of sensitive data without the considerable baggage involved in the use of active bundles, which constitutes a major hindrance in terms of scalability. This problem is not restricted to privacy management in cloud computing. More generally, in computer networks, the addition of a security layer on top of preexisting architectures and protocols is often very difficult. Clearly, the best way to proceed is to take security imperatives into account from the earliest stages of the design process. As this approach has not widely been taken in the past, we often encounter stalemate situations, involving a compromise between the implementation of a genuinely secure system and the need for simplicity, which would considerably increase the possibilities of mass uptake, and consequently, standardization.

5.7. Conclusion

The principle of on-demand access to all types of services provided by specialist external suppliers has become widespread with the remarkable expansion of cloud computing. In terms of digital identity, this transformation of the computing domain can notably be seen in the generalization of identity federation.

Identity federation technologies are now sufficiently developed to allow simple adaptation to the context of cloud computing. In terms of mechanisms, authentication to cloud providers presents no major differences to authentication with more traditional service providers. The radical change lies in the number of servers needed to respond to the demands of cloud computing, most notably the property of elasticity. This leads to considerable traffic of data within the network, to the point where users now have no way of knowing where their data are physically stored. This dispersion of data across the network goes alongside the increase in complexity of connections between different actors involved in cloud computing, implicated in trust circles that continue to be multiplied and refined.

The main element of digital identity in which cloud computing is not currently able to treat is logically user privacy. To understand this, we simply need to consider the loss of control over the traffic and storage of data in the cloud, in association with the fact that identity federation technologies are not always implemented in a way that allows users to precisely control the disclosure of their personal details. Until a satisfactory standard is established for this domain, users and companies generally have no choice but to trust cloud providers not to carry out abusive collection and retention of sensitive data.

It is often said that the future of computing lies in the cloud. The emergence of mobile cloud computing and cloud gaming provides additional proof that the current trend supports this vision. However, individuals remain free to choose how far they wish to participate in this development, and to what extent they consent to give up the physical possession of their data, in turn, for the advantages offered by cloud techniques.

5.8. Bibliography

[AHR 10] AHRONOVITZ M., *et al.*, Cloud Computing Use Cases, White Paper, version 4.0, Licenced under Creative Commons Attribution Share Alike 3.0 Unported License, 2010.

[ANG 10] ANGIN P., *et al.*, "An entity-centric approach for privacy and identity management in cloud computing", *Proceedings of the IEEE Symposium on Reliable Distributed Systems 2010*, pp. 177–183, 2010.

[BER 12] BERAUD P., BRASSEUR S., GRASSET J.-Y., *La fédération identité, une nécessité pour le Cloud*, Microsoft Tech Days, 2012. Available at http://video.fr.msn.com/watch/video/la-federation-didentite-une-necessite-pour-le-cloud/zqqxgk4s.

[BHA 13] BHANDARI R., BHOI U., PATEL D., "Identity management frameworks for cloud", *International Journal of Computer Applications*, vol. 83, no. 12, pp. 25–31, December 2013.

[CAI 13] CAI W., LEUNG V.C.M., CHEN M., "Next generation mobile cloud gaming", *Proceedings of the IEEE Seventh International Symposium on Service-Oriented System Engineering*, pp. 550–559, 2013.

[CAI 14] CAI W., LEUNG V.C.M., HU L., "A cloudlet-assisted multiplayer cloud gaming system", *Mobile Networks and Applications*, vol. 19, pp. 144–152, 2014.

[CAS 10] CASOLA V., RAK M., VILLANO U., "Identity federation in cloud computing", *Proceedings of the Sixth International Conference on Information Assurance and Security (IAS)*, pp. 253–259, 2010.

[CEL 10] CELESTI A., TUSA F., VILLARI M., *et al.*, "Security and cloud computing: intercloud identity management infrastructure", *Proceedings of IEEE Workshops on Enabling Technologies: Infrastructures for Collaborative Enterprises*, pp. 263–265, 2010.

[CHE 12] CHEN J., WU X., ZHANG S., *et al.*, A decentralized approach for implementing identity management in cloud computing, *Proceedings of the Second International Conference on Cloud and Green Computing*, pp. 770–776, 2012.

[CHO 11] CHOUDHURY A.J., KUMAR P., SAIN M., *et al.*, "A strong user authentication framework for cloud computing", *Proceedings of the IEEE Asia-Pacific Services Computing Conference*, pp. 110–115, 2011.

[DEU 11] DEUBY S., *Outsourcing Your Identity with IDaaS*, Windows IT Pro, 2011. Available at http://windowsitpro.com/identity-management/outsourcing-your-identity-idaas.

[DIN 13] DINH H.T., *et al.*, "A survey of mobile cloud computing", *Wireless Communications And Mobile Computing*, vol. 13, pp. 1587–1611, 2013.

[DRE 13] DREO G., GOLLING M., HOMMEL W., *et al.*, "ICEMAN: an architecture for secure federated inter-cloud identity management", *Proceedings of the IFIP/IEEE International Symposium on Integrated Network Management (IM 2013)*, pp. 1207–1210, 2013.

[ELU 11] ELUDIORA S., ABIONA O., OLUWATOPE A., *et al.*, "A user identity management protocol for cloud computing paradigm", *International Journal of Communications, Network and System Sciences*, vol. 4, pp. 152–163, 2011.

[GEL 09] GELLMAN R., *Privacy in the Clouds: Risks to Privacy and Confidentiality from Cloud Computing*, World Privacy Forum, 2009.

[GOP 09] GOPALAKRISHNAN A., *Cloud Computing Identity Management*, vol. 7, no. 7, SETLabs Briefings, pp. 46–53, 2009. Available at http://cis.cau.edu/cms/files/CIS509-OAUTH/cloud-computing-identity-management.pdf.

[GUN 12] GUNJAN K., SAHOO G., TIWARI R.K., "Identity management in cloud computing – a review", *International Journal of Engineering Research & Technology*, vol. 1, no. 4, pp. 1–5, June 2012.

[HEL 14] HELMER F., *Architecture Cloud eEtreprise*, training by Pythagoras F.D., May 2014.

[HUA 10] HUANG D., ZHANG X., KANG M., *et al.*, "Building secure mobile cloud framework for mobile computing and communication", *Proceedings of the IEEE Service Oriented System Engineering*, vol. 1, p. 27–34, 2010.

[IDA 14] IDaaS, available at http://searchconsumerization.techtarget.com/definition/identity-as-a-Service-IDaaS, 2014.

[KON 10] KIM I.K., PERVEZ Z., KHATTAK A.M., *et al.*, "Chord based identity management for e-healthcare cloud applications", *Proceedings of the 10th IEEE/IPSJ International Symposium on Applications and the Internet*, pp. 391–394, 2010.

[MAR 09] MARINELLI E., Hyrax: cloud computing on mobile devices using MapReduce, Master Thesis, Carnegie Mellon University, 2009.

[MAR 10] MARX R., FHOM H.S., SCHEUERMANN D., et al., "Increasing security and privacy in user-centric identity management: the IdM card approach", Proceedings of the 2010 International Conference on P2P, Parallel, Grid, Cloud and Internet Computing (3PGCIC '10), pp. 459–464, 2010.

[MEL 11] MELL P., GRANCE T., The NIST Definition of Cloud Computing, NIST, 2011. Available at http://csrc.nist.gov/publications/nistpubs/800-145/SP800-145.pdf.

[NIR 13] NIROSHINIE F., LOKE S.W., RAHAYU W., "Mobile cloud computing: a survey", Future Generation Computer Systems, vol. 29, no. 1, pp. 84–106, 2013.

[OPE 07] OPENID AUTHENTICATION 2.0, http://openid.net/specs/openid-authentication-2_0.html, 2007.

[OTH 09] OTHMANE L.B., LILIEN L., "Protecting privacy of sensitive data dissemination using active bundles", Proceedings of the CONGRESS'09, pp. 202–213, 2009.

[PAR 13] PATRIOT ACT USA, http://epic.org/privacy/terrorism/hr3162.html, 2013.

[PAT 13] PATEL S., A Survey of Mobile Cloud Computing: Architecture, Existing Work and Challenges, Computer Engineering Department R.K. University, India, vol. 3, no. 6, June 2013.

[RAN 10] RANCHAL R., et al., "Protection of identity information in cloud computing without trusted third party", Proceedings of the IEEE SRDS 2010, pp. 368–372, 2010.

[REN 14] RENAUDVENET, http://www.renaudvenet.com/cloud-computing-avantages-et-inconvenients-2011-01-26.html, 2014.

[SAL 14] SALESFORCE, http://www.salesforce.com/fr/socialsuccess/cloud-computing/les-10-avantages-du-cloud-computing.jsp, 2014.

[SAN 12] GUERRERO R.S., CABARCOS P.A., MENDOZA F.A., et al., "Trust-aware federated IdM in consumer cloud computing", Proceedings of the IEEE International Conference on Consumer Electronics (ICCE'12), pp. 53–54, 2012.

[SAT 09] SATYANARAYANAN M., BAHL P., CACERES R., et al., "The case for VM-based cloudlets in mobile computing", IEEE Pervasive Computing, vol. 8, no. 4, pp. 14–23, 2009.

[SHE 13] SHEA S., LIU J., NGAI E.C.-H., et al., "Cloud gaming: architecture and performance", IEEE Network, vol. 27, no. 4, pp. 16–21, July/August 2013.

[SIM 12] SIMANTA S., LEWIS K., HA G., *et al.*, "A reference architecture for mobile code offload in hostile environments", *In Proceedings of MobiCase 2012: Fourth International Conference on Mobile Computing, Applications and Services*, Seattle, WA, pp. 274–293, October 2012. Available at http://www.cs. cmu.edu/~satya/docdir/simanta-mobicase2012.pdf.

[STI 12] STIHLER M., SANTIN A.O., MARCON A.L., *et al.*, "Integral federated identity management for cloud computing", *Proceedings of the 5th International Conference on New Technologies, Mobility and Security (NTMS)*, pp. 1–5, 2012.

[URI 10] URIEN P., KIENNERT C., MARIE E., "An innovative solution for cloud computing authentication: gids of EAP-TLS smart cards", *Proceedings of Conference on Digital Telecommunications 2010*, pp. 22–27, 2010.

[XML 08] XML Encryption Workgroup, 2008. Available at http://www.w3.org/ Encryption/2001.

[ZHA 10] ZHANG Q., CHENG L., BOUTABA R., "Cloud computing: state-of-he-art and research challenges", *Journal of Internet Services and Applications*, vol. 1, pp. 7–18, 2010.

List of Authors

Amira Faiza BENKARA MOSTEFA
SIR lab
Université des Sciences et de la
Technologie d'Oran Mohamed
Boudiaf
Algeria

Samia BOUZEFRANE
CEDRIC lab
Conservatoire national des arts et
métiers
Paris
France

Augustin DE MISCAULT
Arismore
Saint-Cloud
France

Julie DENOUËL
CNRS Praxiling Lab
Université de Paul Valéry
Montpellier
France

Mathieu JEANDRON
Direction Interministérielle des
Systèmes d'Information et de
Communication
Paris
France

Christophe KIENNERT
CNRS LTCI lab
Télécom ParisTech
Institut Mines-Télécom
France

Maryline LAURENT
CNRS SAMOVAR lab
Télécom SudParis
Institut Mines-Télécom
France

Claire LEVALLOIS-BARTH
CNRS LTCI lab
Télécom ParisTech
Institut Mines-Télécom
France

Pascal THONIEL
NTX Research SA
Paris
France

Patrick WAELBROECK
Département Sciences économiques
et sociales
Télécom ParisTech
Institut Mines-Télécom
France

Index

Printed in the United States
By Bookmasters